Shadowmancer

G. P. TAYLOR

REALMS
A STRANG COMPANY

Most STRANG COMMUNICATIONS/CHARISMA HOUSE/SILOAM products are available at special quantity discounts for bulk purchase for sales promotions, premiums, fund-raising, and educational needs. For details, write Strang Communications/Charisma House/Siloam, 600 Rinehart Road, Lake Mary, Florida 32746, or telephone (407) 333-0600.

Shadowmancer by G. P. Taylor
Published by Realms
A Strang Company
600 Rinehart Road
Lake Mary, Florida 32746
www.realmsfiction.com

Library of Congress Control Number: 2004105100

International Standard Book Number: 1-59185-665-5 (paperback)

05 06 07 08 09 — 987654321

Printed in the United States of America

To Kathy, Hannah, Abigail and Lydia,
the golden girls—
it wouldn't have been possible
without you and Riathamus

© 2004 John Freeman

Contents

Foreword

THE people, places and spirits you will read about in *Shadowmancer* are drawn from the Yorkshire coastline. This is a countryside of cliffs and moors, richly steeped in history and folklore. If you choose to follow the *Shadowmancer* trail from Wyke Woods to Whitby, as centuries of souls have done before you, you will quickly become aware of their echoes.

Wyke Woods is to be found nestling around the bay of Hayburn Wyke. The trees are tightly packed, and each pathway to the rocky beach is said to be haunted by the ghosts of smugglers caught by the excise men and hung at York. The sound of water is never far away. The sea echoes through the trees, and the stream picks its way through them before dropping over the cliff onto the rocky beach below. The bay is haunted with the memory of wreckers, merciless fortune hunters who would light lamps to bring the unwary sailor crashing to the shore. If you listen carefully, voices of smugglers and whispers of thulak can still be heard.

The North Road leads you past the high stone circle now hidden by trees, and rises quickly. It runs past Bell Hill Farm, which is built on the site of an ancient Templar church, around Rudda Gallows, where many a man was hung by the crossroads as a warning to others, and then on to the village of Ravenscar, set high on the cliff top. The Vicarage dominates the horizon here. Its long drive with two raven pillars guarding the entrance takes you to the fine Georgian building now known as Raven Hall Hotel. It has been called one of the most beautiful views in the world, where on any day of the year the sight of Robin Hood's Bay and the village of Thorpe inspire the soul. It is easy to see why Obadiah Demurral wanted it so badly.

In the grassy fields below once stood an alum mine, and to the west are the deep gouges of the alum quarry that look like blisters in the earth. High above are the Crags and White Moor. It is said that you must never ask directions on the moor from a stranger, for he may be a boggle who will send you the wrong way. That's what boggles always do, especially when they know your journey leads to Boggle Mill, set deep in the valley below, hidden by a small wood cut in two by a ravine where the angry waves of the German Ocean break on the beach. Boggle Mill is now a youth hostel, and yet it doesn't take a great deal of imagination to see Rueben Wayfoot and his children working the mill and refining the flour.

Are there really boggles? Well, in these parts every village has a boggle or hob. Sometimes they are helpful and will work the land for free or heal the sick, even guard the herds. But wobetides if you upset one . . . they will smash your plates and your cow will go dry, your wife will look uglier by the day, your children will never hear a word you say and every drop of beer you drink will be soured. Hobs are hobs and are best left to those who know how to deal with them. If you should see one from the corner of your eye as you cross the bridge at Boggle Mill, it is best that you greet it with a smile and leave a bright penny under the sign that takes you to Baytown.

Baytown is a beautiful place, and yet so much has happened here, including murder, smuggling and treachery. From the quayside to the top of the village runs a smuggler's tunnel that connects to many of the cottages as a handy escape route, or a safe place to store contraband.

The road to Whitby climbs the cliff and on over Hawsker Moor. This is not a place to be alone at night. The gnarled, wind-beaten trees are spoken of as the fingers of the witches that frequent these paths.

If you manage to arrive safely in Whitby town and make your way through the narrow ginnels leading to Church Street, you may rest a while at the Griffin Inn. The food will warm the heart and the company is always plentiful. It is in this street that *Shadowmancer* comes to its conclusion. Kate, Thomas and Raphah walked on these very cobbles past the ancient bookshop where the redheaded bookseller lures the customer from the street to sample the delights of the written word. Onwards and upwards to the church of St. Mary, where Hilda and Caedmon set their seal on history with poems and peacemaking.

If you believe in angels, then this is the place to be. Sit in the boxed pews, close your eyes and listen to the proclamation of the centuries that has burnt in the hearts of so many people. In these seats, people have lamented over the loss of a loved one, given thanks for new birth and the joining of lives. Some, they say, have even sat in the company of angels who come to this place dressed as strangers, bringing with them a light to the world that the darkness will never overcome.

This is the place of *Shadowmancer* . . .

G. P. Taylor

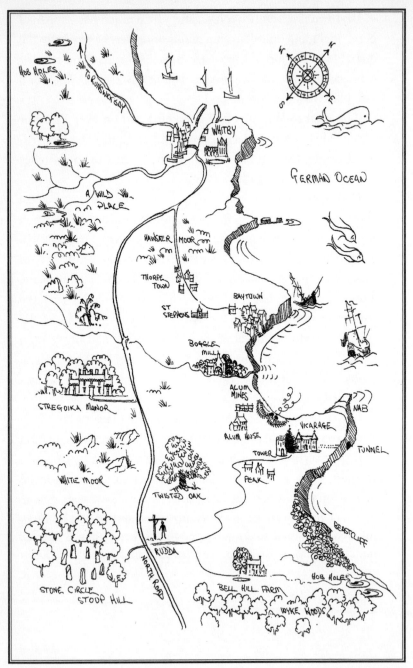

The Dark Storm

It was a still October night. On the cliff top the harvest was gathered in and sheaves of corn were stacked together to form peculiar straw houses. A bright silver moon shone down on a calm sea. In the distance the silhouette of the *Friendship*, a collier brig, could be seen picked out against the waves. The sails of the ship looked like the flags of a small army preparing for war.

The brilliance of the full moon penetrated the darkest depths of the wood that gripped the tops of the cliffs. A small, darkly clad figure in a frock coat and knee boots stumbled along, carrying a long black leather case, timidly following a tall, confident man with long flowing white hair.

Nearby, a fox lay hidden in the undergrowth, dreaming of fresh rabbit, when suddenly it was woken by the panic of a deer bolting from the cover of a holly bush and running deeper into the darkness of Wyke Woods.

"What was that?" The small man was startled and his voice jumped and quivered. He dropped the leather case in fright and clutched at the cloaked figure that he had followed so closely through the autumn night. *"It's there,"* he squealed. "I can see it, it's in the trees."

His companion grabbed him by the ear. "Keep quiet, Beadle. The world doesn't need to hear your voice."

The small man pinched his eyelids together as he tried to peer into the darkness and hide in his companion's cloak at the same time. Beadle didn't like the darkness and he hated the night. Bravery was for other people, and the night was to be spent by the fire of the inn, listening to stories of faraway places, the news of war in other lands and of smuggling, while drinking warm, frothy beer.

Here in the wood on the top of the cliff was a different world for Beadle, a world where he did not belong. The wood was the place of boggles, hedge witches, hobs and *thulak*. Beadle feared the thulak more than anything. They were strange, invisible creatures of the dark. They could steal upon you at night, smother you in a dark mist and take from you the will to live. There were stories that they would creep through open windows and come into houses to cover an unsuspecting sleeping victim like a dark blanket. Once the victim was seized, he couldn't move. They would take his strength and fill his mind with horrifying, hideous thoughts. These were the thulakian dreams that would be with him for the rest of his life. They would leave their victims listless and heavy-limbed, with sunken eyes from the sleepless nights spent fearing their return.

Beadle grasped his companion's cloak even tighter as a gentle breeze rustled the brown, crisp leaves in the trees.

"Is it a man or is it . . . them?" He could hardly say the words; his right leg shook, his eyelids twitched, his mouth went dry and his tongue stuck to the roof of his mouth.

"Them?" hissed his companion in his face. "Who are *them*? Can't you say the word? What are you frightened of?"

Beadle hunched his shoulders and buried his face in the musty black cloak of his tall, angry companion. "Thulak," he whispered feebly, trying to muffle his voice so they would not hear him.

His companion raised both his hands and cupped his mouth like the bell of a trumpet; he took in a deep breath and with a voice that came from the depths of his soul, he bellowed: "Thulak. Thulak. Thulak." The voice echoed around the woods; the fox scurried from the brush and ran deeper into the undergrowth.

A roost of the blackest rooks lifted from the trees above their heads and their *caw-caw-caw* filled the night sky as they circled above the branches, dancing in the moonlight.

". . . *No*," whispered the now terrified Beadle. "Please, Parson Demurral, don't say that word, they will hear and they will come and get us, my mother said—"

He was hastily interrupted.

"*Us*, Beadle? Did you say *us*?" Demurral towered over the cowering, frightened form of his servant. "I fear nothing and no one, and they have every reason in the world to fear me. Tonight, my little friend, you will see who I really am and you will not say a word to anyone. I control creatures that are far more frightening than the thulak. One word of what you see tonight and you will never dare to close your eyes again, or want to see the sun go down on another day. Now, come on, we have work to do; a ship awaits its fate and I await mine."

Demurral took Beadle by the collar and lifted him to his feet, dragging him down the path towards the sea. Beadle could not refuse. He had been servant to the Vicar of Thorpe for twenty years. On his eleventh birthday he had been sent to work for a penny a week, a bed in the barn, fresh straw and a Sabbath rest once a month. People said he was lucky—stunted, one leg withered, he was not much use to anybody. Demurral was a harsh master: He had a harsh tongue and an even harsher hand. Sometimes Beadle would creep into the back of the church and listen to his ranting from the pulpit. Hellfire, damnation, boiling cauldrons of molten blood, serpents and all things horrible that would await the unbeliever.

Beadle muttered to himself: "Blast, bother, boiling blood, this isn't a job; too dark, too cold, too many—"

Demurral butted in. "Stop your mumbling; there are things to be done. Drag that leg of yours a little faster. Maybe then we'll get to the stone before the ship passes." Beadle slipped in the mud as he tried to obey his master's command. "Be careful with the box, it took me a long time and a lot of my money to find what I've been looking for. Now be careful: We have to get down the waterfall before we find the stone."

Beadle knew that it had not been Demurral's money that had been used to buy the black box. Sunday by Sunday he had stolen from the villagers in rents and tithes.

He thought back to the night when the long black leather case had arrived at the Vicarage. Beadle had peered through the open crack of the study door, which hung very slightly ajar. For the first time in his life he had seen a man with a skin so black that it shone. Never before had such a trader been in these parts. The landlord of the Hart Inn had said that he had come from Whitby by carriage, the sole passenger on the brig *Whitehall*, which had docked the day before from Spain.

Beadle had watched carefully as the man opened the case and in the glimmering candlelight brought forth a long, shining pole as tall as Beadle himself. From the case the man then took a solid jet-black stone hand in the shape of a clenched fist. Into the grip of the fist he placed a silver dagger encrusted with two pieces of darkest jet.

It was then that Beadle saw something so beautiful that its image was impressed on his soul forever. The man brought out a black velvet bag from beneath his cloak and placed it gently on the desk. As the trader opened the bag, Beadle could make out two gold wings stretching back over a small statue. Before Beadle could see any more, Demurral quickly got up from the desk and slammed the door shut. He and his guest spoke in hushed tones. Beadle pressed his left ear to the door and listened.

The visitor spoke to Demurral in fluent English. "I have risked many things and come many miles to bring you this. It has powerful magic and they will stop at nothing to get it back. You are a brave man, Demurral. Either that or a rich fool."

Beadle heard his master laugh. "What I am, is what I am. Now take your money and go, and not a word to anyone. Fear not that which can destroy the body, but that which can destroy the soul." Demurral paused and then continued. "When does the other Keruvim arrive?"

Demurral's guest spoke softly. "It will not be long; they cannot be separated. The Keruvim will find you." Beadle heard footsteps coming to the door and hid himself behind the large curtain of the hall window.

Now, many nights later, Beadle and Demurral came out of the wood that covered the cliff path. The noise of the waterfall and the smell of the sea filled Beadle with a sense of excitement tinged with trepidation. Demurral lowered himself down the rope ladder at the side of the waterfall and then onto the shingle beach. Beadle tied a length of hemp cord onto the case and gently lowered it down to his master.

"Yes," cried Demurral. "It is almost time. Hurry, I can see her sails."

Beadle almost dropped the twenty feet to the shingle beach; he did not want to be left behind on the edge of the wood. A shudder ran up and through his spine and the hairs on his head stood on end. Thulak could be anywhere.

Demurral made his way to a large flat rock only a few feet away from the gently breaking waves. In the full light of the moon everything had a dark blue and silver glow; everything looked so cold.

He noticed that the rock was in the shape of an open palm, cupped to receive the sea. In the centre was a small carved hole. Three steps were cut into the side of the rock. The steps were too small for his feet, so he scrabbled up the stone on hands and knees.

"Come on, man!" shouted Demurral. "We have only minutes, then it will be too late." For the first time he allowed Beadle to see all that was in the case. "Stand back, Beadle, this is holy work. . . ."

Demurral took out the golden staff and placed the shaft into the hole in the centre of the rock. It was a pole made from the finest acacia wood and wrapped in bands of beaten gold. He quickly screwed in the black stone hand and placed the silver dagger in it. He knelt down and opened a long, narrow, concealed lid within the case. From the baize he took out a solid gold winged figure. Beadle giggled with excitement. In the light of the full moon the figure glowed with a ghostly radiance.

Demurral looked at Beadle and lifted the gold statue from the box. "This is a Keruvim. There are only two in the whole world. Now I have one and tonight I will have the other."

Beadle gazed at the beautiful creature as Demurral held it in his hand. It was the size of a barn owl, and had golden wings folded back along the length of its body and the head of a beautiful child with eyes of purest pearl.

"Stand aside, Beadle. Our work begins," Demurral said. He took hold of the golden staff and placed his left hand on the stone fist. He raised the Keruvim with his right hand, pointing it towards the sailing ship that silently cut through the night in full sail. Beadle saw the red and green lanterns for port and starboard bobbing up and down as the ship dipped and peaked in the gently rolling sea.

Demurral shouted out into the night. "Waves and wind, fire and water. Thunder, lightning and hail, hearken to my desire, hearken to my words. Come forth from the north and from deep below. Tempest, storm and ravaging wind, crash this boat to this shore, bring the Keruvim to me."

A single flash of the brightest, whitest light appeared to shoot out of the mouth of the Keruvim. It hit the sea and then deflected upwards until it touched the sky, making a loud crack like a bolt of lightning crashing to Earth.

Beadle jumped back in fear, lost his footing and fell from the stone to the shingle beach, landing on his back with a thud and a crunch.

For a moment he lay motionless. "What are you doing, Beadle? There is no time for resting. Get up, get up," Demurral snapped angrily.

Beadle lay on the shingle and quietly moaned. He placed his hand in the pocket of his frock coat and felt the broken shards and soft mess of the cold boiled egg that he had been going to eat for his supper.

All was silent. At first there was nothing. No movement, just the same calm as before. The sailing ship moved majestically through the rolling waves, cutting further and further to the north.

Then it began. First quietly, then louder and louder, from the depths of the sea a shrill and piercing singing was heard. At first it was faint like a whisper and then it grew stronger and stronger, heard not through the ears, but through the soul. From the deep black sea came a choir of Seloth. Graceful, flowing, feminine creatures that sang and swirled around the ship, woken from their sleep by the call of the priest.

Through the rigging, the sails and ropes, they swept around and around, singing louder and louder. Their sea-green hair trailed out behind them, long and billowing; their sightless eyes stared into the darkening night.

From behind the stone Beadle could hear their voices as they chanted and sang over and over again in ever more frightening tones. Beadle was too scared to look out from the safety of his hiding place and covered his ears, trying to stop the singing of the Seloth from driving him mad.

"What are they singing? It's piercing my brain like a hot knife. Tell them to stop."

Beadle pushed his face into a pile of damp seaweed, hoping to hide himself in its depths.

"It is the song of the deep. They are calling the dead to come to the feast. The Seloth will not stop until the ship is broken on the rocks. They want a sacrifice, not mercy," Demurral shouted above the wind and the waves, his eyes devouring the spectacle set before him. As they sang, the sea whipped higher and higher. Waves washed back and forth against the cliffs of Baytown, three miles to the north. Thick black clouds grew in the night sky and lightning exploded into the swell.

As the storm grew, the fishing boats anchored in the bay were dashed against the rocks that jutted out of the surf below the high cliff. The slipway of the town was awash; high into the main street the waves beat against the doors of the houses like the fists of the press-gang searching for menfolk to drag off to sea.

As the sea smashed against the steep rock, the cliff suddenly gave way and tons of mud and rock fell into the raging water. With the pounding of the storm the houses and shops of King Street crumbled and tumbled into the sea. As the buildings slid and toppled into the maelstrom, men, women and children were thrown from their sleep. In the dark of the night they cried out to be saved, but their screams for mercy could not be heard over the terrible thundering of the German Ocean.

Wisps of grey and blue fire broke through the swelling surf. Ghostly figures like giant white horses leapt from the waves that began to crash upon the shore.

The sky grew darker and darker and the full moon was blotted out by thick black clouds as streaks of lightning flashed from sky to sea, exploding in the water. A lightning sword hit the ship. The mainsail cracked, then crashed to the deck, sending startled crewmen bolting from their hammocks.

As they rushed on deck, another sail crashed down, splitting the deck in half and sending shafts of splintered wood into the air. The ship lifted and dropped with each wave; a crewman was thrown through the air and into the cold sea, never to be seen again.

"A direct hit," shouted Demurral, laughing and rubbing his hands together in glee at the sight. "One more strike and the Keruvim will be mine."

He raised the statue into the air and chanted more magic. "Wind, hail, lightning, thunder and wave." The sea rose at his command, each surge growing higher and higher. Breakers like black fists smashed against the ship, almost engulfing the vessel.

On the ship, the captain shouted to the crew: "Tie on. Tie on. We'll run for the beach. It's the only chance we have." He spun the ship's wheel and the brig lurched towards the shore.

The first mate struggled through the waves breaking on the

deck. He grappled with the broken rigging, pulled himself along the deck to the rear hatch and pushed it open.

He looked down into the darkness. There, staring back at him, was a young man with dark skin and bright white eyes.

"Take the empty barrels and tie yourself on, we're going down." He could just be heard over the roaring of the sea and the screaming of the Seloth.

As he spoke, a wave hit the stern of the ship, throwing the first mate crashing down into the hold. His head smashed against the floor. A large beam of wood slid the length of the hold and pressed him against a locker. As he lost consciousness, his face was submerged in the water. The youth took the barrels and with discarded rope from the sail-mender's locker tied them to the first mate. Thick salt water splashed against his feet as gallons of spray showered down through the open hatch.

"You all right down there?" the captain yelled into the hold. Then he turned to see a large wave looming above him. The sea was rising like a large mountain, higher and higher, coming closer and closer.

The biggest wave he had ever seen lifted the ship from the stern and tipped it over, end upon end, ripping out its very heart and spinning it through the spray towards the beach. It crashed the ship upon the rocks, splintering it like matchwood. The vessel cracked in two as the keel snapped. The sound of the breaking beam cut above the noise of the waves, echoing into the heart of the wood.

Seeing the ship in such distress, Demurral jumped up and down on the hand stone: "It's mine, all mine, I will have it tonight. Tonight, Beadle . . . tonight, I will have the Keruvim." Beadle looked up at Demurral and saw his face change. His eyes began to glow as wisps of green mist swirled around him.

"I will have both the Keruvim. They will be mine," Demurral repeated over and over. The black hand on the acacia pole began to glow brighter and brighter.

He thrust the pole towards Beadle. "See. The hand tells me

the Keruvim is coming closer. When I have it in my grasp, then the power of God will be mine. No more begging for a favour, clucking like a chicken at his altar. When I have the Keruvim, then he will have to listen to me."

Demurral shouted into the sky and jumped down from the stone to the gravel beach. In his hand he held the acacia pole. "Come on, Beadle, let us await the arrival of the Keruvim!" With that he grabbed Beadle by the ear and pulled him along the beach.

In the distance the *Friendship* lay broken on the rocks. The masts had snapped off. The sails and the rigging were torn from them, hanging like a gallows in the calming waters. The ship was broken open, exposing every deck to the torture of the sea.

The captain floated facedown in the water, gently buffeted by the waves. He was dead, like all the crew, including the first mate, although he had been kept afloat by the barrels. Their broken bodies bobbed in the ebbing tide as the Seloth gathered their souls, taking them back into the deep. The storm faded into the night, the dark clouds parted and the moon dulled as it set behind the hills to the west.

In the bay, pieces of the *Friendship* were washed ashore by the now gentle waves. Demurral walked up and down the beach, becoming ever angrier.

He screamed at the sea, "Come to me, my pretty, come to me." In his hands he held the acacia pole. The glow of the divining hand was beginning to fade.

Beadle followed his every step. "How do you know it was on the ship? How do you know it will be here?"

"It has to be here. It has to be tonight. There are only two Keruvim in the whole universe and they must be together. They will always find each other, that is the Law." Demurral looked out to the ship.

"What if it's gone down with the wreck? Gold doesn't float," Beadle asked.

"Then you, my friend, will have to learn to swim or you will go the same way as they have and the Seloth will feast on your soul as well." He pointed a long bony finger to the ship lying slaughtered on the rocks.

"Where are you? Come to me, come to me!" the priest shouted at the waves. The sea gave no reply. The wind was silent and the waves babbled over the shingle. Beadle followed Demurral along the beach, both men searching the tide for the Keruvim. It was nowhere to be found.

The Poisoned Angel

The following morning, as the waves crashed and rolled against the beach, a bright amber glow appeared to the north just above the horizon. The clouds were edged with a green tinge, and the fresh morning sun was glowing bloodred. It was as if the sky had been recoloured.

The villagers from Thorpe filled the beach, looking over the wreckage and taking whatever they thought useful. Obadiah Demurral, Vicar of Thorpe and all lands to the south, rushed into the centre of the gathering and jumped up on a small rock. He was now higher than the crowd that picked over the boxes, sails and smashed barrels littering the beach. Beadle, his servant, followed on behind, even more pained from the fall of the night before. The *Friendship* lay broken open a hundred yards from the shore in a gentle swell.

"Gentlemen, ladies, we stand in the midst of a great tragedy. Many fine men have lost their lives in this vessel, and we have to bury the dead of Baytown. Let us not become grave robbers." The crowd gathered around him and began to mutter and moan. Demurral spoke even louder.

"As Vicar of the parish I have the right of salvage. All this belongs to me."

"The whole world belongs to you, Vicar," a young boy with a pair of old boots hanging around his neck shouted out from the crowd, then, laughing, ducked down behind a burly fisherman.

The fisherman took him by the collar of his torn and tattered jacket and held him in the air. The collar ripped and the fabric split around the neck; the boy kicked at his shins. "Put me down, you barrel of fish bones!" he cried.

The fisherman spun him around by the scruff of his neck, released his grip and the boy slumped to the beach, slipping and falling backwards into a rock pool directly in front of Parson Demurral.

"Thomas Barrick," he roared. "I should have known it would be you. You're not only wet behind the ears, you're wet behind the rump as well."

The crowd laughed at the boy as he got to his feet and brushed the damp sand from the back of his trousers. He turned and began to walk away. Demurral continued to speak.

"Friends, let us treat all these things with great dignity. Take all you find to the Vicarage and I will make a correct record. We will hold a wreck sale on the quay at Whitby on All Souls' Eve. We will divide what we sell by the number here today." Demurral smiled as he spoke, but his face was closed and secret.

Like an obedient congregation, the villagers all nodded. The fisherman shouted up, "I agree with the Vicar, let's take what we can find and sell it on the quay." As he spoke, he nodded in approval of himself.

Thomas turned back and shouted at him: "You'd agree with the hangman before he dropped you through the trap. What you collect will not be what you sell." He looked across to Demurral. "Are you going to steal a tenth of this, like you do everything else?"

"Ignore this little vermin, he is only too lazy to help and too stubborn to want to. He'll be the one who loses, when all he's got is the bread dole." Beadle had surprised himself. He hadn't intended to speak; the words had just appeared in his mouth. The crowd cheered and Beadle pushed out his chest, suddenly feeling important. His ears began to glow and he twitched his nose with great glee.

Thomas picked up a smooth round stone from the beach.

"I don't mind work, Beadle. One more word from you and I'll knock that wart from the end of your nose. Where were you the night my mother was burnt out of the cottage?" He pulled back his arm, closed one eye and aimed the stone.

An old woman spoke softly and motioned with the back of her hand for Thomas to walk on.

"Be off with you, Thomas, this isn't the place and it isn't the way. Leave the Vicar to his business or you'll find yourself before the Magistrate."

"I'll be off, but you mark my words, that man has a plan and it's not one from God. It'll cost each one of you more than your life." His eyes filled with angry tears and he smashed the stone against the cliff.

Demurral smiled complacently at Beadle and said quietly: "He may throw stones, but he will find that I can cast shadows. It will not be long before the darkness gathers on his life."

Thomas turned and walked along the shingle towards a finger of mud and shale that jutted out of the cliff into the sea, separating the bay from Beastcliff. He scrambled up the shale, over the rock and into the cover of the wood. His anger burnt inside his head and he coughed back tears that he didn't want to cry.

Thomas Barrick was thirteen years old. He had lived all his life in Thorpe and had never been any further than Whitby. His father had been lost at sea in a great storm when Thomas was seven years old. He and his mother had lived on in the cottage rented from the church. It was more a stack of rooms than a house. It had one room down and another up, with a dry privy in the yard that they shared with three other cottages. The Vicar owned the villages of Peak and Thorpe. Every house, hostel, farm and shop paid him rent and tithes: One tenth of everything went to Demurral and the villagers never saw a penny back.

Thomas was now homeless. The death of his father and the sickness of his mother had left them unable to pay the rent, and with Demurral there was no charity. As he walked along the path through Beastcliff, he remembered how Demurral and his men had threatened that she would be out within the week if she couldn't pay.

Two nights later, just after dark, he had left the cottage to pick sea coal from the beach. From the shore he had seen the smoke. He ran back to the village and found the cottage burning brightly in the night air. Demurral and Beadle had just happened to be passing. His mother was sprawled in the back of Leadley's cart, covered in a blanket. Mrs. Leadley was by her side.

"Don't worry, Tom, she's all right. We'll take her to the infirmary. They'll look after her," she said.

Demurral had butted in. "Sorry, Thomas, you should have taken more care of my property. I'm afraid this is a clear breach of tenancy. You will both have to find somewhere else to live." He raised one eyebrow higher than the other. The side of his mouth twitched a pleasing twitch. "There is always room with my pigs."

"Pigs!" Thomas had shouted. "There is only one pig around here and that is the Vicar himself."

He grabbed hold of an old bramble to pull himself up. The spines stuck into his palm, but his bursting anger dulled the pain. He found the path through the wood that led across the back of the nab and then down into the bay.

He loved the bay. It was a place of adventure, with the finest sand and no shingle. It was shaped like a giant horseshoe set in the sea. At low tide there were wonderful rock pools full of seaweed, small fish and red crabs. It was a place of legend—chilling stories that went back to the dawn of time, tales of King Henry and Robyn of Loch Sley—framed by the high moor and the great sea.

For the past few weeks the bay had also been his home. Since the fire he had lived in a hob hole, a large cave in which the villagers believed the Hob of Thorpe lived. Every village had its own hob: a spirit that would take on the form of a small man. Hobs were little dark brown creatures with large eyes, small ears and tufts of black stubbly hair—just like Beadle. They possessed magical powers and would play tricks on the unwary and those who didn't leave them food or money.

15

The villagers at Peak said that Beadle was the son of a hob, that he had been conceived when his mother had fallen asleep on Beastcliff.

The hob always lived in a hole or cave in the sea cliff. It was said that they could cure all things from belly spots to whooping cough. The whooping cough had killed Thomas's older sister when she was two years old. She had whooped and coughed for several days and nights, then finally died. His mother had said it had smothered her spirit, taking away her life. Next time, she said, they would take a child to the Hob.

When Thomas was five, he had coughed his way through his fourth winter and fifth birthday on Lady Day and by Maundy Thursday was so sick, he couldn't walk. His father had carried him over to the Hob at Runswick Bay.

Thomas was covered in goose grease and brown paper and wrapped in a thick blanket. His father had set out to cover the eleven miles on foot with Thomas strapped to his chest. When they arrived at Runswick Bay, it was midafternoon. His father had stood on the beach in front of the hob hole and shouted the spell into the darkness.

"Hob! Hob! Lad's got hicky cough. Tak' it off, tak' it off, tak' it off." With that he threw a penny coin into the hole, lifted Thomas from the ground and slapped him on the back three times before pushing his head into the hole.

Thomas could still remember the sickening, musty smell. It was dark, damp and almost full of rotten food thrown in by the old woman who looked after the Hob. Thomas took in a deep breath and began to cough and cough and cough. He felt as though his breathing would stop. He coughed until he was sick. But he never coughed again.

Thomas had felt cheated. All that way and he hadn't even glimpsed the Hob. Surely it couldn't have been that small. There was barely enough room for his head down the hole, never mind a hob as well. By Easter Eve he had convinced himself that hobs did not exist—but he wondered why his cough had gone.

Now he was returning to his makeshift home deep in a real hob hole near the bay, thoughts of his mother's illness replacing the memory of his own. He had all that he needed: driftwood for a fire, bracken for a bed, candle stubs that he had stolen from Demurral and dole bread. As a pauper, he was allowed to collect the dole bread from St. Stephen's. Each week one loaf of bread was left for him in the cupboard at the back of the church. This was the only charity he got; the only charity he wanted. Thomas promised to himself that now he was settled, he would visit his mother.

Thomas knew that none of the villagers would come near the cave until All Souls' Day, for fear of the Hob. He hurried down the track and through the wood. It was a gentle slope to the beach. Soon the tree cover would break open and he would have a view of Baytown and the coast.

Suddenly he heard the sound of scratching against wood, like the noise of a large animal sharpening its claws. It rasped and chaffed at the bark of a tree to his right, higher up the cliff. He looked but could see nothing. Thomas knew there were no wild dogs in these woods, yet the sound came again, this time from behind him and getting closer. Whatever it was moved from tree to tree and scratched each one as it went by. It was like the sound of a farm cat scratching for mice at the barn door, only this time it was a louder and far bigger creature.

He shrugged his shoulders and pulled up his torn collar against the wind blowing through the trees. Then he heard the scream. It was a scream that almost burst his ears and took the breath from his body. Thomas began to run in fear to the caves.

Whatever was stalking him was getting closer. The path of Beastcliff was slippery from the morning frost, and as he ran downhill, he went faster and faster, jumping the knots of tree roots that burst through the path. Twenty yards ahead the path forked. To the right it went to the beach and the caves, straight on to the top of the nab and then the sea. He grabbed the bow of a small sapling and it flung him round and onto the beach path.

He laughed to himself and thought, I'll never be caught, by man or beast.

Suddenly in front of him, only a few feet down the path, he heard the scream again. Immense, unseen claws frantically rasped at the wood, gouging deep wounds into the soft flesh, shredding the bark of an oak tree to his left. All around him the light of day was being transformed into a deep black, sucked into a dark shape that now blocked his escape. The light of the sun was being stolen from the sky and pulled into a black shadow. A shadow that slowly and meticulously began to take the form of a large black animal.

Thomas felt that his feet were rooted to the ground with fear; beads of sweat dripped across his forehead. The animal began to take on form and substance, becoming almost solid in appearance, towering frighteningly above him. An aura of power surrounded the creature as the pulsating shadow reached out towards him.

Digging at the last of his strength, he turned and ran towards the nab. He was soon out of the trees and onto the narrow path that ran along the top of the rocky outcrop separating Beastcliff from the bay. He looked back to the wreck of the ship. The beach was now empty apart from a solitary figure dressed in clerical black, holding both arms above his head, in his hands a small figure that glinted in the morning light.

From the wood Thomas again heard the scream and the shredding of wood as the shadow creature got closer and closer.

There was no escape. He was trapped on the cliff top. Behind him were the creature and the forest; in front was the sea a hundred feet below. High above his head were the battlements of the Vicarage, the home of Demurral.

The bushes at the side of the path began to shudder as their branches were torn from the trunks and thrown into the air. The invisible beast was at the edge of the wood and only feet away from Thomas.

Thomas could feel the energy and life being sucked from his body. A thick mist surrounded him and began to wrap him tighter and tighter. His eyelids became heavy and all he wanted was sleep. He began to dream with his eyes wide open, yet he could no longer see the world or hear the sea. Dark shapes appeared, then vanished; disfigured faces in black cowls lurched at him, laughing and chattering through broken teeth. In his stupor he felt as if he was being lifted from his feet by the mist. A dark hand was squeezing his body so that he could hardly breathe. In his dream he could see his father on the night of the great storm. He was struggling in the sea as waves crashed over him, taking him deeper into the depths.

Through the blackness he saw something reaching out to him.

"Come to me, Thomas. Come to me. Take my hand; it will free you from the darkness." It was the rich, warm, loving voice of his dead father. "Fight, Thomas, like I told you how to fight."

Thomas limply raised his hand, fighting against the thick black cords of mist that gripped him in his weakness.

"I can't. . . . I want to sleep. Just to sleep." His voice ebbed away. He had no strength. He was being emptied of his life as the shadow creature swirled around him, binding him tighter and tighter.

There was a sudden thunderous explosion. The mist disappeared and Thomas felt his arms drop to his side. He could see the sky, then the sea, then the cliff. He was falling, crashing the hundred feet to the sea below.

The sea swiftly engulfed him and the ice-cold water burnt against his skin. Down and down he sank, surrounded by the swirling green of seaweed. He could feel the breath bursting in his lungs as he lashed out frantically with his arms and legs, grappling for the surface and the fresh October air. But he couldn't reach it. His feet were gripped in a mass of seaweed that covered the rocky seabed. He held his breath for as long as he could until his lungs threatened to burst. When he could hold his breath no more, he closed his eyes and breathed out, knowing there was no air to breathe in. He stopped struggling in the weed and rested in the waves, his long hair covering his face like a watery mask.

The Triptych

Thomas woke up in his hob cave. A warm fire glowed in the darkness and the smell of cooked fish greeted him. His clothes were hanging against the wall, drying by the heat of the fire.

"How?"

He spoke out quietly, his eyes looking around the cave he knew so well and where he had lived for the past few months.

"Who?"

There was a crunching on the shingles in the mouth of the cave and footsteps crept stealthily towards him. A dark shadow moved over the wall of the cave, growing larger. Thomas slid back under the tatty grey horse blanket and hid his head.

"You're awake, aren't you?" It was more of a statement than a question. Thomas slowly pulled the blanket down from his face and stared into the eyes of a young man with deep black skin and long hair that had been rolled into shoulder-length locks, glinting with drops of oil.

"Who are—?" But Thomas was interrupted by the smooth voice of the young man, who replied in perfect English.

"I am Raphah. I realized you were in trouble when I saw you fall into the sea. I pulled you from the weed." There was peace in his voice. He paused, smiled and said, "Welcome to my home." His bright eyes wandered around the firelit cave.

"This isn't your home," snapped Thomas. "It is my cave. I

found it before you. I've been coming here for years." He pulled the blanket closer to himself and stared at Raphah through narrowed eyes.

"Maybe I should have left you to the sea, then I could have lived here alone. I hope that not everyone in this place is as ungrateful as you; or are they worse?" Raphah laughed and turned the fish that was slowly cooking on long sticks held over the fire. "Do you want to eat, or are you still full of seaweed?"

Thomas was just glad to be alive. He thought back to what he had endured that morning and the forces that had tried to take his life. He thought of the creature that had chased him through the wood, and the sight of Parson Demurral on the beach. Raphah saw the distant look in his eyes.

"You think a great deal for someone so young. Why are you living here and not with your family?"

Thomas could feel tears welling up. "I can't live with them. I lost my home, my family, and I've no money, so I live here." He buried his face in the horse blanket and the smell filled his nostrils. Thomas had never seen anyone like this before. Raphah could have been fourteen or twenty. He had a glow of youth and an incredible smile that burst onto the world. He was dressed in a thick black smock coat, white shirt and knee-length boots. He looked like a highwayman or smuggler.

"Where are you from? I have never seen a . . ." He paused, not knowing what word would best describe him.

Raphah had seen that look many times before. It was the embarrassed, sometimes angry look as the onlooker surveyed the colour of his skin before speaking to him brusquely or ignoring his presence completely.

"I may not be the same on the outside, but I speak English . . . and many other languages." He paused. "I am from Cush. It is in a land that you call Africa. I want to return there as soon as possible."

He turned the fish on the spike again. The skin spat and hissed in the flames of the fire. "I am here to find something that

21

was stolen from my family; then I will return. Your sea is cold and your sun is too weak. That is why you must be so pale. Eat the fish and then I will show you a secret."

While Thomas was eating, Raphah pulled on a cord around his neck and took out an embroidered gold bag. He opened the top and from inside gently removed an ornate piece of dark jet, like a huge almond-shaped eye. He held the object towards Thomas.

"Where I am from, we are told that if we know the Spirit of Riathamus, our old men will dream dreams and young people will see visions. Look inside, little fish, and tell me what you see."

Thomas gazed into the depths of the stone. He saw the blackness slowly begin to transform into the brightest blue, like the opening up of the night sky at dawn.

His eyes were drawn deeper until the solid gold edges became the horizons of a new world. He could clearly see large stone build-ings like cathedrals rising out of thick forests. Enormous red and green birds circled round and around above the tall trees. Hundreds of people all like Raphah were gathered on the steps of the largest building. They were dressed in white linen robes with bright gold bands around their necks. The strands of their hair dripped with golden oil that glistened in the morning sun.

"These are my people." Raphah smiled as he spoke. "They are at the Temple. Meeting with Riathamus. He guides us in all things. It is he who has sent me here and he has brought you to help me. Caught like a fish." His laughter echoed around the cave, his shadow flickered against the walls and his face glowed in the amber light of the fire.

Frightened, Thomas broke his vision from the eye-stone and looked at Raphah.

"What are you? Are you a witch? Only witches can do that sort of thing." He raised himself up. "How do you know I will help you; and help you do what? I want nothing to do with witchcraft. They'll hang you for that." Thomas had a sudden swell of bravery. Raphah may have been older, but Thomas didn't care.

He decided that if Raphah were a witch, he would make a run from the cave, even without his clothes. He had begun to feel that this day was a dream from which he would soon awaken; a day in which he had been chased and half drowned and rescued by an African who could make people appear from jet stones.

Raphah smiled again. "I am not a witch, or a warlock, or a sorcerer. They are filled with wickedness. All I have is that which is given to me by Riathamus." Raphah looked into Thomas's eyes. "Look again, my little fish. This is the power of all goodness. He who is will show you."

Thomas could not look away. He felt the heat of the fire grow more intense; the driftwood burnt brighter. The warm blackness of the stone drew his eyes in. There, within the swirling dark mists, he saw two men, one white, the other black. They were running from the entrance of the Temple, down the steps and into the forest. The white man carried the most beautiful golden figure that Thomas had ever seen. As he ran, he wrapped the creature in his sweat-stained shirt and clutched the bundle to his chest. The forest then became awash with white breaking foam as the scene suddenly changed. Thomas was able to see the sails of a ship that blew back and forth in a full gale. Waves grabbed and plundered at a tall masted ship. The two men huddled in a cabin below deck, holding on to each other against the sea's rage. Again the stone changed the scene as the cabin faded to be replaced by a candlelit study. Thomas gasped. There, appearing in the eye of the stone, was a face that he knew too well.

"Demurral." Thomas shouted out the name. "Demurral."

"Do you know this man?" Raphah had an urgency in his voice. "Tell me—I must know. Do you know him?"

For the first time in their brief encounter, Thomas noted a change in his companion. Raphah looked as if he was waiting for some urgent and unwelcome news.

"He is the man that I seek, he has something that was stolen from my people." He tried to remain composed, but it was easy for Thomas to see the concern that burnt through his eyes.

"I know him," Thomas replied. "He has stolen from so many people, so many times, that it comes easily to him." There was bitterness in his voice for the years of misery that Demurral had inflicted on his family. "I hate him, I hate him so much that I could kill him like he tried to kill my mother." He spat out the words. "He calls himself a man of God. Anyone who knew God wouldn't act that way. With all his cheating and lies, I say he is the spawn of Satan. He has the whole village in his power and wants to control every one of us."

Raphah was quick to reply. "It is more than this village that he wants to control. If he has his way, and if what is stolen is put to work, then he could control the world and even the power of Riathamus for himself."

Thomas knew nothing about Riathamus, neither did he care. But he had waited a long time to get his own back on the Reverend Demurral, and he sensed that here was an opportunity for revenge. Thomas prided himself on his ability to fight, catch fish and plunder the hiding places of the smugglers of Baytown without them knowing. He knew every inch of the village and the passages under the Vicarage. Whatever Demurral had stolen, he would steal back. Thomas gazed into the embers of the dying fire, trying to keep his thoughts to himself.

"So you will help me, I know you will." Raphah was excited. "Who is this Demurral? Tell me all and then we will plan." Raphah thrust out his strong black hand, grabbed hold of Thomas's wrist before he had time to reply and stared into his eyes.

"First we bind ourselves to the thing that we do. This Demurral is not a servant of God, and he will do all in his power to destroy us both. We fight principalities and powers, spirits and demons. Demurral is more than just a man, he is a speaker to the dead—a Shadowmancer."

The grip on Thomas's arm grew tighter as Raphah's smile grew wider.

"Now I will speak with Riathamus. Close your eyes."

Thomas was given no option. This was a command and not a request. There was something powerful about Raphah, something that Thomas could not resist, nor did he want to. All he cared about was the increasing numbness in his hand from Raphah's strong grip and the smell of his scorching trousers on the fire. To obey would mean that he could save his hand and, with any luck, his trousers. He crunched his eyes shut, but tried to keep them open just a crack so he could see what would happen.

Raphah began to speak in a voice deeper and stronger than before. "Lord Riathamus . . . Creator of all that is good . . . fill us with your Spirit."

He shouted out and the cave echoed with the power of the words. Thomas opened his eyes to see what looked like tongues of fire leaping around the chamber. A whirlwind blew round the cave, blasting his bedding and supplies into the air. It was like standing in the eye of a storm, whilst all around was chaos. In the centre of the cave floor the fire burnt even brighter, whilst all around, his books, candles, bread and blankets danced and swirled in the air. He held on to Raphah for as long as he could, then without thinking stepped back into the tornado. He was lifted from his feet and thrown back against the damp, slimy wall. His body shook.

Tears welled up in his eyes and he began to sob. As he lay motionless on the floor of the cave, it was as if unseen hands untwisted the knot of emotions in his chest that he had carried for so many years. All the anger for his father's death, his hatred towards the world and his fear of dying—all began to melt and leave him. Thomas could not understand what was happening. The musty smell of seaweed, damp walls and fish skins was replaced by the overwhelming fragrance of the meadow harvest. In the darkness of the cave he felt as if the heat of the summer sun was gently warming him.

He could hear Raphah speaking to him from far away.

"Don't fight this. Allow Riathamus to touch your heart, he knows how much you hurt. He knows the sadness of your life. In Riathamus we can all find peace."

Thomas felt the warmth of Raphah's hand on his forehead. It soothed like the nettle bandages that his mother made. The heat from Raphah's palm became more and more intense; it radiated through Thomas's whole body. He didn't fight; he allowed the experience to go on and on for what seemed like hours of blissful peace. Is this more witchcraft? he thought to himself, half-dreaming.

As if he knew Thomas's thoughts, Raphah replied, "No, there is no fear in this. This is not made by man or conjured from the darkness. There is no power within me; it is a gift from the Creator to you. Take it. . . . Breathe it. . . . Allow this time to last." His words echoed deep into Thomas's mind. They were restful, bringing with them sleep and dreams.

Raphah covered him with the horse blanket, put more driftwood on the fire, sat back and closed his eyes.

The noise of the crashing sea pulled them from their dreams. Thomas woke first and in the half-light of the embers of the fire, he got dressed. His trousers were crisp and hot and smelt of salt water. Raphah opened his eyes and his smile exploded like the sun. "Did you dream?"

Thomas could hardly contain his newfound feeling of joy. "I dreamt of many things, my father . . . mother . . . yesterday. It was all so real. I feel as if my body has wings." Thomas paused, his smile drained from his face as he remembered the vision. "I dreamt of Demurral. I know why you are here and what you are looking for. He has the creature I saw in your stone. . . . He tried to use it against you."

"Fear not, it was only a dream, but we are given dreams to warn us of what is ahead and also what is in our hearts." Raphah got up from his makeshift bed of bracken on the floor of the cave. "Dreams are a shadow of the future or of ourselves; they are never to be feared but embraced and used for our good." He placed his hand on Thomas's shoulder. "Where does Demurral live? Is it near?"

Thomas thought of the quickest way from the cave to the Vicarage. "It's about three miles, but if you don't mind the dark, we can make it two if we go through the tunnel from the wood."

He knew the tunnels from the nights when he had helped his father load casks of smuggled brandy, silk and tobacco that had been brought ashore by small boats. His father had been a fisherman, a hard and poor life that he supplemented by the occasional trip offshore to a French schooner from which he would return with wonderful things. Demurral had taken his cut, even from this. "Storage fee," he called it. There was no brandy for the parson or baccy for the clerk. No. Demurral wanted his cut in hard cash, in gold or silver.

Tonight, thought Thomas, Demurral's greed will lead to his downfall.

"Then it's through the tunnel," said Raphah. "Not a moment to waste."

In the entrance to the cave the soft blue light of the full moon illuminated the stones that led out onto the sandy beach. In the northern sky Thomas could see the amber glow; although he thought it was bright, it didn't cast much light, leaving the night dark and menacing.

The air was fresh and clear—such a change from the must and smoke of the cave. They walked quietly through the wood. Thomas avoided the path where he had met the thulak and took Raphah along the edge of the cliff.

They began to climb the slope away from the bay and towards the Vicarage that dominated the cliff top on the headland at Peak. The trees reached over their heads like the knotted fingers of old hands. Crisp leaves dropped to the floor in the gentle breeze of the night and rustled in the undergrowth. The call of an old owl, deep and husky, broke the silence and the dry branches of the trees clashed against each other.

Thomas stepped from the path and dropped into a small gully that was blocked by a holly bush. He pulled back the spiky growth, revealing the entrance to a tunnel. It had been cut into the rock just wide enough for a man to carry a brandy barrel through without tearing the flesh from the back of his hands.

"This way." Thomas spoke as quietly as possible, but the owl burst from the tree with a loud shout. Without any warning, a small figure leapt out of the darkness at Thomas and Raphah, grabbing them both by the throat and pushing them facedown onto the ground. They lay side by side in the wet bracken and grass, the smell of cold earth pushed up their nostrils and the heel of a boot embedded in the back of their necks. They had been ambushed and were now captured.

"Stand and deliver, your money or your life. What's it to be, musket ball or knife?" There was the familiar click of the hammer of a pistol being pulled back, and Thomas felt the cold ring of the steel barrel pushed against the back of his head.

"Give us yer money, Barrick, or your friend takes the lead." It was a girl's voice and one that Thomas knew.

"Get off my back, Kate Coglan, or I'll whip your backside from now till next Friday and harder than your father does." He tried to move, but the full weight of the girl fixed him to the floor.

"Where have you been, Thomas? It's Monday. I bring you supper on a Monday. I've been waiting for hours." There was another click as the hammer of the pistol was allowed to fall without igniting the powder.

"I've had a visitor. I'm taking him to see Demurral. Now, are you going to let me up?" Kate Coglan jumped from their backs and sat on a tuft of broken-down bracken.

"Who's your friend? He's not one of us."

Raphah got to his feet and brushed the dirt from his tunic.

"I am certainly glad I am not one of you. I've been in this country for less than a day and have had welcome that has been neither gracious nor friendly." He stopped speaking and looked her up and down. "May I say that for a girl you look incredibly like a man." Raphah pointed in the moonlight to the trousers and boots she was wearing. Kate Coglan was definitely a girl, a defiant girl, a brash girl, but nonetheless a girl.

Thomas stood between them. He knew that Kate would be on her feet, with her fists ready to bring dark bruises to dark skin.

"What's with the pistol, Kate? Taken to highway robbery?"

"Borrowed it from my father—he'll be as drunk as a skunk by now, so he won't know it's gone. Brought it to blast any of them shadows or boggles, or anything else that may get in the way." She aimed the pistol at Raphah. "Are you a shadow or don't you wash? Never seen one like you before."

"He's from Africa and he has saved my life, so that's enough of your piggery." Thomas felt the sharp edge of her words. They were reckless words that pierced like a sword. He looked at Raphah.

"Don't worry, Thomas, I have heard much worse and from far more frightening people than a girl in man's clothing." Raphah grinned. "Take pity. From the way of her dress she has problems of her own." Raphah winked at Thomas and they both bowed to Kate.

"Enough," Kate shouted at them both. "Let's start again." She paused and then smiled. "I'm Kate; you know Thomas. So who are you?" She stood up from the bracken, put the pistol in her belt and held out her right hand.

"My name is Raphah. I am from Africa. It is good to start again." He reached out. Kate felt the soft warmth of his hand, and their eyes met. Thomas broke the moment.

"We're going thieving from Demurral. He has got something from Raphah's family and I'm going to help him get it back. Are you up for coming? That pistol of yours would be a handy signal—you could keep watch here so we can make our escape."

Kate reached into the holly bush and threw a muslin bag at Thomas. "Maybe. First, here's your supper. Bread, cheese and ginger cake—better eaten now than later."

They sat in the hollow and shared the food. Raphah spoke of the voyage and the shipwreck. Kate chattered and filled the night air with her questions. The full moon slowly began to set behind the distant hills. The three shadows sat in the grassy hollow of the woodland glade. Thomas got to his feet and went to the base of the holly bush. He dug the toe of his boot into the earth. The soil gave way to wood as he uncovered the top of a barrel buried near to the entrance to the tunnel.

"We need some light, so let there be light." He bent down and squeezed his fingers under the tight lid, pulling back the wooden flap and reaching in.

"Sorry, Kate, there are only two lamps in here. Never mind, you have eyes like a cat." He set the wick and fired the tinderbox that he had found in the very bottom of the barrel. The forest was lit with a brilliant amber light from the storm lamps.

Kate placed the lid back on the barrel.

"We don't want to leave any tracks and I don't want my father to know I have been here." Her father was the Revenue man. He patrolled the coast from Whitby to Hayburn Wyke, looking for smugglers; at least for those who had forgotten to pay him his cut of brandy. Such was the life of the moors and the coast. A thin veneer separated law from disorder, good from evil, and this world from the next. At least for tonight she knew her father would be so drunk that he would neither know nor care where she was.

"Don't hang about; I don't want to be here all night." Kate gestured for them to get going. She drew the pistol from the belt and cocked the hammer.

Thomas replied, "Keep your powder dry and the muzzle trained and shoot anyone that tries to come in after us."

He was beginning to feel that this was no longer a game; it was real. This was life or death.

Raphah and Thomas set off into the dark of the tunnel. They could hear the water dripping from the roof. With each step the air got colder and colder; the light from the lamp shone only a few feet and cast eerie shadows on the wall. Thomas listened to each noise, fearing the creature from the wood, or finding the secret hiding place of a hob or boggle.

"Do you know the way, little fish?" Raphah spoke in a whisper.

"We keep to the left-hand tunnel. That is where we always put Demurral's money. There's an empty stone jar by an iron door. When we find that, we find the way into the cellar of the Vicarage and then our problems begin."

Raphah was quick to whisper his reply. "Be sure of this: The wicked will not go unpunished, but those who are righteous will go free." The words, though spoken in a whisper, echoed through the tunnel. They walked through the biting cold for ten minutes. The dark smell of dankness grew stronger and stronger. Thomas's feet crunched through the rubble on the tunnel floor. He looked down and realized he was walking on the bones of a dead deer. Its head and antlers fell to one side of the floor.

"It must have got lost. There are miles of caves and tunnels down here. That's why the smugglers use them; once in here, if you know your way, you will never be caught."

"Ah yes, but if you don't know your way, then you may become as dead as the deer." Raphah spoke, hoping that his words would never come true. He felt the weight of the task firmly on his shoulders. It was he who was responsible for Thomas and now Kate. They had been brought into his life to help him. He had to keep them safe.

High above, in the Vicarage, Obadiah Demurral sat at the large oak desk of his study, surrounded by dusty books. Across the front of the desk was the acacia pole, wrapped in bands of pure gold. To the right was the winged figure of the stolen Keruvim. In the gentle candlelight of the room, the jet hand began to glow. At first it glowed softly and was hardly noticeable, but with each second it pulsed brighter and brighter.

There was a knock at the door. Demurral awoke from his snoozing. "Yes, come in."

Beadle entered carrying a tray of neatly cut pieces of meat, the end of a loaf of bread and an exceedingly large chalice of red wine. "Your supper, Master."

"On the table over there, then go." He spat the reply at Beadle.

"Master?" whined Beadle.

"Go, Beadle, now!" he shouted.

"Master . . . it's the hand."

"There's nothing wrong with my hand. Get out, before I slam it on the back of your head." He picked up the bread loaf and launched it at Beadle, hitting him in the left eye, sending crumbs across the room.

Undeterred, Beadle tried again, but this time put both arms over his head for fear of wine, or cheese, or both being launched at him. "Master, the . . . black . . . hand . . . is . . . glowing."

"What!" cried Demurral as he launched the wine into the air above his head. He turned to see the hand, now burning, now almost white-hot.

He ran to Beadle and hugged him into his waist, rubbing the wart on Beadle's nose into his belt buckle. "Quickly, let us prepare a welcome for our guest. I knew it didn't go down with the ship and now it has come here. Blessing be to Pyratheon, dark god of the universe."

"What shall I do, Master?" Beadle scurried around the room, picking up pieces of the shattered loaf and using them to mop up the wine.

"Go to the cellar and bring me the Hand of Glory. Quickly— we haven't got much time." Demurral could not wait and they both raced to the cellar. From a large oak chest Beadle removed the hand, wrapped in a black silk cloth. It was the severed hand of a hanged murderer dipped in wax so that each finger could be lit like a candle. Once it had been lit, anyone in the house would be put into a deep sleep until the candle was blown out. All were affected except the one who carried the hand. Demurral took it and lit the little finger. "Leave, Beadle, or you too will fall under the spell."

Demurral turned and went towards the metal door that led to the tunnel. From a lamp on the wall he lit the thumb and the remaining fingers. They hissed and spat as the spell began to charm the darkness. He pulled open the stiff metal door and the light from the hand broke through the blackness. Demurral stepped into the tunnel.

"Welcome, my friends, welcome to my home. Come, eat with me and we will share the wonders of this night."

Thomas and Raphah pressed themselves to the side of the tunnel walls and tried to merge with the dampness.

Demurral spoke again. "Come, come, now, don't be so shy, I know you are near. I will never harm you." He gave a one-sided smile and raised his eyebrow to cover the lie. From their hiding place they tried not to breathe for fear he would hear them.

"If I can't find you . . ." He paused and thought. "Then maybe a thulak will prise you from your hole."

In the cold of the tunnel, beads of sweat dripped across Thomas's forehead. Raphah sensed his fear and reached across to hold his hand. He looked down and noticed that the lamps were beginning to fade. Soon they would be plunged into darkness.

The Oak King

Kate Coglan was hidden in the holly bush, waiting for them at the entrance to the tunnel, surrounded by the darkness. She always said that she feared nothing. She didn't believe in ghosts, creatures of the night or God himself. Her father had beaten all her belief from her. To her father she had to be the nearest thing to a son. The son who had died two years before Kate was born. It was a death that was never spoken of and only marked by a small stone high in the cliff-top graveyard, mother and son together in death as in life.

Kate always wore thick knee breeches, long boots and a heavy jacket, topped with a tricorne hat. Her long hair was tied back in a ponytail, but her wide blue eyes and glowing skin gave away the fact she was a girl.

As for ghosts, well, Kate was convinced they didn't exist. In her fourteen years she had never seen a single one and what she had never seen could never hurt her. Why fear the invisible when all the hurt and pain in her life was caused by those around her? She had often asked her father about life and death. This had been ignored, either by silence or the back of his hand. He had told her over and over that all that you can see in life is all there is. When she was a young child, he would shake and shake her if she asked about her mother. He would shout drunkenly that she was dead and that was it, never to be seen again, covered by the sod of earth and left to the worms. He would scream: "If there was a God, why would he take my son, then my wife? Loving God . . . God of the imagination . . . Crutch for the weak . . ."

Kate would cover her head and curl up in the corner of the room as in his anger he threw what furniture they had around the house. He would then sob and sob and hold on to Kate in his grief, but she could never cry. All the crying was locked away, buried deep in her soul like the distant and faded memories of her mother. Kate had set her face like flint. She would allow nothing and no one to harm her, and now with a pistol in her hand she wanted to take on the whole world.

Looking out from behind the holly bush, she aimed the cocked pistol into the darkness. She could hear the echoing, muffled shouts of Demurral cascading through the murky blackness and out of the mouth of the tunnel. She knew his voice well. In her hiding place she thought of Thomas and Raphah, and with each shout from high inside the labyrinth she grew more concerned.

In the gloom of the forest her eyes began to make strange shapes out of everything she looked at. A tree appeared to change into a giant's head, a cloud looked like a swan fixed against a star and a small tuft of grass took on the shape of a hedgepig that seemed to crawl through the wood. Kate stared into the night. Then froze. The night was staring back at her!

There in the glade, just several feet away from her, five pairs of bright red eyes were gazing towards the holly bush. Kate felt the palms of her hands begin to sweat as sudden panic gripped her tightly. She dared not move for fear that they would see her. She dared not swallow for fear that they would hear her. Even at such close a distance, she could not make out any shape of the creatures, just red staring eyes. If they were smugglers, then this was the best disguise she had ever seen. She had certainly not heard their arrival; they had simply appeared.

As she looked on, Kate saw a silver outline begin to appear around each figure, like millions of tiny sparks jumping in a fire. Brighter and brighter they glowed. Then all the sparks began to draw closer together. They rolled around each other as if propelled by some unseen wind blasting the embers of a fire. As they burnt brighter, they changed from silver, to red, to green, to blue. Finally, and as quickly as they appeared, they vanished. Kate stared fearfully into the night. Her gaze was transfixed by what was before her.

There, standing in the glade, were five tall figures dressed from head to foot in metal armour. Each wore a burnished helmet in the shape of a snake's head, with glistening eyes that shone like diamonds. Two large ivory fangs stabbed down to the front of each helmet like the sabre teeth of some long-extinct creature.

The breastplates of the armour outlined every muscle; a long metal spine ran to the elbow of each arm, where it was joined to a thick leather gauntlet. In between each piece of metal, Kate could see the skin of the creatures. Dark green and lifeless, it had an eerie glow that almost merged with the night. Around each waist hung a thick black leather belt, onto which was strapped what looked like a short sword with a black leather grip. The smallest of the creatures carried a round shield studded with silver, inset with glowing red jewels.

From her hiding place she could not make out the features of their faces. She could see only the bright red eyes still staring towards her. Kate aimed the pistol directly at the head of the largest creature. She took in a slow and silent breath. She was terrified. A voice inside her head screamed, *Pull the trigger!* She was unable to move, rigid with fear, petrified as a statue.

The voice screamed at her again. *Pull the trigger!*

Again she could not move. The weight of the gun began to tug against her hand as if it was being pulled from her grip. All Kate wanted to do was run and scream. She knew she would get only five paces before being caught. She knew that if she moved her hand or lowered the pistol, the creatures would hear her. Kate summoned every ounce of strength to hold the pistol in front of her. She could feel the muscles in her arm begin to ache, the pain reaching from the tips of her fingers to her shoulders. She wanted to cry, she wanted to go home. Again the voice cried in her head.

Pull the trigger. . . . Pull the trigger.

Now trembling with fear, Kate tried to squeeze the trigger, but her finger wouldn't move. A numbing coldness began to claw its way up her arm, as if she were being slowly turned to stone.

The creatures gathered together and began to mutter and chant in a language she could not understand. They snorted and grunted to each other, drawing closer to form a circle.

She knew that she had only moments before she would drop the pistol. Suddenly from within the depths of the tunnel came an earsplitting scream. Kate knew that this must be Thomas. The scream was quickly followed by the sound of someone running frantically down the walkway back to the entrance.

As he ran, Kate could hear his echoing screams. *"No, no, no!"* They were the shrieks of someone in fear of his life, of someone running from the presence of evil. They were getting closer by the second.

Kate was not the only one to hear the screams coming towards them. The creatures turned and faced the entrance to the tunnel, their eyes glowing even brighter than before, with gusts of green steam vaporizing in the cold night air as they blew out each expectant breath through their nostrils. Without any word of command they drew their swords at the same time. Then, they silently melted away and hid in the thick cover around the glade, their piercing red eyes shining like large fireflies in the under-growth.

Kate could hear Thomas shouting for help as he ran towards her. The shrill echoes of his cries billowed out of the tunnel like the sound of some sleeping monster awoken from its sleep. There was no way of warning him of what lay in wait. Kate felt that he was escaping one nightmare to be captured by another.

Thomas fell out of the mouth of the tunnel and into the cold grass of the glade. He rolled over, then stood up panting and shouted out urgently.

"Kate, come out, Demurral is coming. He's chanting some kind of magic. Come on," Thomas called into the night. Kate did not reply. From where she was, she could see the eyes of the creatures looking at Thomas from their hiding places. She wanted to speak, but an even stronger fear gripped her throat like some dark cold hand.

Paralysed, she looked at Thomas, only a few feet away. He was her friend whom she had known since she was a young child. They had grown up together, played together, fought together. She was closer to him than any living thing. Beyond, she could see the creatures waiting for their moment to strike.

"Come on, Kate, stop your fooling. I know you're hiding," Thomas said. "We've got to be quick, Demurral isn't far behind. Come out, Kate," Thomas shouted desperately.

He saw a dark shape in a small clump of grass close to the edge of the glade. He could see the outline of a shoulder and the side of an arm. In the bright starlight he could vaguely see the glinting of polished metal.

"Got you this time. Put the pistol away. I know it's you."

The figure did not reply or move. He took a step closer and kicked at the clump.

"Get up, you vagrant, we've got to be going—sharpish. He's only a couple of minutes behind. We've got to climb up to the Vicarage."

Thomas, wanting to get Kate to follow quickly, kicked at the clump again.

A pair of bright red eyes flashed upon him, lighting up his face in a dim glow. The armoured figure began to rise up, higher and higher. Thomas followed the eyes, transfixed, as the creature began to tower above him until it reached eight feet in height. He heard the sound of the other creatures as they stepped from their hiding places in the wood and moved in the crisp grass towards him. He saw that the glinting metal was a short sword. The spectre quickly raised the sword above its head and gave a loud, shuddering roar. Thomas could feel himself being pushed to his knees by an unseen force as he dropped to the wet grass. He waited for the sword to come crashing down.

The forest fell silent, a strange peace descended upon him. All around was still. In his heart there was no fear. Thomas no longer wanted to run or to struggle. He bowed his head and awaited the blow. The moment lasted a lifetime. He never thought that this would be the place where he would die. He had always believed that he would be given to the sea, like his father before and so many of his family. To die at sea was an expectation. He had worn a caul from an early age, given to him by his mother. It was a sign of great luck and a protection from drowning. It was the only thing of value that Thomas had. Worth six guineas and not a penny less. But how could a dried-out membrane of his birth mask, kept in a silver locket, have any power over swords?

He could hear the short breaths of the creature and he was surrounded by the cold mist that fell from its nostrils. With each of its breaths, like the ticking of a clock, he waited for the sword to fall and take his life.

He felt that they were waiting for the perfect moment for his execution, as if in the silence someone would issue the command and the blade would fall. Thomas waited. The presence of the beast brought with it a chilling grip and the slow paralysis of numbing cold. All around he could see the dew-covered grass turning to thick hoarfrost. Each leaf and blade of grass was being outlined in white ice crystals as the creatures breathed the icy mist into the glade.

The cold grew so intense that Thomas could hardly breathe as he felt the moisture in his throat turning to ice. He crumpled forward and fell at the feet of the beast, his hands taking hold of the twisted metal of the bronzed leg armour. Here, at the moment he touched the creature, he could see into its world. In a few brief seconds it was as if his mind had been opened by some unseen key.

Thomas suddenly knew their name and their purpose. These were the Varrigal! In his mind's eye Thomas could see the cold barren land that they were from. It was a place of darkness and storm, blizzard and thunder. A grey, formless world of waiting. They were neither dead nor truly alive, but just being, awaiting the control of some unknown master. The Varrigal were a race of warriors, bound in time and charm to the awaker of the dead. Bound to him who knew the forgotten incantations.

A sudden explosion shook Thomas from his trance. Its thunder went on for an eternity, blowing heat across the back of his neck and filling the glade with brilliant light. He heard the loud and sudden thud of lead against metal and felt a tremor that shook the Varrigal from head to foot. The short sword dropped to the ground, missing his head by an inch, landing crisply into the now frozen ground, cutting through it with ease. The creature buckled at the knees and began to fall forward.

"Thomas, run!" Kate shouted from her hiding place in the holly bush.

The Varrigal crashed to the ground as Thomas quickly rolled away, grabbing the sword from the earth with numbed fingers as he got to his feet, pulling himself from the cold earth. He lashed out into the darkness with the sword, landing a blow to the back of the beast that had stepped towards the place where Kate was hiding. The sword cut through the armour like a hot knife through butter. The Varrigal fell to the ground howling and hissing. The other spectres turned to Thomas, raising their swords to strike at him.

"Kate, come on. We'll run for Boggle Mill," Thomas shouted as Kate crashed through the bush and into the glade. "Run, Kate, run."

A Varrigal thrust at Thomas with his sword. Thomas struck a blow, sword on sword, green sparks flashing into the night. He and Kate began to run. He had never run so swiftly. He dragged Kate by her arm to pull her faster. They both crashed through the bracken as it grabbed at them like so many sharp fingers.

From the glade they could hear the Varrigal screaming to each other. Then there was silence. It was a silence broken only by the pounding of their feet as they fled along the path, deeper into the wood. They ran blindly through the trees along a small deer track that took them from the glade towards Boggle Mill. They had covered nearly a mile. Thomas stopped, his lungs bursting as he gasped for air; he could go no further. Together they slumped against the trunk of a large oak tree. Here in the wood the only thing that Thomas could hear clearly was the *thump-thump-thump* of his beating heart. He looked at Kate, who tried to smile and hold back tears at the same time.

"What were they, Thomas? They had me frozen," she whispered, gulping for breath and fearful of being heard.

"Whatever they were, I know that Demurral had something to do with them." He tried to smile at Kate. "It was a good shot, it saved my life." Thomas gently touched her face. She was still so cold. "Come on, we're only a couple of miles from Boggle Mill, we can hide out there."

"What about Raphah? Are you going to leave him behind?"

"No. It was all part of the plan," he panted, still short of breath. "When we got to the secret entrance to the Vicarage, Demurral appeared holding some kind of burning hand and muttering curses. The lamps were flickering out, so Raphah hid and I made as much noise as I could to get the old codger to chase me. With luck, Raphah will be safe inside, finding what he has to find. If he's not back by tomorrow, I'll go and look for him."

Kate took hold of his hand. "I'm frightened, Thomas. I've never seen anything like them before. I shot one . . . dead."

Thomas knew he had to show no fear.

"Life has changed, Kate. It may never be the same again. There is no going back and what has happened tonight can't be put right. There's a madness. Something is altering the world. In the tunnel you could almost feel it. There was a sense of something very evil and wrong. It twisted my stomach." Thomas took hold of the sword he had stolen from the Varrigal and rolled it from side to side, looking at the blade now stained with a purple smear of Varrigal blood.

Kate whispered: "What are we going to do? My father will be looking for me in the morning. I can't go to the Mill—I'll have to go home."

"Home? If Demurral gets his way, none of us will have a home. When I touched the creature, I saw the place it had come from; I could see inside its mind." He paused and looked at Kate. "You don't realize, Kate. Demurral has a plan for the future. If he succeeds, this world will be transformed beyond our understanding. Raphah told me that Demurral has a power that can call up the dead, control the wind and sea and make those beasts in the glade follow his every word. There's no going back; it is beyond our control. We have to help Raphah because he is the only one who can stop Demurral."

"How do you know? You've only just met him." Kate began to sob. "I want this to stop, I want to go back to how it was. I wish I'd never met him with all his stupid talk. Has he bewitched you as well?" Kate spoke through her tears. "I killed something tonight . . . I saw it die. It tried to kill you. Please, Thomas, make it stop, make it stop."

She pulled her knees tightly up to her chest, making herself as small as she could. If she closed her eyes, she thought, maybe she could shut everything away, like a bad dream that vanishes in the first light of morning. Thomas put his arm around her. He had never seen her cry before. She had always been so strong, always in control of every emotion. Now she was weeping like a child, like someone who had boasted of her own strength only to be beaten by someone stronger and more powerful. In the black wood they held on to each other, not speaking. Thomas also felt afraid, but dared not say so. How could they fight against Demurral? He was the Vicar, the owner of the alum mine, the Magistrate. He was everything powerful in Thomas's world. Thomas was powerless—a child, homeless and poor, and now an outlaw.

He leant back against the oak tree and looked up through the bare branches into the night sky. The Oak King had lost its glory;

it was now the season of the holly. The oak tree had lost its strength; it had been drawn back into the earth. All around lay decaying leaves; the broken acorn cups lay waiting for the Jack-in-the-Green to wake them in spring, to wave over the land the flag of new life, the never-ending genesis.

Thomas spoke in a soft voice above Kate's gentle crying. "We'll stay here until dawn, then we'll go to the Mill. Try to sleep. I'll keep watch."

Kate didn't reply, but buried her face into his shoulder to keep warm. Thomas pulled up the rough, torn collar of his coat. He held the sword in his hand and stared into the night. Through the trees he could see the small lights of Baytown to the north beneath the glowing cloud. He tried to keep awake, but the call of sleep pulled his heavy eyelids closed, as its warmth numbed his mind to the fears of the day. His thoughts turned to dreams, and reality gave way to reverie.

The earth was like the soft bed at the end of a long road. The gentle and rhythmic bickering of the branches soothed his mind. He snuggled into Kate, her hair pressed against his face. She smelt of soap, earth and gunpowder. Thomas breathed softly, feeling safe, knowing he had a friend.

The Golden Altar

Thomas was dreaming. It was pitch-dark; he was in a cold stone chamber. The blackness pressed against him and wrapped him like a tight shroud. Far away in the corner, a candle burst into flame, sending shards of light across the chamber. He could see that it was a large, vaulted stone room, as big as any building he had ever seen. The ceiling hung high above him and was held in place by seven stone columns topped with carvings of rams' horns. At the far end, Thomas could see a golden altar with a tall jewelled cross standing on it. It was encrusted with jasper, chalcedony, sardius, topaz and chrysolite, which completely covered the surface. A golden circle looked as if it hovered in the air behind the cross. It was set with seven fine emeralds. He began to walk towards the altar. The large blue stone at the centre of the cross turned to black, then as he stepped closer, all the jewels changed to crisp, blue, human eyes that followed his every step.

From the wall stepped seven tall, winged figures dressed in long, white, flowing robes. The wings of each creature curled forward and covered its head as they walked towards the altar. They had long golden hair, each strand shining like thick wire. Their skin was deep brown and had a richness that glowed. They were strong and bold, at least seven feet in height, with wide shoulders and piercing dark eyes. As they walked in step, they began to chant, their powerful voices filling the chamber. Every word was like music. It pulsed and pitched, echoing around the vast hall, filling every inch with a deep sense of peace. Thomas started to shake as each wave of sound vibrated through him to his soul. He clasped his hands to stop them from shaking, linking his fingers together and knotting his hands. He listened to every word.

"Holy. Holy. Holy. Lord of Hosts.
Heaven and earth are full of your Glory."

The words echoed through his body. They spoke the words again and again as they walked to the altar. One of the figures carried a large sword, another a shield, another a helmet. Thomas was drawn closer, as if it was his right to be a part of this ritual. It was as if he was being drawn to a moment in his life that would change him forever. He neither knew nor cared if the creatures could see him.

They were half-human, half–something else. With each step they took, the chamber vibrated. Their white robes shone with a purity that Thomas had never seen before. He could not believe this was a dream, it was so real, so true. A voice in his head called to him.

Wake up, wake up.

He had never felt so awake, never felt so alive. In this chamber, among the brightness, in the presence of the winged creatures, was more life than he had ever known. Thomas felt that someone was looking at him, that he was not alone in watching the ritual. He turned and noticed that a man was standing to his right. He was dressed in a linen tunic, long baggy trousers and a pair of the finest, yet the strangest, silver-tipped pointed shoes that Thomas had ever seen. The man was neither white nor black, but had the appearance of being burnished by the sun. He had hair that was very dark, and curled and twisted like a tangled hawthorn. The man smiled and spoke to Thomas in a rich warm voice, calling him by name.

"Fear not, Thomas. This is all for you." He motioned towards the altar.

"The powers that you will fight against are not of flesh and blood. They are the rulers of darkness and the spirits of wickedness."

The man held Thomas by the hand. Thomas looked into his eyes, and he realized they were the eyes of the cross, deep blue, warm, all-seeing, all-knowing. He felt naked before him, as if this man knew all about his life. Every secret, every lie, every ugly thought was on display. Yet all of this was greeted with a smile as the man softly squeezed Thomas's hand.

He spoke to Thomas.

"Fear not. Whatever you have done can be put right, blotted out, forgiven." Thomas turned his face away, unable to look at him. He felt ashamed. Thomas saw for the first time that he was dressed in filthy rags that hung from his body like grave clothes. He hung his head lower, unable to look up.

"Who are you?" Thomas could hardly say the words. He kept his eyes fixed firmly on the pattern of the stone floor and awaited the reply.

"I am a king. Have you not heard of me? Don't you know my voice?"

"Our king is fat, greedy and mad," Thomas said. "He would never speak to a thief like me. You cannot be my king." He continued to look down, not wanting to look upon the man.

"I am King, but not of the world. All you have to do is believe in me. Thomas, I can be your king." He touched Thomas gently on the forehead.

"How can I not believe in you when you stand before me? I have seen you with my own eyes. I can never doubt what I see."

"Do you believe only in those things that you can see? There is more to life than what we are told by our eyes. I have known you since you were knitted together in your mother's womb. Before the beginning of time I set all your days before you."

He looked at Thomas and smiled.

"You can believe in things and yet you do not have to follow them. It is easy for you to believe in me when you stand in my world. But what will you believe when you return to your world? What will you believe when you cannot see me?" The King placed his hand on Thomas's shoulder.

"I will believe, here and in the world to come." Thomas reached out to the King. He took Thomas's hand.

"Thomas, if you believe in me, will you follow me?"

Thomas could hardly speak; he had never stood in the presence of someone like this before. He could feel the unspoken majesty and authority. The man's face began to radiate pure white light, filling the chamber and bathing Thomas in its glow. It was so bright that Thomas closed his eyes and looked away.

"My Lord. You will be my king. I will follow you." Thomas spoke out the words slowly, his head bowed low.

"Do you really know what you are saying, Thomas?"

"I do." Thomas was certain in his reply.

"Then look up and see." The man lifted Thomas's face by the chin. "Open your eyes. This light has never blinded anyone who looks upon it in truth. It is the light of the world. A light that the darkness will never understand."

Thomas opened his eyes. The chamber was full of winged creatures bowing before the man, their chanting growing louder and louder.

"Holy. Holy. Holy. Lord of Hosts.
The Heavens proclaim you King.
The earth is full of your Glory!"

Thomas did not understand. "Who are they?" he asked, with disbelief in his voice.

"They are the Seruvim, they are the army of the Mulkuth. Come to the altar. There is something important that must be done."

He escorted Thomas to the altar. In the powerful radiance of the King the chamber echoed with light. There were no shadows, no dark places, no secrets. The Seruvim circled around Thomas and the King. The chant grew louder and louder. At the altar, Thomas stood before the cross, the eyes illuminating his soul. At his feet was an old book, with a cover of hammered gold, its pages made of thick parchment. The book opened by itself. Thomas could see that it was full of names. One by one the pages turned and there on the final page his name began to appear, written by an unseen hand without ink or quill.

"This is the Book of Life. Everyone whose name is written in here need not fear death." The King smiled as he spoke. "Thomas. Today I will give you two gifts. Carry them with you always. They will be of use to you in the time to come."

With that, one of the Seruvim stepped forward to the King and handed him a thick leather belt with a golden buckle. The King placed it around Thomas's waist.

"This is the belt of truth. Your enemy will use lies and deceit. He is the father of all lies. Beware. He is a devouring lion and will destroy your soul. Keep my truth and you will never fail."

The King looked at the tallest and strongest of the Seruvim and beckoned him towards Thomas. The creature had the most beautiful face that Thomas had ever seen. It was neither male nor female, young nor old. Its features were almost transparent and yet were of great strength.

Thomas noticed that the Seruvim's white robe was woven with thread that gave off a beautiful gold and silver light from each strand. It was tied with a thick belt that was made of living wood. Fresh buds and green shoots intertwined with dark rowan twigs, growing around the waist to form a strong buckle and scabbard for the sword that hung from it. The wings of the Seruvim shimmered and glowed. The wings were neither bird nor reptile and did not look out of place attached to so human a creature. They appeared to pulsate, fractionally changing in size as if given life by every heartbeat of the creature. The Seruvim drew the golden sword from his belt, held it by the blade above his head, then slowly lowered it, offering it to Thomas. The King looked into Thomas's eyes.

"Azrubel will give you his sword. Before you take it, think of the battle that must be fought. Don't take hold of the sword unless you are prepared to fight. Today you come of age, today you become a man. Remember, Thomas, it is harder to believe in me when you cannot see me, and to follow me when you are on your own. Remember this night. All you have to do is speak and I will answer. I will be with you always, even to the end of time."

Without any hesitation, Thomas reached out and took the sword from Azrubel, gripping it tightly by the handle. The chamber was suddenly plunged into darkness. Thomas could feel the sudden drop in temperature as a cold wind blew around him. He could see nothing, his eyes frantically searched for the merest fragment of light. He was in total darkness . . . total silence.

Then the whispering began. First it sounded like the scratching of rats in the distant corner of the chamber. Then it grew into the sound of young voices, laughing and mocking. He could hear a child start to sob, then cry and cry in the black dark.

Very slowly, Thomas edged his feet along the stone floor. As he did so, he could feel dankness with his bare feet. From all around he heard a scurrying and scratching on the floor, the familiar sound of long tails sweeping in the dust. Everywhere he could hear rats.

Edging his foot further, he felt the warm, moist fur that made up the living floor he was now trying to walk on. With every footstep they scattered, jumping across his bare feet, gripping his ankles and biting as they jumped from him. This was Thomas's worst fear, a nightmare beyond nightmares. All around the sound of whispering grew louder. He could see no one. He could hear only the lost voices crying for help, sobbing and restless. In the darkness a hand touched his face, another grabbed his leg, others took hold of his hair. He could feel the cold fear rising from his stomach. Fear that made his mouth dry and his lips tremble. Fear that knotted him up and took the strength from his limbs.

He heard the striking of a tinderbox, and the light of a candle

49

appeared in the distance. There was no altar, no Seruvim, just the single light. He struggled free and walked slowly towards it, holding the sword out in front. It had no weight and even in this blackness had an ethereal glow, like the golden dawn of the darkest night. He could see the squat shape of a small creature cowering by the candle.

"Who are you?" Thomas shouted, but there was no reply. "Who are you?" Thomas smashed the sword against the stone floor in anger. The chamber began to shake with the sound of the earthquake beneath him that shook him from his feet.

The stone floor broke open and from the rubble emerged the dark wood of a church pulpit. It thrust its way through the broken stone until it soared above Thomas. A solitary red pulpit candle slowly dripped wax onto the stone floor six feet below. Demurral stood in the pulpit, looked at Thomas and began to speak.

"I will capture the heavens, I will be more important than God. I will sit in judgment of the earth. I will be higher than the heights of the clouds. I will be the most high. The whole world will worship me." Demurral began to laugh and laugh.

Thomas looked to the base of the pulpit. Kate and Raphah were tied to it with thick ropes that resembled a coil of thin snakes. Each strand of slithering rope moved and swirled around their feet and wrists, binding them tighter and tighter to the pulpit. Thomas stepped forward and lashed with his sword at the pulpit. It shattered like black glass, sending sharp broken crystals across the chamber floor.

Demurral fell to the ground and was immediately surrounded by several black foxes that jumped from the shadows and stood like sentinels protecting their master.

"Come on, boy. If you want to fight, take another step if you dare." He mocked Thomas as the foxes slobbered and barked in concert with him.

Thomas stepped forward and raised his sword, aiming a blow at Demurral's head. The stone beneath him began to crumble into sand. He could feel his feet begin to slip as a cavern began to open beneath him. He was falling.

"Thomas!" Kate screamed, woken from her sleep. She saw the Varrigal step from the darkness of the wood and loom over them. It drew back its arm to strike at Thomas with its sword. *"No!"* she screamed into the darkness as the red eyes of the Varrigal burnt brightly in the faint light of dawn.

Thomas was thrown from his dream back into reality. Without thinking, he lashed out at the falling sword, and metal struck metal only inches above his head.

"Run, Kate. To the Mill." Kate shot up from the oak tree and ran downhill along the track. The Varrigal struck again at Thomas, who jumped clear so that the sword embedded itself in the trunk of the tree. The mighty oak became stiff with frost, each contour of the bark instantly outlined in bright white ice that froze each branch and limb. As the creature pulled at the sword, Thomas slashed at its leg, then, seeing his chance of escape, ran after Kate.

Thomas ran as fast as he could and within half a mile he could see Kate ahead of him on the path towards Boggle Mill. In the breaking dawn the world appeared to be cast in grey. It was a shadowless time, colourless with half-light. He looked behind. He was not being followed. He was angry with himself for falling asleep, for being caught by the creature yet again and for being saved once more by Kate.

"Hey, Kate," Thomas called to her. "Wait for me, I can't run as fast as you," he panted out, trying to get her to stop.

"You'd run faster if you knew the devil was after you," she snapped back and kept on running along the track that led to the Mill brook.

"He is, Kate. He is. But he won't catch us." He took hold of Kate by the shoulder. "Stop. We need to talk."

"Every time I talk to you, I end up with someone trying to kill me."

"Listen." Thomas put his hand over her mouth to stop her

speaking. In the distance was the familiar sound of horses being led up the path from the beach to the moor. They could hear hoofs clashing against the stones.

"Smugglers. Into the wood, we don't want to be seen by them." Thomas pushed Kate from the path and into the bracken. They crawled through the undergrowth until they were out of sight. One by one, the horses passed by, each attended by a man on foot. At the front of the procession rode a man on a large black horse. Thomas peered above the bracken. He spoke in a whisper to Kate.

"It's Jacob Crane, back from Holland."

"Killer Crane, escaped from the gibbet more like." Kate had no time for smugglers. She knew they were not to be trusted and would sell their own mothers for a quart of gin. "Keep down or he'll see you," she whispered at Thomas, and pulled on his shirt.

Jacob Crane was a neat man who always dressed in the finest clothes. Soft, black leather riding boots, the whitest shirts, neatly cut jackets, always covered by the heaviest oiled-cotton overcoats that money could buy. He carried two of the best flintlock pistols, double charged, one with shot, the other with a single lead ball.

He turned his head, unsure if he heard voices. He pulled his horse to a stop and looked into the mist rising from the under-growth. The man leading the first horse realized what Crane was looking at.

"Dragon's breath, Mr. Crane, that's what it is. Comes from the earth every morning, rises with the dawn. It's the Earth Dragon." He nodded to Crane as he spoke, trying to get him to agree.

"Dragon's breath? These are the 1700s. Dragons are all gone and the only spirits in this wood are the ones we carry in these barrels. Now, come on, it's twenty miles to the inn and the brandy is getting warm."

Crane stopped and looked again towards the place where they were hiding. The bracken tops moved slowly backwards and forwards.

"Mr. Agar, I think we are being watched." He drew a pistol from his belt and took aim into the bracken. "Come out, or I'll blast you from your hiding place."

Thomas and Kate looked at each other. Thomas signalled for her not to move.

"You're a braver man than I am. This is your last chance before I shoot." He turned to Agar. "If it's Captain Farrell, then we'll string him from the tree; if it's the dragon, then you can have it for breakfast."

At that moment something leapt in the half-light from the bracken. Crane fired the pistol, the shot echoing through the valley and towards the sea. The old deer screamed and kicked out with her back legs, jumping through the bracken and into the small wooded valley and the safety of the trees.

"There's your dragon, Mr. Agar, buckshot to the rump." Crane laughed and pulled on his horse to go forward. Agar smiled and looked to the place where Thomas and Kate were hiding. Under his breath he made his reply.

"There's your Revenue man. Someone so clever wouldn't have missed the two fawns, Mr. Crane." With that he slapped the front horse and it kicked off up the track.

From their hiding place Thomas and Kate listened to the fall of the hoofs going into the distance. On the other side of the brook was Boggle Mill. Fresh smoke from a new fire blustered from the chimney. They waited in the bracken until the sound of the horses faded into the distance. Kate was the first to speak.

"He was going to shoot us." She gave Thomas a stern look and pinched him on the leg.

"He would've missed." Thomas tried to ignore her worries.

"It was Jacob Crane; he's a killer, and a smuggler. He doesn't want anyone to know what he is doing." Kate was angry. She pinched Thomas again to try and get some reaction.

"He's not a smuggler, he's a free trader, and there's nothing wrong with that." Thomas paused, peering above the bracken and looking down the bank across the brook to Boggle Mill.

"Anyway, we have more to worry about than him." Thomas stopped and began to sniff the air.

"What about Raphah? He could be caught by Demurral." She pinched him again, even harder than before.

"Will you stop it." Thomas pushed away her hand and again sniffed the air.

"You're not listening to me, you're thinking about something else." She prodded him in the chest with a pointed finger. "What is it, Thomas, why aren't you listening?"

"I am listening, but not to you! Can you hear it?"

Kate strained her ears. Slowly, the sounds of the first call of morning lifted from the trees. A woodpecker beat against the side of a large ash, a thrush sang out loudly from the branch of an oak. Thomas looked at her and smiled.

"It's morning. We made it through the night, we are alive." He began to laugh and then suddenly stopped as he saw the sword by his feet. Kate noticed where he was looking. The purple blood of the Varrigal stained the blade. In the first light of the safety of morning, it could still hold them both in fear.

Kate looked to Thomas and grabbed his hand.

"Do you think they will come after us again?" The worry was engraved in her face.

"I think they will come for us again, but not by daylight."

Boggle Mill

oggle Mill had stood by the side of the brook for one hundred years. Its rough-cut, three-storey stone walls supported a red tiled roof, which was covered in places by thick green moss. A large wooden mill wheel jutted out and turned slowly, creaking as it went round with the pull of the water, moaning at the work that it had to do. It rolled on without stopping, the newly cast metal and fresh blue paint churning the water of the brook. It was a wet-damp place by the mill wheel, with a strong smell of freshly milled flour, cattle feed and curing beef. Each of the twenty windows on the front of the building had a curious little carving of a frog in the corner of its frame. In the growing light of morning the windows reflected the gold of the sun, like so many large square golden plates hanging on the stone wall.

Across the brook was a small stone cottage, set higher up the bank and away from the water. It had a little vegetable garden to one side, and several chickens scratched away in the dirt. A fat black calf pressed its nose against the low wattle fence that struggled to keep it in. The door to the cottage was so small that a grown man would have to stoop to gain entry. It was made from one solid piece of oak. The dark, knotted, weathered wood formed strange patterns that led the eye to see many shapes within it.

Boggle Cottage looked an inviting and friendly place, a whiff of smoke indicating the presence of a warm fire in the hearth. In the fresh morning light it called Kate and Thomas to safety. They could hear the sound of a man singing from within. It was a song of the sea, a tale of adventure and great gain.

He sang with a heavy inflection, and a strong foreign accent that sounded like someone with a heavy cold. The man's voice pitched and tossed like the rolling tide. It would stop, then quickly start again, missing out the words of a verse and then repeating them out of place and out of time. The singing, which was definitely not in tune, was interspersed with high-pitched laughter, as if the man was sharing a joke with himself.

Thomas and Kate could hear the man beating time with what sounded like a wooden spoon on the side of a jam pan. The loud clanging broke the morning air; the chickens and the calf gathered close to the door as if they were waiting for the man to make a grand appearance.

With a click of the latch the oak door swung open and from the shadow of the cottage there was a loud shout of "Coohmahn," followed by the throwing of the contents of the pan onto the garden. The chickens fought with the calf to get there first. The calf snuffled with its nose in the mixture of grain, bread and milk, as the chickens jumped on its back and head, pecking at its nose to get it out of the way.

The man didn't notice Thomas and Kate standing by the fence. He scraped the rest of the chicken feed out of the pan then began to sing again, closing the door behind him as he went. Thomas stepped up to the door and knocked three times on the dark wood. There was no reply. Thomas knocked again, this time hammering at the door with his fist.

"Hello. Can you spare some bread?" he shouted.

The small window to the side opened and the man's nose appeared and sniffed the air.

"Dead. Who's dead?" He spoke in an enquiring, deep and throaty voice.

"No one is dead," Kate shouted back. "Please, could we have some bread?"

The man looked at them through the leaded glass of the window, his eyes searching their every feature carefully.

"Well, if it is bread you want, then bread you'd better have. Can't go to a mill and not find any bread, and some roast beef too. What about some tea?"

The window slammed shut, and the door opened. The man stared at Thomas and Kate. They were covered in mud and stained with bracken. He couldn't help but notice the apprehensive look in Kate's eyes. Thomas quickly hid the Varrigal sword by the side of the wattle fence.

"Come in, come in. You can't stand on the doorstep all day long. Come in out of the cold and warm yourselves by the fire."

The man spoke quickly and ushered them both into a large kitchen. It was neat and clean with a black range set into the far wall. Two leather chairs snuggled up to the fireplace, with a pair of trousers drying over one arm. A peat fire lit the whole room in a warm orange glow, and scented the house with the smoky fragrance of rich earth. There was a strong, sweet smell of yeast, fruitcake and baking bread, which reminded Thomas of his mother's preparations for Christmas. The room was long and low with a dark-beamed ceiling and white plaster walls.

Above their heads, two dead pheasants hung by their necks from a hook in one of the beams, their red, brown and gold feathers catching the rays of sun that came in through the window. Next to the pheasants hung a large crusted piece of salt beef that looked as if it had been covered in a thick brown wax.

"Sit yourselves down, you both look like you've spent the night outside. What are you doing here so early in the morning?" He stopped and put his hand to his mouth. "How rude of me. I am Rueben Wayfoot—the miller—and this is my home. Welcome." He held out his hands in a gesture of friendship.

Rueben Wayfoot was a large-framed man built like an ox. He had sturdy forearms and broad shoulders. His hands were the size of coal shovels, and yet were held in a dainty, careful way. For his size he did not appear to be a clumsy man.

Everything about him was very neat.

Even though his clothing was well worn and twice turned, he had the appearance of a gentleman. He wore a pair of old worsted trousers, a once white shirt and a thick leather apron stained with flour. In fact, everything about Rueben Wayfoot was stained with flour. His long white hair, his large ears and even his thick, bushy eyebrows. All carried the appearance of fresh fallen snow. It was, however, his big green eyes that attracted the most attention. They were soft, smiling and warm. They were the eyes of someone who could be trusted, someone good.

"Now let me get you that tea and some bread. Both you lads look like you can do with something to warm you up. I have two boys myself. They'll be up in an hour or so. A bit younger than you two, but big boys all the same." Rueben opened the door of the small side oven and took out several thick slices of well-roasted beef. He placed the hot meat on a plate and presented it to them.

"Eat up and I'll get you some bread. You can tell me what you've been up to. We never get many visitors, this being a bog-gle mill." Rueben took hold of a loaf of bread and held it before them, then with his large hands broke the loaf in half.

"Here you go. There's nothing like warm bread first thing on a morning." He put the bread on the plate then clapped his hands, filling the air with a cloud of flour.

They both began to eat, filling their mouths with the hot beef and bread as Rueben carried on with the morning's chores. They watched as he swept the floor and set four places at the long wooden table that was in front of the small bay window. Rueben noticed that Kate followed his every move. She was just about to speak when he said:

"Before you ask, I do have a wife. She's called Isabella, and she is out collecting from the wood, while the twins are asleep." He noticed another question come into her eyes. Her mouth full of food made it impossible for her to speak.

"They're called Bealda and Ephrig. You'll hear them before you see them." He motioned with his eyes to the beamed ceiling and the floorboards several inches above his head.

"Now you answer me a question. What are you doing out so early in these parts?"

He had taken in every aspect of their appearance. The dirt on their boots, the sweat stains and mud on their faces, and most of all their deep-set look of unease. His deep voice and broad accent made him sound like a stranger to that part of the world.

They both knew of Boggle Mill, but it was a place that people would rarely visit, and never wanted to talk about. It was believed that boggles lived in the valley. These were strange creatures that could take on the appearance of a man or an animal. They would never really harm people, but it was well known that they would steal everything they could from you.

If you were lost and asked a boggle the direction, it would always send you the opposite way. Ask for the road to the sea and a boggle would direct you to the moor top and the treacherous Fyling Bog. Ask for the road to Whitby and before you knew it, you would be standing on the old south road that in places had long since fallen into the sea. As no one was ever sure if they had seen a boggle, no one could ever really say what one looked like. The rumour of boggles was enough to keep both villagers and strangers away from the Boggle Mill, and the long valley that connected it to the sea at Boggle Hole.

Rueben sat down, pulling the wooden chair closer to the fire. He looked at them both and waited for a reply to his question. Kate gulped down the bread and was about to open her mouth to speak when Thomas butted in.

"We got lost in the dark, as simple as that. Got on the wrong track, couldn't find our way back." He looked at Kate to confirm the story. Thomas didn't want to lie, but he didn't want to share the truth either. Kate tried to nod but could feel herself getting hotter and hotter. Rueben looked at them. He noticed Kate's embarrassment.

"There are a lot of things out in these woods at night. It's a dangerous place for two young lads on their own." He spoke in a hushed tone.

Kate replied quickly: "I'm not a lad. I'm a girl. My name is Kate and this is Thomas. We weren't lost, we were trying to get away from—"

"Free traders, smugglers," Thomas butted in. "We were on the track and came across them going up to the beacon, so we hid to get out of their way. Didn't want them to catch us." He sat back in the leather chair, pleased with his reply.

Rueben nodded as if in agreement with him. Thomas breathed a sigh of relief and reached out for some more bread.

"Looks to me like that is alum mud on your boots." Rueben pointed to the thick red clay that coated Thomas's soles. "You don't find that around here. You must have come from the other side of the bay. That's a long walk in the dark, especially if you don't know where you are going."

Thomas couldn't think of a reply. He breathed in and looked around the room for some kind of inspiration. Lying had been a part of his life; the lies would drop from his lips like honey. Now he groped in his mind for something to say, some sentence that would cover the truth.

Suddenly there was the noise of a great excitement at the front door. The chickens could be heard running and squawking around the garden. The calf moaned loudly, and could be heard pushing against the wattle fence. The oak door was flung open, and it was as if the house had been hit by an unexpected storm. Rueben jumped up from the chair and flung open his arms, shouting, "Isabella. Isabella!" He took from her the large basket that she carried over one arm. Thomas and Kate almost laughed at this strange and loud way of greeting.

"Isabella, we have two guests. This is Kate, and this is Thomas. They've been lost in the woods and have found their way here." He made a small gesture to them both with his hand. "I've been feeding them up to get the cold out of them." Rueben spoke excitedly and looked so happy to see his wife again, his eyes sparkling and every part of him seeming to be filled with joy. It was as if he would explode if he didn't share it in an expression of welcome for his wife. He put his arms around her and they squeezed each other, Rueben lifting Isabella from the floor.

Thomas noticed that Rueben had five fingers and a thumb on his right hand. He counted his own fingers in disbelief, thinking he had made some mistake. He was right. He had four fingers and one thumb, and yet Rueben had five fingers and one thumb. Thomas looked at Kate, hoping that she too had noticed. She stared at the floor, not wanting to look at them. He realized that, like him, she had never seen this kind of love between two people.

He thought of his own parents. His father had always been at sea, and on his return he had come home by way of the Dolphin, the Old Mariner and the Nag's Head Pub. He would come into their tiny, cramped, untidy cottage, pat Thomas on the head as he would some young dog and then fall into a deep gin-sleep in the chair by the fire.

Rueben and Isabella finished their embrace and turned to Thomas and Kate. Isabella was as tall, if not an inch taller than Rueben, and was different from any women either of them had ever seen. She wore a long green dress with a white apron and a black oiled-cotton coat. Her long hair was the purest silver, each thread like a shining strand of a spider's web caught in the winter frost. She had a rich, deep brown skin from hours of working in the summer sun, her eyes and mouth were lined with the marks of laughter, yet Thomas couldn't guess her age. Isabella and Rueben stood together, their outlines framed by the sun now beaming through the bay window.

Isabella looked at Kate. "You look like you've lived in those clothes for a long time. Come with me, I may have something warm you can wear."

She took Kate by the arm and led her upstairs. The size of the cottage was deceptive. Thomas noticed it had two staircases that led from the kitchen to separate parts of the upper floor.

Rueben looked at Thomas. "It must have been a long night for you in the wood."

Thomas felt he didn't want to reply without thinking what he was going to say.

"I'm quite used to it. I've been living out for some time now." He stopped speaking and looked out the window. He could feel his lip begin to quiver and tears well up inside him. He took in a deep breath and dug his nails into his hand.

"My father is dead. Mother is in the infirmary." He reached out to the fire to warm his hands.

"Sad thing, that." Rueben paused and thought. "I think I've heard of you. You must be the lad from Baytown. I was told about you by some free traders. Quite a fighter, I hear." Seeing that Thomas was upset, Rueben half laughed and smiled at the same time, tried to get Thomas to smile. "What brings you to the wood? I thought you were a sea boy."

"A friend." He paused. "We met with a friend."

"And this friend of yours is still in the wood?" Rueben moved his chair closer to Thomas. He leaned forward, drawing nearer to him.

"Dangerous place is this. Never know what kind of trouble you can get yourself into. It's not just the smugglers that will cut your throat in the dark."

Thomas could feel Rueben's breath against his face. Rueben rubbed the growth of beard on his chin.

"Tell me, Thomas, who did you see last night?" he whispered.

"We saw no one. I never see anyone I shouldn't. I've learnt to turn my face at the right time and to walk another path when the free traders come by. I don't see anyone, ever." He sat back in the chair, trying to pull away from Rueben to give himself space.

"Good. Sometimes it's best to see no one, and to hear nothing, especially around Boggle Mill, young Mister Thomas."

With that came the rattle of feet upstairs. The floor shook as a fight broke out in the room upstairs. Dust fell from the kitchen ceiling. The sound of shouting filled the cottage. There was a thud to the floor and a loud yell, which was quickly followed by the sound of a smashing pot.

Rueben looked at Thomas. "My two boys are awake. They will be down in a moment."

With that, the sound of the fighting drew nearer. Down the far staircase fell the joined mass of the two boys, both still wearing their nightclothes. They were punching and kicking in the air, and at each other, as they tried to get to the foot of the stairs first. As they came they screamed and shouted. The threats of what they would do filled the air.

"Let go or I'll pull out your brains through your nostrils—that's if there's any to find," Bealda was shouting.

"Think you're funny, do you? Well, laugh at this," Ephrig replied, aiming a punch at Bealda.

"Boys!" Rueben shouted. His voice boomed around the kitchen louder than anything Thomas had ever heard. The two boys froze and pointed at each other.

"It was him." They both spoke at exactly the same time and almost in the same voice.

Bealda protested, "I caught him trying to pull my tooth while I was asleep. That's the third time this week."

"Enough, you two. Can't you see we have guests?" Rueben stepped to one side to reveal Thomas standing by the fireside. "Now sit at the table and I'll get you some breakfast, and be careful what you say—we have a young lady in the house."

"He looks like a lad to me," Ephrig shouted, and elbowed Bealda in the ribs. They both laughed.

Rueben motioned for them to be quiet and sit at the table.

"This is obviously not a girl, this is Thomas. The girl is upstairs with your mother, getting changed. They're our guests, so don't be too rough."

"Yes, and don't try to pull his teeth out, Ephrig." Bealda pushed Ephrig towards the table.

Rueben tried to stop himself from laughing at the boys. They both jumped onto the long bench at the side of the table and waited. Bealda smiled at Thomas, a toothless smile.

"Don't worry, Thomas, they won't try to steal your teeth; yours can't be sold to Old Nan like Bealda's and Ephrig's." Rueben continued to make breakfast, setting the table and taking more roasted beef from the side oven.

Thomas looked at both the boys. They were nearly identical. Bealda was slightly larger than Ephrig, and had a wider face and longer hair. They were large children, and even though they looked no older than nine or ten, their size was easily that of a sixteen-year-old. They wore similar knee-length nightshirts made of thick cotton and buttoned to the neck. On their feet they had large sheepskin bed-boots that came up past the ankle. These were worn on top of knitted green knee-length socks. They looked well cared for and from the warmth of their appearance were well loved.

Rueben looked at Thomas.

"Come and join us for some of this hot tea; it's fresh in from Holland."

Thomas did not have to be asked again. This was a drink he loved. It was a drink that was fought over, and even murdered for. Every ounce of local tea was smuggled into the county to avoid paying the duty; many a man had lost his life to bring in a chest of tea. He loved to watch the hot vapours rising from a freshly made pot, and then to savour that first taste of the bittersweet drink.

Thomas sat at the table and waited for the tea. He smiled at the boys, who sat next to each other eating hot greasy beef with their fingers and mopping up the fat from the plate with their bread. He looked at Ephrig.

"Do you really sell teeth to Old Nan? I thought she was a witch."

From the staircase Isabella spoke. "They do, and yes, she is a witch."

Thomas looked up and was taken by surprise. In front of him was a completely transformed Kate. Her hair had been let down and was brushed through. She wore a long, dark blue dress with a white collar and a small red jacket covered her shoulders. Kate was smiling. He had never seen her look so well.

"If you really want to know, Thomas, we sell the boys' cub teeth when they fall out. Old Nan believes they have certain qualities—"

Ephrig butted in: "She thinks we're boggles."

It was then that Thomas noticed that both of the boys had the same number of fingers as their father.

"Are you boggles?" Thomas asked, unsure if he really wanted to know.

Isabella was first to reply. "I don't think that what we are really matters. Just take it that we are your friends." She walked closer to the table and stood with Rueben. "People think we are many things. Wherever our folk have been, we have been persecuted and driven away. They even blame us for bad weather, cows going dry and the poor price of grain." She paused and looked at Rueben.

"My wife is right in what she says. We are different, yet we are the same as you. For the last two thousand years our people have been scattered to the four corners of the earth. We get work where we can, harm nobody and try to live in peace. The problem is, Thomas, people get jealous when we do well. Because we look different and have our own language, people often blame us when we are not to blame. I'm not saying we are perfect, but do we really look like monsters?"

Thomas thought that Rueben Wayfoot could not be described as a monster. In the short time that he knew them, they had been so kind. Rueben patted Thomas on the back and then ruffled his hair. Isabella put her arm around Kate and pulled her close to her.

"From what Kate tells me, you've been awake most of the night. You can both take a sleep in the boys' room. Then you can decide what you are going to do."

Isabella went to the fire and pulled a pot of steaming water from the hot embers. From a side cupboard she took two plain white pot beakers. She took down a dried sprig of green herbs that hung behind one of the beams. She rubbed some of the leaves into each beaker, then covered them with the hot water. Isabella handed the beakers to Kate and Thomas. The smell of mint, lavender and camomile swirled around him. The hot vapours filled his nose as he breathed in the strong scent. He closed his eyes and allowed the powerful fragrance to wash over him.

"Drink this. It will take away all those thoughts that will stop you from sleeping. Don't worry, it won't poison you; they don't call me Old Nan."

Thomas and Kate knew that it would be pointless to argue. He felt comfortable with Isabella. He always thought he could judge someone by their eyes, and she had the eyes of someone filled with love. Isabella turned Kate by her shoulders and pointed her to the stairs.

"Now go on, you two. We have work to do. We'll call you when it's time to get up."

Thomas followed Kate to the boys' bedroom. It was large and clean, with two wide, wooden, handmade beds. It was so different from the corner of the cave where Thomas slept on a worn-out horsehair mattress under a thick, stiff old blanket. He sipped from the beaker and looked around the room, taking in all that he could see.

The walls were of the same plaster and wood as the rest of the cottage. In each square of plaster was painted a small picture of a lamb or a fox. On the wall around the window was painted an incredible tree that looked solidly rooted into the floor. Its trunk and branches rose up and surrounded the window, and its rich green leaves looked as if they could be picked.

On each branch were painted golden spheres that hung like fruit. Within each sphere was written, in fine blue paint, a word in a language that Thomas could not understand. He sometimes found it hard enough to recognize the King's English, but these words looked as if they were from another world. The painting filled the whole wall and made him feel as if he were a part of the tree. The brightness of the vivid gold, green, yellow and blue vibrated against the eye.

Every branch of the tree was interconnected, every golden sphere linked by a thread of silver vine leaves. On the left was a full moon setting in the hills, on the right a golden sun rising from the sea. At the base of the tree was painted a man and a woman holding hands. Between them stood a young lamb. Crawling through the painted green grass was a black leviathan, half-lizard and half-snake. Its purple eyes stared out at Kate and Thomas, following them around the room.

They stood mesmerized by the painting, their eyes searching out each and every detail that they could find. Hidden amongst the leaves were the faces of children. Small birds and fruit filled each bough. With each second of looking more and more was revealed, as if the picture were being painted before their eyes.

Thomas felt envious that these two boys had such a beautiful room. By each bed was a small table, and set on each was a candle in a hand-carved wooden holder in the shape of a small green boat. The floor was made of wooden floorboards, and a small peat fire was set in the neat fireplace.

Neither Thomas nor Kate spoke. They sat on opposite beds and then lay back into the soft mattress. Within moments they were both asleep.

In the kitchen Rueben and Isabella sat by the fire and waited until there was no more sound from the room above. Bealda and Ephrig continued to eat breakfast at the table by the window. Isabella looked at Rueben and with her hand, beckoned him to move closer.

"They're in trouble, Rueben. The girl told me that they had been chased through the wood by some strange creatures. She has a pistol that she stole from her father, and when I came back to the cottage, I found a sword hidden by the cow fence." She spoke quietly so that the boys wouldn't overhear. "She said there's another lad who is trying to get into the house of Obadiah Demurral, the priest. She said the lad was black as the night. From Africa." Isabella continued to speak in a quiet, yet excited, voice. "The boy is called Raphah. You know what his name means. He is a child of The Book. Kate told me he has come here to find something stolen by Demurral."

Rueben rubbed his hands together and looked at the boys and then back to Isabella.

"Raphah is the name of a healer. I hope this lad can live up to his name. I knew there was more fear in Thomas's eyes than just running from smugglers. If the old goat Demurral is involved, then it's not the work for two lads and a girl, but we can't stop them."

Rueben took hold of Isabella's hand. "They will want to do what they will do. We must pray for them, they will need the help of all heaven if they are in conflict with the priest."

Dagda Sarapuk

The Vicarage was always a dark place. Even on the brightest autumn morning it had the feeling that night still clung to its portals. It had a strange, rugged beauty, and looked as if it was hewn from the rocky headland high above the bay.

Demurral had cheated his way into being the Vicar of Thorpe. Many years before, he had been the guest of the Parson Dagda Sarapuk. Demurral had been a visiting preacher, earning his keep with penny sermons that he preached from haystacks, carts or wherever he could summon a congregation. From the moment he stood in the cliff-top garden of Peak Vicarage and looked out across the three miles to Baytown, he had been ensnared by the powerful charm of the house and the beauty before him. In the bay the waves broke against the rocks, the dawn-tinted heather stretched into the distance and the green of the hills rolled out like some luscious carpet for miles and miles. He knew that he could never leave this place. Whatever happened, he had to become the possessor of each stone and blade of grass that was Peak Vicarage. As he stood on the battlements that towered over the sea, he was overcome by a sudden greed.

Darkness and desire had consumed him, washing from him all his light and charity. Demurral was changed in the twinkling of an eye. Every ounce of goodness, every drop of mercy and every speck of joy were suddenly and powerfully transformed in one shudder of his bones. In that instance he had given over all that was good to that which was corrupt.

On his first night as guest of Parson Sarapuk, when Sarapuk had drunk far too much wine, Demurral had persuaded him to wager all that he owned on the outcome of two cockroaches racing across the large kitchen table. Sarapuk had chosen the biggest and fattest cockroach he could find. Demurral had selected the slightest creature from the scurrying mass that ran across the stone floor; it was the only one his wine-numbed fingers could catch. The mini-beasts were placed next to each other, and to start the race Sarapuk dropped his handkerchief to the table. Demurral closed his eyes and began to pray. For the first time in his life he could feel a power coming from within him. He felt as if he was not alone, that he shared his body with another being. It was like being a god, with the power to make all the elements of earth, wind and fire obey him.

To his surprise his scraggy, thin, long-legged cockroach attacked its fat rival, biting off its head and leaving it like an upturned, six-legged black saucer. The conquering cockroach then waddled to the other side of the table, winning for Demurral the Vicarage, and the living from all the land as far as the eye could see. Sarapuk had begun to sob, realizing his stupidity. He had lost everything. Demurral leapt from the chair, lifting the victorious cockroach in his hand.

"Praise you. Praise you, my little dark beast," he shouted as he leapt around the kitchen, waving his hands in the air and then falling across the table. He was again overcome with the force of powerful desire. He looked at Sarapuk and began to laugh. "And you, my stupid friend, you will be out of here in the morning."

Demurral leant over to Dagda Sarapuk, holding out the cockroach towards him.

"Do you want to change your luck? Go on, take it. I'll race you again with the odds in your favour," he said mockingly.

Sarapuk gave out a sharp squeal, tears filling his eyes, lip quivering. He reached out with a shaking hand for the beetle. Demurral snatched the cockroach back towards him. With a sharp squeeze he crushed the creature in the palm of his hand. It gave out a gratifying crunch as its hard shell crumpled in his fingers.

That night was twenty-five years ago, and the wickedness of Demurral's heart had grown with each passing season.

Raphah hid in the damp cellar of the Vicarage, amongst some stored apples that had been stacked in wooden trays and covered in sackcloth. He had wedged himself between two crates, and covered himself with the musky cloth. He had been there for several hours, trying to breathe as quietly as he could, hoping not to be found. In almost complete darkness, he had listened from his hideout as Demurral and Beadle had searched for him. They had returned after many hours to slam shut the metal door that led from the cellar into the tunnels, and to curse the fact that the young invaders had not been captured.

Raphah had no way of telling what time it was. From the kitchen above he could hear the clanging of pans and the footsteps of the cook as she hobbled across the floor. He listened to each footfall. From the way she walked he could tell she had a severe limp and was of a great weight. He could hear the uneven steps that she took across the floor, and the straining of the floorboards above his head. He knew it was a woman from the high-pitched voice that screamed at Beadle to get out of her kitchen and never to darken the door again. All this had started about an hour before, so Raphah presumed it must be early morning. He had spent most of the night trying to stay awake and pray. He had inwardly cried out for Thomas's protection from Demurral. Their plan had worked; he was inside the Vicarage, but Thomas's fate was unknown. The last he had seen of him, Thomas was running down the tunnel in the light of the doorway, being chased by Demurral. Raphah had then slipped into the cellar and hid.

In his hiding place he thought of what he had to do. He knew that recovering the Keruvim would not be simple. It was far too precious an item for things to go well. He also knew that Demurral's desire to possess the Keruvim would mean that he would stop at nothing to keep it in his grasp.

He couldn't tell if the door to the cellar was locked; he had not heard a key being turned. He realized that at some point soon he would have to venture forth and find the Keruvim.

Raphah slid his hand into one of the apple boxes and pulled out a large firm apple. He took a bite, but it had the taste of damp wood. He spat it out and put it back in the box. Crawling along the side of the wall, he made his way in the darkness to the doorway. He could see a chink of light flooding in from under the door. There was no key in the lock. Raphah took hold of the metal handle and slowly pressed down. The door gave a loud clunk as it jumped off the catch.

Outside the cellar a flight of ten stone steps went up to a bright passageway. He climbed carefully, stopping and listening on each step. He could still hear the woman's voice moaning about her life and wishing all the ill luck on Demurral that her thoughts could muster. At the top Raphah could see that the doorway to the kitchen was open. The smell of boiled fish and cabbage filled the air, as steam swirled around the dark oak kitchen door. He could see the back of the cook. She was facing a tall window, washing up pots in a stone sink. She was large and round and wearing a dark blue frock and grey pinafore tied at the back. He crept past the door and slowly walked along the passageway. At the far end he could see the large front door. Above the door, stretching from the lintel to the ceiling twelve feet above him, was a gold-framed mirror with a large statue of a raven carved into the frame. The raven was at least six feet tall. Its long, sharp talons gripped the mercurial glass, and its even longer outstretched wings swept down to each side. It had green painted eyes that seemed to follow Raphah as he walked towards it along the passageway. Raphah looked up again, unsure if he had seen the raven move. For a moment he thought the bird had shaken its golden feathers, then frozen again into its position. He felt as if at any moment this great bird could swoop down and grasp him in its thick, spiked talons.

Raphah continued to edge his way along the passage. He knew that in an instant one of the dirty oak doors could open and Demurral would catch him. He listened for the smallest turn of a handle, and the slightest squeak of a floorboard. Far behind him he could hear the sound of the cook as she moaned and threw pans across the kitchen. He got to the front door, the raven dominating the wall above his head and looking down on him as if to strike. To his right was a doorway, and to his left a stairway that led to an upper floor and then sharply twisted back upon itself. Raphah closed his eyes, and slowly and purposefully breathed in. He began to calm himself and softly spoke out.

"Riathamus, lead me."

He opened his eyes and looked across the passageway. From beneath the door opposite there was a billowing of thick dust, rising up like a small cloud. He knew that he had to try the door. Putting his hand to the large brass lock, he pressed against it and the door began to open. He didn't think for a moment that there could be anyone inside the room. He just knew that this was where he was being led.

Inside was a large desk. Pieces of bread were scattered across the floor, a flagon of wine was standing on the side table and several old books were lying across the desk. A large bay window with faded green curtains dominated the room. From the doorway he could see the sea, and in the distance Baytown. It was a bright day, and yet the room was in dark shadow.

It was a beautiful room made dull by neglect and by the possessions of the owner. He scanned it quickly for the Keruvim, but it was nowhere to be seen. He searched the drawers of Demurral's desk, and a large sea chest that was set into the alcove of the fireplace. It was not there. Suddenly, Raphah heard footsteps coming down the stairs. He knew there was no escape. A second set of footsteps could be heard coming along the passageway. They beat out a pace on the hardwood boards as each heel dug in with each step. They were purposeful, long, confident steps, and they were approaching the room quickly.

Raphah knew he had only seconds to hide.

The door was flung open. Demurral entered the room and went to his desk. He sat in the chair, put his long, thin feet on the table and leant back. He pulled the silk dressing gown around him and shrugged his shoulders. Beadle arrived and, like an obedient dog, stood by his side, waiting for his instructions. The mud from the night before covered his boots, and he rubbed his grubby unwashed fingers as he waited impatiently.

"You lost them, Beadle. Now we will never know who they were."

"Or why they were here," Beadle replied.

"On the contrary. They were here for the Keruvim. They wanted to steal my little golden angel." He rubbed his chin and looked around the room. "They will try again, so we must find out who they are, and who has sent them." He kicked the table with his foot, sending papers scattering across the floor.

"Where shall we start to look? We searched all night and never found them." Beadle spoke as he tried to pick up the papers.

"They will not be too hard to find. No one should know what we have here, unless you have been talking again." He looked at Beadle in an accusing manner, raising one eyebrow. "Drunken talk will cost your life. What we have has to be protected and little people can be sacrificed for the cause."

Beadle gave a visible gulp. He knew that Demurral would be a man of his word, that he would not hesitate to kill him by whatever foul means he could think of.

"Bring the scrying bowl. Perhaps Pyratheon will be able to guide us." Demurral dropped his feet to the floor, stood up from the chair and rolled back his sleeves. Beadle went to a small table and from the drawer took out a black bag. From inside he took out a green china bowl engraved with serpents that coiled around the base, circling upwards to the rim. He placed it on the table. Demurral reached into the top drawer of his desk, took out a crystal bottle of clear fluid and poured it into the bowl. He looked at Beadle.

"Blood, Beadle. We need blood." Beadle looked aimlessly around the room then cast a worried, blank look at Demurral.

"Your blood, Beadle. I need your blood." He beckoned for Beadle to step closer.

"But I only have enough for myself—I can't spare any—I'll dry up," he pleaded as he took a step back away from Demurral.

From the drawer Demurral took out a small knife and held it towards Beadle.

"I don't want a bucketful, just a drop. I promise this won't hurt."

He made a sudden grab for Beadle and managed to get hold of him by the arm. He pulled him to the desk and held his right hand over the bowl, stabbing the small sharp tip of the blade into Beadle's thumb. He squeezed two large drops of blood into the bowl and with the knife blade, swirled them around in the water. The shocked Beadle jumped back from the table and screeched like an owl. He stuck his thumb in his mouth and sucked the wound, looking like a large fat baby.

"You lied. It hurt! And you took it all," he squawked at Demurral, thumb in mouth.

"Come, my friend, and look into the water."

Demurral placed his palms over the swirling water. Closing his eyes, and in a deep voice that was not his own, he began to speak.

"Pyratheon-Kaikos-Theon-Anethean."

As he spoke the words, the water began to turn black and whirl in the bowl like a captured storm. "Show me, Pyratheon, Dark Lord from above, show me," he intoned loudly as the water turned to dark silver, and froze like thick ice. In the reflection Beadle saw a house appear. It was a small cottage, set in the woods by a stream.

"Look, Beadle, they are here—or, rather, they will be. Do you know this place?"

"It's the miller's cottage, where the boggle lives." He looked again into the bowl. "This is two hours' walk; how can it be seen here?" Beadle shuddered as he spoke.

"This is magic, it comes from Pyratheon. I lost so many years following the wrong way. I tried so hard to understand all that I had been taught as a child, but in the end it was useless. There was no power, no glory, only empty words. I wanted God to give me one sign. To change water into wine just for me, but I got nothing. I was taught to love my neighbour as myself, and love God with all my heart. But how can you love someone who is against the true prince of the world? How can you love your neighbour when you don't even love yourself?"

Beadle looked dumbfounded by his words. Demurral continued to speak, staring out of the window.

"One day you may understand, but in this small sign of blood and water I now know where they are and I will stop them. There is only one thing in this world worth dying for, and that is power. Power over people, power over the elements and ultimately the power to be God. With the Keruvim I can control the elements. When I have them both, I will change the world, and I will bring about the death of God. This time he'll be nailed to the tree forever."

He smashed his fist hard into the desk. The water in the bowl jumped. It was no longer ice and there was no vision of the cottage. The reflection shimmered as Demurral dipped his fingers in the water, crossing himself in the sign of a pentagram. He flicked the last few drops of water at Beadle. Then Demurral suddenly stopped and looked at the sea chest. He shuddered, and the dark voice returned.

"Beadle, take the chest out of here, lock it and burn it." He looked sharply at Beadle. "Do it now, Beadle."

His servant crossed the room and took hold of the brass handle on the side of the chest, trying to slide it across the floor. It was heavy and hard to move. Beadle struggled across the room, sliding the chest over the wooden boards. Demurral came to his aid and together they shoved and pushed it through the door and into the passageway. They dragged it through the front door and onto the steps. Beadle began to lose his grip, the weight of the chest pulling at his hand. He let go and it tumbled down the flight of stone steps, crashing onto the driveway below.

Raphah, stunned from the fall, spilt out of the chest and into the mud. Demurral quickly pounced upon him, grabbed him by the throat and lifted him from the ground.

"There is nowhere to hide from me. Do you think I would put the Keruvim where you could find it?"

Raphah could not reply as the priest squeezed his throat harder and harder, lifting him from the ground at the same time.

"You'll kill him, Master," Beadle cried out to Demurral.

"He was dead the moment he stepped into this house. But perhaps now is not the time or place. You never know, Beadle. He may be more useful alive."

He twisted Raphah around and threw him to the ground.

"You have some explaining to do. Now get to your feet and don't think of running. We have dogs that would catch you within minutes."

Raphah got up from the mud and was dragged by Beadle towards the door of the Vicarage. He didn't speak to his captors and tried not to look at them as they hauled him back into Demurral's study. Beadle locked the door and from a large empty plant pot took a cane walking stick. He twisted the shaft and pulled a long sharp blade from inside the cane. Demurral sat in a battered leather chair and looked at Raphah. His eyes scoured every inch of Raphah's body, taking in every detail of his appearance, searching each line or contour for some clue as to who he was, and why he was there. After several minutes of his staring, Demurral finally spoke.

"What's your name?" he demanded. Raphah made no reply. "It won't harm you to tell me who you are. Then we can at least be civil to each other." He tried to smile. "I can tell from your skin that you are not from these parts. Are you a slave?"

Raphah stared at the floor. The room smelt of sweat and damp books. It was messy, cold and brutally unfriendly. The floor was several years unswept, and littered with pieces of broken glass, pottery and dry bread. In the corner by the door were the scratch marks of a large rat that had torn at the wood and eaten the edge of the skirting board. On every surface the dust lay winter-thick like a covering of grey snow. The beauty of the room had been overlaid by years of neglect that provided Raphah with a wonderful distraction from Demurral's questioning.

"Come on, man, tell me who you are," he barked at Raphah, the smile gone, the deep, dark voice rising from his stomach like the outflowing of a sewer. "I can get you to talk in ways that you wouldn't like. If there is one thing I hate, it is the arrogance of silence. Are you here to steal the Keruvim?"

Raphah took in a deep breath of the stale air. He looked up at Demurral, who sat protected by his desk in front of the empty fireplace.

"Steal? I have not come here to steal, but to take back that which belongs to me. That is the truth." He stared at the priest, and for the first time noticed the man's thin bony face and sharp features.

"Truth. What is truth? It is all relative. You are here, hiding in my sea chest, spying on me. The only thing of value I have was brought to me by one of your kind. And I'll have you know I paid a fair price for it," Demurral snarled. "So I can only presume that you are here to steal it from me. Did Gebra Nebura tell you it was here?"

Demurral reached into a drawer of his desk and pulled out a knife, pointing the blade towards Raphah.

"Nebura is a thief. He stole his name, and he has stolen the Keruvim. There will be no rest for him, not even in death," said Raphah. Beadle jumped at this sharp reply and lashed out with the swordstick, missing Raphah by a fraction of an inch.

"Don't play games with me," said Demurral. "We hang people for stealing, and there is plenty of rope still left on the gallows to go around your pretty little neck. Now tell me the truth. Who are you, and what do you want in this place?" Demurral stabbed the blade into the desk.

"I want what's mine and will leave you to whatever you are

78

planning to do. Just give me the Keruvim and I'll be gone. You will have no more trouble from me," Raphah replied.

"You, my friend, are not going anywhere. You will be here until you die. That may be tomorrow or the next day, but it will be soon. One Keruvim is now mine, and before long I will have the other. At that time the world will be changed beyond your wildest dreams." He pointed out the window to the sky. Since the storm it had glowed with strange colours that billowed out of the sea to the north. The horizon was tinted with orange and green that shimmered in the first light of morning.

"Look at that, my friend. Even now the world is beginning to change. The Keruvim has a power that you would never understand. We are coming to a time when the sky will grow dark and the moon will turn to blood. There will be signs in the sky that will make the strongest of men fear for their lives. Not even your God can stop what is about to happen." Demurral got up and walked from behind the desk, past Raphah, to stand in the bay window. "And it is all because of me!"

Raphah continued to face the fireplace, and Demurral's empty chair, as he spoke.

"You flatter yourself. Don't you know that you will never understand the power of the God whom you fight against? . . . Don't you realize he is just allowing you this tiny piece of vanity? You talk about rope, but the only one who will hang is you. God is coming, but he is coming to judge, and you have been held in the balance and found wanting."

Demurral picked up an empty bottle and in two paces crashed it into the back of Raphah's head. The blow came silently and unexpectedly. Raphah dropped to the floor, hitting his head against the side of the desk and landing in the dust and dirt, amongst the dry bread and mouse dung.

"Get him out of here, Beadle. All this talk of God makes me sick. Get me the branding iron: We'll leave him with a mark that he will never forget."

Brimstone and Cold Cabbage

It was the intense smell filling his nostrils that convinced Raphah that he was not dead. It was a caustic, tear-bringing smell that inflamed his eyes and tore at his throat. As he breathed, he could feel himself being choked by the rotting fumes welling up around him. It was the smell of brimstone and sulphur, burnt seaweed and dog pee.

In complete darkness he lay facedown, struggling not only to breathe but also to regain consciousness. The wound at the back of his head throbbed and throbbed, and the blinding agony set every nerve in his body on fire. His right shoulder burnt with an excruciating pain. It was as if his flesh had been torn from the bone, and slashed with a thousand cuts. If he could feel pain, then he was still alive, he thought to himself as he tried to spit out a mouthful of sodden straw and mud that had somehow got embedded in his teeth. A strong taste of ammonia now filled his mouth; he gulped back the urge to be sick as he realized that his hands had been tied firmly behind his back.

Raphah could hear the sound of running water and the voices of men somewhere outside. One man with a deep gruff voice was shouting orders, barking like a zealous guard dog. He could hear the wind blasting at the window shutters, which were smashing back and forth against the wall with a heavy *thud-thud-thud*. In the distance came the clang of a hammer beating against metal, ringing out cold tones. He opened his eyes and searched the darkness for the slightest chink of light. The gloom swirled around him like a thick mist that neither eyes nor light could penetrate.

Raphah twisted himself around and managed to sit up, leaning back against the cold, wet, slimy stone wall. His hands pressed against the damp floor and he tried to feel his wrists to see how he was bound. From somewhere in the blackness of the room he could hear the quiet sound of someone softly crying. Raphah called out.

"Peace to you. Speak so that I may know your name."

There was no answer, but the sobbing continued. Raphah heard the rattle and crash of metal chains being dragged over stone stairs. The door of the chamber burst open, and two men in sea boots and long, dirty frock coats bustled in. A small, thin man with crimped feet carried a storm lamp. The other, a large, tatty fat man, carried a pair of iron manacles and a riveting hammer. In the light of the lamp, Raphah saw that the sobbing had been that of a young boy huddled in the corner of the room, wrapped in damp straw. He was dressed in a torn shirt and ragged trousers; his hair was matted with dirt and stuck to his face.

The man with the hammer and chain grabbed Raphah by the hair and pulled him to his feet. He smelt of beer and cold cabbage. His face was rough with a reddish tinge, and silver bristles stuck out from his chin.

"Come on, boy; Demurral wants these on you so you don't run away." He laughed and rattled the chain in front of Raphah. "Just don't think of doing anything stupid. The only way out is through the front door and that's locked."

The man dragged Raphah by the hair across the room, tumbling him into the wall, and then tripping him so that he fell to the floor. Raphah screamed with pain as the wound on his shoulder scraped against the stone wall.

"Oh dear, oh dear. Looks like he's had too much to drink. Better cool him down."

With that the fat man grabbed the slop bucket that was by his feet and tipped the sordid liquid over Raphah's head.

"That'll make you smell nice for the ladies. Now come on, let's get these on yer."

The small, thin man looked at Raphah in disgust. He could not understand why Raphah was so quiescent. He did not speak or put up a struggle. In the dim light of the storm lamp, Raphah smiled back through his pain. The two men looked at each other, both wanting to gain some reaction from the young man they so much wanted to torture, wanting to hear him scream for mercy. They looked at each other for a second time, and then at Raphah as he knelt in sodden straw that was scattered over the stone floor.

Before they could do anything, the boy in the corner of the room jumped up. He kicked out with his bare feet at the backside of the fat man, knocking him to the floor and his head into the slop bucket. The fat man grappled himself to his feet and spun round, the bucket still on his head. He let out a muffled yell and shook it off.

The boy gave a satisfied grunt that was cut short by the back of the thin man's hand as he was slapped across the head, sending him spinning to the floor. The boy cowered in the corner of the room, trying to make himself as small as possible against the cold stone, holding his arms tightly against the side of his ribs. He knew that at any moment he would face a deluge of blows as sharp fists and blunt feet poured down on him like winter rain.

The boy looked across at Raphah. The expected blows came swiftly and forcefully; both men kicked and punched the boy as he lay helpless on the floor.

"Stop—it—now!" Raphah shouted, his voice so loud that it shot echoes around the room. "If you want to fight with someone, then fight with me. Or can you only win against children?"

The thin man gave one last kick that lifted the boy from the floor. They both turned and faced Raphah, who had got to his feet and tried to stand as tall as he could. The thin man looked at him and laughed.

"We would love to give you something to think about. The problem is that Parson Demurral has got other plans. He doesn't want a hair of your head to be out of place. So we can't touch you." He paused and gave Raphah a nasty look. "Well, not yet, anyway."

They walked towards Raphah. The fat man began to swing the chain in his hand. Raphah bowed his head, waiting for the blow. The fat man grabbed him by the throat and pushed him against the wall, pressing his face as close as he could to his. He breathed beer-sodden breath into his face and rubbed the sharp stubble of his chin into Raphah's soft cheek.

"Listen, boy, there is nothing I'd like more than to squeeze the life out of you, but you are a lamb for slaughter and he wants you without speck or blemish."

He spat out the words, and Raphah tensed the muscles of his throat against the strong hand that attempted to stop him from breathing.

"Why pick on children? Is it because they can't fight back?" he managed to say as the man's grip grew tighter.

"Why are you so concerned for such a boy? He can't hear you. He can't speak. He's a deaf-mute. He's completely worthless, should have been drowned at birth." He stopped, thought, smiled and said: "Just . . . like . . . you."

With that the man let go and Raphah fell to the floor. He took in a deep breath, trying to hold back the tears.

"You don't know what you are doing. You are like sheep without a shepherd. You don't even know what's good anymore, do you?" Raphah looked at the boy. "What has he ever done to you? Yet you treat him like an animal."

The fat man was silent. He bent over and drew out a long thin knife from his belt. He pushed Raphah's face into the straw. With a quick slice of the blade his hands fell free from the wrist binding. Both men took hold of him and lifted him from the ground. They pressed the bracelets of the manacles over each wrist and hammered in the locking rivets. The thin man took hold of the chain.

"Now, come on, my little lamb. Come to see all the other lambs for slaughter. We'll even take your little friend with you and you can dig shale together. Then we'll see how much you love one another."

He led Raphah out of the room and down a flight of stone stairs, followed by the fat man dragging the young boy by his hair. Together they were tumbled out of the Alum House and into the bright afternoon. The mine was like a small village, two hundred feet below the Vicarage on a flat ledge of land between the sea and the cliff, surrounded by thick woodland. Two large, gouged quarries dominated the western skyline. They had been hacked from the alum shale by a million ulcerated hands over the past hundred years. They stood out against the beauty of the vale like two giant sores, blistering through the skin of the earth. The dirty red stone scar was incongruous against the soft green and brown of the tree-covered hill. The air was filled with a heavy smoke from the smouldering mounds of alum. This was mixed with the deep scent of stale urine, burnt seaweed and sulphur.

Raphah stared at the devastation that had been wreaked on the land. He could feel a rising anger as he looked across at the dirty terrace of miners' cottages with their broken windows and mud-stained walls. Everywhere he looked was filthy and broken-down.

High above, the sound of pickaxes chipping away at the stone in the quarry was a constant reminder of the reason for all this decay. As he was being dragged down the muddy path, all he could think of was Demurral's greed.

The pain in his shoulder grew more intense as the cold of the day dug into his flesh. He couldn't see what was causing this pain, but he could feel the burning ache penetrating to the bone. The man dragged him faster by the chain, almost pulling him from his feet. He looked at Raphah eye to eye. Raphah smiled in return, but his look was met with contempt.

At the end of the terrace of cottages was a large stone house with three floors and a grey slate roof. It was dark and forbidding, the windows to the upper floor painted black. Around the faded green front door were scattered the remains of several uneaten meals. Two fat crows pecked at the food and reluctantly flew away as the men approached.

With their usual impudent style the men kicked at the door and pushed Raphah and the boy into the building. Inside was a large room with a long wooden table and bench seat. At the end of the room was a fireplace set into the stone wall. A small fire crackled in the grate. Around the sides were wooden beds, stacked four high with just enough room to squeeze in between them. Each was covered with a dirty blanket over a straw mattress placed on frail wooden slats.

At the end of the table sat a wiry redheaded woman. She had a long thin face that was thickly powdered with white lead. Her lips had been dyed bright red by cochineal, which had smeared across the side of her mouth. A black beauty spot had been crudely, almost drunkenly, drawn on the side of her chin. Raphah looked at her and thought it resembled some kind of giant black fly crawling across her face.

She sat in the oversized wooden chair with her feet resting on the table, and a long clay pipe smoking in her hand. Wisps of grey smoke danced about her face and clung to the strands of red hair that fell untidily over her eyes. By her feet was a small, dark green bottle made of thick glass, half full of liquid.

She leapt to her feet unsteadily as a shudder of excitement vibrated through her body. Quickly, she patted her long skirt and tidied her collar.

"Mr. Consitt, Mr. Skerry, to what do I owe this unexpected . . . pleasure?"

Mr. Consitt, the fat man, smiled, and made a pretend bow, touching his forelock as he bent forward. He always thought he could impress with his fine manners.

"Just the usual, Mrs. Landas. This young man would like to sample the finest living accommodation with the most beautiful hostess in the district." He brushed the wisps of hair across his bald head. "This fine young man is the guest of Parson Demurral, and awaits your pleasant hospitality." He slobbered as he spoke, each sarcastic word prefixed by a piece of white spittle.

"Leave him with me, Mr. Consitt, I'll make sure he has a wonderful night before he starts work." She placed the pipe on the table and bid the two men leave with a smile and the waving of her hand. They went with a quick good-bye. Mrs. Landas, grinning a white-faced grin, scurried to the door, closing it firmly behind them.

It was when she turned that Raphah noticed the complete change in her mood. Gone was the charm, and gone was the smile. She seemed to grow in stature as anger poured from her. Her chest swelled up, rage spilling across her face, digging deep white furrows into her brow and, looking at Raphah and the boy, she began to scream.

"Don't think this place is going to be easy for you. You are here to work, my boy, and work you will. Any slacking and it will be the store for you."

She pointed to a small wooden door on the opposite wall. The young boy could not hear what she said, but looked as if he understood. He cowered away from her, trying to hide behind Raphah.

"Just because you're deaf and dumb, doesn't mean you'll get off lightly this time. I know you're not stupid, boy, and there'll be no running away from me again."

With that she picked up the brush-broomstick from beside the door and lashed out at him, catching Raphah a glancing blow on the shoulder. He winced with pain, clutching at the wound. Mrs. Landas stopped suddenly. Dropping the broomstick to the floor, she stepped towards Raphah, putting her arm around him.

"You're hurt. What have they done to you?" Her voice changed yet again. It was kind, gentle and almost soft; the brashness had vanished. "Let me look, my lovely."

She pulled his jacket from his arm and opened his shirt, trying to pull it from his shoulder.

"Better leave it like this," she said. "I'll have to get a damp cloth, the wound has stuck to the shirt."

Raphah could smell the strong scent of cheap gin and tobacco on her breath. She had crooked, yellow-stained teeth and a bristly white moustache. Her reddened lips were dry and cracked, the whites of her eyes bloodshot. She helped him to a chair and beckoned to the boy to get a wet cloth, gesturing for him to go to the bucket by the window.

She pulled Raphah's jacket back as far as she could, the manacles preventing him from slipping out of the sleeves, and then dampened his shirt with the wet cloth the boy had brought her, teasing the material away from the wound. She looked at the fabric of the shirt. "This is fine, very fine. I've never seen such a fine weave, and expensive too. You must be a very good thief."

"I'm not a thief; I was shipwrecked," Raphah replied.

"You can say what you like, but if you're in here, it is not for doing good. Now let me see what they have done to you."

Mrs. Landas pulled back the shirt. On the back of his shoulder was a deep and blistered burn in the distinct shape of the letter D.

"My goodness, my goodness. He's given you the brand. When did he buy you?" she shrieked in her seagull voice, surprised at the severity of the wound.

"He didn't buy me. I really was shipwrecked. Two nights ago in a bay just south of here. I am not a slave."

"As far as it goes around here, if you carry that mark, then you're Demurral's property. That's his mark and no one will ever dispute that you belong to him. You better start thinking like a slave or life will get harder for you."

She bathed the wound with a wet rag and dressed it the best she could with old strips of cloth gathered from around the kitchen. Raphah realized that the place must be some kind of hostel for the workers in the mine and that Mrs. Landas was in charge. In between searching for bandages, she would help herself to large gulps of gin from the green bottle. The deaf boy stayed out of her way, curling himself up into the corner of one of the bunk beds, staring out with the large round eyes of a little owl.

She tied off the final bandage and looked at Raphah wistfully.

"Oh, I wish I had a man of me own. Someone for me to look after when they need it, and someone to look after me when I'm too old. . . ." Her top lip began to quiver. "I've got nobody—not a single soul." She put her face into her hands and began to cry. Her feelings could change faster than the tide. Anger welled up in her voice. "If it hadn't have been for him dumping me here, I could have been a real lady. Wouldn't have had to be nice to every drunk that walks down here for a good time."

She stopped, sat back in the chair and lifted up the nearly empty bottle of gin. "If it weren't for this, I wouldn't know what to do. This is the best friend you can ever have, warms the heart, brings you cheer and—"

"Who is he?" Raphah interrupted her, motioning towards the boy.

"He's nobody, got no name—got no voice, can't hear you." She paused. "He's good for sweeping and carrying washing." She looked at the lad. Raphah noticed that her eyes were now gentle towards him, no anger, almost compassionate.

"Where are his mother and father?"

"From what I know, his father could have been one of five men. His mother was very popular with the men, she always wanted to be in love, but never knew who with." She spoke almost dreamily.

"So you knew her?"

"Knew her very well, but her life came to an end eleven years and five months ago and he's been here ever since." She looked at the boy. "I have a soft spot for him. Drives me bloomin' mad half of the time, love him to bits the rest. Just wish he could hear my voice." She stopped and looked at Raphah suspiciously. "What is it with you? Why should I tell you these things? Come on, you need to rest and I need some more gin." She took the bottle and poured the dregs into the cup. "This is going to be the easiest day you'll ever have in this place." She pointed to the wall. "Pick a bed, they've all got fleas. The higher you climb, the less they bite and the better you'll sleep."

She helped Raphah out of the chair and gave him a hand to shin up onto the top bunk. He lay on his good shoulder, hands still chained, and rested his head against the wooden headboard. The straw mattress stuck into his back and itched like nettles.

He lay to one side and looked across the room as Mrs. Landas began to prepare a meal. The light outside began to fade. One by one she lit the lamps around the kitchen and put a candlestick in the window. The deaf boy scurried around after her, collecting wood and carrying flour. She dropped a wooden spoon to the floor, he jumped in with a smile and quickly picked it up, holding it like a trophy for her. They shared a gentle look between them, unaware they were being watched. Mrs. Landas stroked his hair and with smiling eyes kissed his forehead. Raphah closed his eyes as sleep called him to another world. The sounds and smell of the mine faded into an abyss of dreams.

The Hanged Man

The sound of the slamming front door woke Thomas from his dream. It shuddered through the whole house like a small earthquake, rattling the flame of the candle and juddering the beaker on the small table next to the bed. The crashing door was followed by the sound of a man's voice. It had a powerful confident inflection; it spoke of someone who was earthy and rough. It was a voice that he had heard before, and would never forget. It was Jacob Crane.

Thomas could hear the muffled sound of a conversation coming from the kitchen. Crane was talking to Rueben and Isabella in hushed tones. Thomas got up from the bed and pressed his ear to the floor, trying to listen to what was being said. Kate slept on, unaware. No matter how hard he tried, he could not make out what was being said. He could only pick out certain words: tonight . . . the bay . . . hanged. . . .

It was the last word that especially caught his attention. As a young child he had been taken to Whitby to see the hanging of Charles Mayhew. He had been a highwayman, caught by the militia after robbing a coach from York. The whole town had turned out by the pier to see the makeshift gallows and the condemned man. Thomas remembered that it had been a bright June morning, the sun had been warm and the smell of fish and drying nets had filled the air.

Mayhew was dragged screaming from the Customs House

with his hands firmly tied behind his back. He was pulled out onto the gallows, where the noose was forced over his head. From his screams and the way he fought it was obvious how desperate he was not to die. Thomas had been pushed to the front of the crowd. A young drummer boy began to beat out a solitary beat on his drum. The crowd went silent. Mayhew screamed and sobbed, shouting curses at the hangman and the Magistrate. Thomas had tried to press himself back into the crowd but found it was like pushing against a human wall. With every beat of the drum Thomas had waited in expectation for the highwayman to be pushed from the platform of the gibbet and crash to his death. The moment lasted for a lifetime. The drumbeat pounded away like a sea cannon. Mayhew screamed at the crowd.

"You won't see the last of me, I'll be back to haunt every one of yer." He had glared at the Magistrate. "As for you . . . before the cock crows . . . you will be dead."

The priest had shouted for him to repent before he died, but before Mayhew had been given the chance to speak, he was pushed from the gallows. The rush of his falling body and the crack of the knot had sent a chilling gasp through the crowd. It was like a wave crashing on the sea wall sending spray into the air as the crowd, hit by the gasp, jumped back, fell silent and then moments later began to roar savagely.

His body had twitched and jumped at the end of the rope as the last ounce of life was squeezed from him. Some women beat at his hanging legs with long sticks and children threw stones at the dangling warm corpse. Thomas stood silently. He looked at the body of the man and wondered where the life had gone. What kind of a world was this that in one moment all the energy, all the substance of life itself, could be snuffed out like a candle? Thomas thought it was a cruel God who could give him life, no matter how hard, and then in the twinkling of an eye take it from him and condemn him to nothingness.

It was Kate getting up from the bed that roused him from his thoughts. She kicked at him with her foot, scrunched up her eyebrows and made a face. Thomas placed a finger over his mouth and whispered, "Shhh."

He looked to the floor and signalled that he was trying to listen to the conversation downstairs. Kate got down beside him, pressing her ear to the crack in the floorboards. The conversation carried on below. Even Bealda and Ephrig joined in. Kate heard her name mentioned by Rueben, his deep liquorice voice easily carrying above the rest. It was then that Thomas heard the sound of footsteps crashing up the stairs. The bedroom door was flung open and Bealda crashed into the room, falling over the two bodies on the floor between the beds.

Bealda began to laugh in the only way he knew how. It was the kind of laughter that started in the belly and welled up like the eruption of a large volcano, spilling out of his mouth in torrents of deep belly grunts. He was a large child for his age, with hands the size of a man's. He got to his feet and, still laughing, took hold of Kate and Thomas, lifting them both from the floor.

"My father wants to talk to you downstairs," he said. "We have a visitor. He wants to see you. He has news of your friend."

They knew that Bealda was speaking about Raphah. In their sleep they had forgotten about their friend. Now the memories of the night before came flooding back. Thomas looked to the window. The painted tree framed a scene of complete blackness. It was now night. He felt as if the time of peace and safety was drawing to a close, like the tide rising on a man stranded on the rocks. He knew that they would both have to leave the sanctuary of Boggle Mill to challenge Demurral.

Reluctantly, they followed Bealda downstairs.

The kitchen was bathed in a beautiful amber light from several large candlesticks that adorned the mantelpiece and window ledge. Thomas looked around the room anxiously. There were Rueben, Isabella, the twins and . . . Jacob Crane.

Crane was sitting closest to the fire, dressed in the deepest black from head to mud-stained boots. He leant forward and looked at Thomas and Kate through his narrow, piercing eyes.

Thomas could feel a lump growing in his throat, a goitre of fear making it hard to swallow. He knew that Crane was not a man to be spoken to without good cause. Now Crane was right there in front of him, perched on the oak chair, eyeing him like a large, black, menacing raven waiting to jump down and tear at a dead carcass.

Thomas nodded to Crane as Kate tried to stand behind him in his shadow. Crane was the first to speak.

"Sit down, you two. I have news of a friend of yours who is in very deep trouble." Crane emphasized each word as he spoke. Isabella got up and pulled two chairs from the table for Thomas and Kate to sit on. They faced Crane and the glowing embers of the fire. Thomas stared into the red-hot depths, his eyes soaking up every drop of light.

"You two have bitten off more than you can chew and your friend is as good as dead." He clapped his hands together, rubbing his dry palms. "What you did last night could have made me a very poor man." He looked at Thomas.

"All we did was try to get into—" He was quickly interrupted by Crane.

"All you did was run around in the tunnels, where I had fifty casks of brandy and twenty-four cases of tea, all fresh off the boat and awaiting a good price." His voice grew louder and louder. "Demurral didn't know it was there until he went looking for you and your friend. You have cost me a fortune. All for storing tea and brandy overnight. Two hundred pounds is a very expensive lodging." He glared at Thomas. Kate could feel the tears welling up in her eyes and her heart beat faster as she wondered what Crane would do to them.

Crane's thin face twitched with anger. It was as if every muscle moved by itself. He rubbed his hands together harder and harder, and they scraped like sandstone against wood. "So, what is it going to be then, Thomas? How are you going to pay me back?"

"What about our friend? Is he alive?" Thomas gulped

down the lump in his throat as he spoke.

"Your friend is as good as dead. Demurral told me himself this morning. He's had him branded as a slave, with a letter D burnt into his shoulder. He'll be digging alum shale until he drops, and that'll be either from exhaustion or from the gallows."

Thomas opened his mouth to reply, but Rueben butted in. It was a voice that brought a sense of peace.

"Mr. Crane has a plan. We have told him all that we know of you and he would like to help." He paused and looked at them both. "It may save Raphah's life and your own."

"Who told you about Raphah? We never mentioned his name." Thomas looked at Kate.

"I told Isabella," she said. "I had to tell someone. It was the creatures. They frightened me." Kate began to cry and she wiped the tears on the sleeve of her dress. Isabella put her arm around her and held her close.

"I'm not frightened by Demurral's witchcraft." Crane spoke in a scornful voice. "He can have all the hordes of hell and I will not let it stand in the way of my brandy. He can have Old Nick himself trying to stop me, but we'll see how he takes a ball of lead and the swipe of a cutlass." Crane laughed. "I have twenty men and a fast ship anchored off in the bay. All I want from you is to be my bait for Demurral, then I'll get your friend and whatever he's after. I want the brandy, tax free, and some of the money I have paid the old dog over the last ten years."

"Don't trust him, Thomas. My father said he's a thief and a murderer." Kate leapt towards Crane like a cat about to lash out with her claws. Isabella held her back as she kicked out and struggled. Crane didn't move or even flinch.

He spoke calmly. "Your father, Kate Coglan, is as twisted as I am. He has helped me smuggle enough brandy and tea to fill Whitby harbour. He's had more money out of my pocket than you will ever know, and it's kept you fed and clothed since your mother died."

"Liar. Liar! My father's an Excise man, he works for the

King. He catches smugglers." She shouted the words at Crane. "He would never work for a thief and murderer like you. He's an honest man and that is a word you will never understand."

Crane sat impassively as she screamed at him. He looked at Rueben and nodded towards the front door of the cottage. Rueben got up from the chair and walked across the kitchen to the door. He opened it wide. The cold night air rolled in, bringing a chill to the room. The light from the candles appeared to dim as they fluttered in the draught; it was as if the darkness outside was sucking away the light from the cottage into the ever-increasing blackness.

Rueben spoke quietly to someone in the shadows. Kate could see the shape of a man illuminated by the escaping light. The man stepped closer to the door. She could see he was dressed in a dirty brown oilskin and a whale-oiled hat that shone in the amber light. He bent down to get through the small entrance and stepped into the cottage. He stood by the door with rainwater dripping from his coat. He began to look up, taking off the oilskin hat. Kate shuddered with surprise as she stared into the eyes of her father.

"I think you two don't need an introduction, do you? Kate Coglan, I hope you can recognize your father even in this light. Come in, Mr. Coglan, and sit down. . . . Doubtless she'll want to slap you around the face or kick you in the shins for letting her down all these years. I think she's old enough now to know the whole truth about you and me."

Kate stared at her father in disbelief. She gulped down mouthfuls of air, trying to stop herself from crying as she squeezed her nails into the palms of her hands.

"He knows you, he knows your name," she shouted at her father. "You told me he was a thief and that you wanted to see him dead."

"Who do you think has kept you fed all these years? It wasn't the money from the Customs House. If it weren't for working with Jacob, we would have been out on the streets long ago."

"If it weren't for your drinking, we'd have had plenty to eat without you having to lie, cheat and steal, Father."

"If it weren't for your brother dying, and then your mother, I would never have turned to drinking or smuggling. But neither of us can change the things of the past, Kate. And from what I hear, you have got yourself in all sorts of bother. It won't be long before Demurral beats it out of your friend as to who was with him, and then both of you will be fitted for the rope. I don't want to see a child of mine dangling from the gallows on Beacon Hill."

He stepped towards Kate and held out both hands. It was something he had never done before in his life. She noticed that they trembled as he held them towards her. He tried to smile at her. His face felt so awkward; he was not a man to whom smiling came naturally. It had been so many years since he had even wanted to smile at anyone. A frown and a sharp word had been the only expression of love that he could muster. That and the tears he had wrung out of his gin-soaked soul every time he had fallen into the drunken melancholy of weeping for his lost wife.

He spoke out the soft words. "I love you, Kate."

"If you'd loved me, you would never have lied to me." Her harsh voice covered her true feelings. She wanted to run to him, to put her arms around him and make all things well again. She felt she was rooted to the floor by her anger. She bit her lip, hoping the pain would make all this hurt go away.

"Everyone lies, Kate. It's a part of life. The truth would have been too much for you to cope with. To share a secret with a child and to ask them to keep it is like trying to keep a butterfly alive in winter."

"But you didn't have to lie to me, I am your daughter, I could have helped you. All you wanted to do was soak up the gin, and when you were out working, you were really helping Jacob Crane."

Crane stood up and walked towards her. It was the first time she had seen him up close. He was tall and thin. A white collar poked from beneath his silver-buttoned black jacket. His blonde hair fell over his forehead. On his right cheek was a long cut that had been freshly salted.

"Tonight is not the time for fighting each other or dragging up the past." He looked at Kate and Thomas and put a strong hand on both their shoulders. "You two have a lot to answer for; and before the dawn you may have a chance to make it right." He paused and stared at them both. "Or by the dawn we may all be dead."

10

The Dunamez

Raphah could not believe his eyes. He had fallen asleep in a dark, almost empty room with Mrs. Landas and the boy scurrying about, lighting the lamps. Now he woke up to a bright, smoke-filled workhouse, a great hubbub rising from the gathering at the table.

He looked down from the top bunk bed and felt like a spectator to some grand opera staring down from the highest balcony. Gathered below him was an assembly of the world's most ragged people. Packed into the room were men, women and children, all dirty and covered in the red dust and mud that overlaid the whole mine.

The noise of their chatter echoed against the stone walls. Empty plates littered the table. Everyone spoke excitedly to each other. This was well-fed conversation, while children played in front of a large fire that had been lit in the fireplace. It was a feast of the shabby and tattered, who ate a banquet of potatoes and turnip with a flavouring bone from an old sheep. The remnants of the meal stuck to the bottom of a large stew pan that hovered over the flames, steaming and spluttering like the mouth of some large black volcano.

He could see that there was an order to the table, with the older and less bedraggled men sitting near to the fire at the far end. Mrs. Landas sat in state at the head of the table, smoking a fresh pipe and drinking gin and third-brew beer from a large mug. Raphah thought she looked like some queen holding court, surrounded by courtiers.

To her right was a large, thickset man in a torn jacket and frayed shirt with a piece of red cloth tied loosely around his neck beneath a strong, bold jaw and deep-set eyes. He never smiled and sat back in his chair with a scowl on his face, listening to those around him.

He spoke to Mrs. Landas through clenched brown teeth. "Can we have the cards tonight, Mary? It would be good to see what will be for the future."

Mrs. Landas nodded to the young woman seated to her left, who pulled out a drawer in the table and brought out a bundle of blue silk cloth. Mrs. Landas unwrapped it and took out a large pack of picture cards.

The whole room went quiet as she slowly and deliberately shuffled the pack. She looked around the room and smiled at each person sitting at the long table.

"Who shall it be tonight?" she asked as she looked into their faces, trying to speak in a solemn and serious voice. "What will the cards tell us about our lives?"

Several of the older children called out, trying to grab her attention. Mrs. Landas shook her head at them as if to say it would not be their turn. Each one turned away with a look of disappointment on their face.

"Do it for Demurral—let's see what the cards say for him. After all, his future is our future," replied one of the men sitting close by as he tapped his pipe on the sole of his leather boot.

A woman butted in. "I can't get out of here until I pay back all that I owe him. Tell us, Mary. What happens to him today will haunt us tomorrow. If his future's good, then maybe he'll set me free without me having to pay seven years' rent and the interest on the loan he gave me to pay him back."

Each person in the room owed Demurral money. When they could no longer pay the debt, they came to the mine to work long hours for little wages. With each year of work they would sink deeper in debt to him. He would charge them for their food, children, board and lodgings and even for the tools they used to dig the shale from his mine.

"All right, all right. Demurral it is then!" Mrs. Landas spoke in a loud voice as she hit the cards against the table. This was the cue for the deaf boy to begin to blow out the candles on the window ledge and fireplace. He turned down the lamps and the room dropped into a dim light, Mrs. Landas outlined by an orange aura from the glow of the fire.

"You must all concentrate on the Parson, picture his face in your mind, and I will ask the spirit of the cards to speak to us all."

In the shadow cast by the fire those facing her could hardly see her features. The light from a small candle flickered across her face, giving the impression that it was changing in appearance. She placed the cards on the table and pulled the shawl over the back of her head. When the evening meal was over and after several glasses of gut-rot gin, Mrs. Landas would often perform her magic. She would turn the divining cards, piecing together fact and fiction, telling people what they wanted to hear and surprising them with secrets of their lives that she had surreptitiously gleaned from other people's conversations. Tonight, she thought to herself, might be her finest performance.

"You're not thinking hard enough, there's nothing coming through. How do you expect me to come into spirit if you don't think hard enough? We have to concentrate to open the door into the afterlife." She spoke quickly, closing her eyes and screwing and contorting her face. "Spirit . . . speeeeak . . . toooo . . . meeee. . . ."

She gave a squeak as she spoke, trying to make her voice sound as if it belonged to someone else. Three loud, strong knocks came from somewhere in the darkness. A shudder went through everyone seated at the table. One woman supped from a glass of gin, whilst another clutched the arm of the man next to her. The children huddled together in the light of the fire, hoping to be saved from the darkness.

Mrs. Landas, shocked at the sudden reply from the spirit world, opened one eye and stared around the room. "Who is it? Do you want to speak to us?" she said timidly, pretending to speak in the voice of a little girl.

The man next to her shivered with excitement, obviously impressed. A single loud and defiant knock came again, much firmer than before. Everyone huddled more closely together.

"We want to know what will happen to Parson Demurral. Will you tell us?"

The knock came suddenly and even more powerfully than before, making everyone, including Mrs. Landas, jump with fright. Her voice went up an octave through real fear. This had never happened before. No real spirit had ever knocked.

Mrs. Landas spread out the cards in front of her and picked several at random from the pack. One by one she turned them over.

"Here, the place where he dwells, to speak of life in heaven or hell." She turned over the first card. It was a picture of a man dressed in the robes of a priest holding a golden cup and standing at an altar.

"Oh!" she exclaimed. "This is Demurral, the magician. The spirits always speak of him through this card. Let us see what stands in his way." She began to turn another card.

"Here be all that comes against thee, sword or tempest, love or honour."

She turned the card. It was the picture of a tower being struck by lightning with a man falling from the battlements. Without speaking, she turned more cards and placed them in a circle around the others. Every time she turned a card, she muttered under her breath, looking even more worried.

"What is it, Mary? Tell us what they say." The man next to her pulled at her shawl, wanting an answer. She turned over the final card to reveal the picture of a gnarled skeleton surrounded by bloodred flames.

Mrs. Landas began to pray as she choked back the tears that

welled up in her. She started to tremble with fear, hoping that what she saw in the cards would never come true.

"What is it, Mary? You can't sit there and not say anything, tell us."

She drew breath and spoke slowly.

"The cards speak of a power coming to take this place. Many will be killed if it is not stopped. There will be a disaster, the land will fall into the sea and the devil himself will walk amongst us. Each one of you is in great danger."

"Only if you allow it to happen," a voice called from the darkness.

Everyone turned and looked to see who had dared to speak and break the magic of the séance. Raphah was on the top bunk, his legs dangling down over the side.

"Do you really believe in the power of those picture cards? There is a far greater law than the one that controls the roll of the dice or the turn of a card." He climbed down from the bunk and walked to the table. "Each one of you is taken in by what you hear. You're quick to believe in spirits when it's really someone banging on the side of the bed. None of you will turn to the one who can truly set you free."

"Who are you to talk about freedom? A lad who is a slave speaking to us about freedom—what do you know?" said the man next to Mrs. Landas.

"What makes you any different from me? I am black and you are white. In so many ways we are the same, but you are captive to more things than I will ever be. I may have chains on my wrists, but not even Demurral can capture the soul of the one who follows Riathamus."

The man was quick to reply. "You speak a lot for a slave. We know what life will be like for you—what's left of it." They all laughed.

"My soul is in the hands of the one who sent me here. He has a plan for my life, a plan to prosper and not to harm. A plan to give hope and a future. These cards speak lies to trap and ensnare you."

Raphah leant over the table and picked up the pack of cards. He knew that he had to speak the truth. Mrs. Landas jumped up from her chair and tried to snatch them back.

He held out the cards. "These are evil, and they will lead you into a place from which you will never escape. These are detestable to the one who sent me."

"Who are you calling evil? I bandage your wounds, make you food, welcome you into my home, let you sleep when you should be working, and you call me evil," she said angrily, almost spitting at him. "These cards are precious, they cost me more than a year's wages. Get your dirty hands off them."

Mrs. Landas grabbed at the cards, but Raphah held them away from her. She felt shocked by what Raphah had said. In her world, Mrs. Landas was always right and answered to no one but Demurral. She had never been challenged about anything like this before. In her own way Mrs. Landas had always thought the cards were a drama and a ritual to entertain and make her feel important because she had knowledge that others would never possess. Now she had been told that the pictures were evil. She looked at the cards in his hand and didn't know whether to snatch them back from him. Somehow they now seemed to be tarnished. She was reluctant even to touch them. A doubt had crept into her mind. They had lost their innocence, were no longer a parlour game taught to her by her mother. She was angry that she had been challenged and confronted by the truth in her own lodging house.

There was something about Raphah that unnerved her and made her feel uncomfortable. He was so sure of himself, with an inner confidence. He had a visible purity, a cleanliness of the soul that shone through his eyes and brought hope into the dirt of her surroundings.

"And just what is this 'one' going to do?" she snapped at Raphah. "Can he make our life any better, take us out of this place? Can he stop Demurral from overworking us, underfeeding us and never paying us?" Mrs. Landas prodded a sharp pointed finger into his chest with each question. "Where is this 'one' that you speak about? Can we see him?"

"He's behind you, Mrs. Landas." He raised one eyebrow as he spoke. Mrs. Landas jumped around to see what was there. "No, Mrs. Landas, he is all around you. You can't see him, but he knows the secrets of all your hearts."

"Who are you? Where are you from?" said Mrs. Landas, angry at his impertinence. Raphah looked at the staring faces gathered around him. It seemed that the whole room waited for him to reply.

"That is not important. Tonight the one who sent me will show you something that will change your lives forever." Raphah stepped towards her, holding out the cards.

"What if we don't want to change?"

"Then he will open your eyes so that you may see the dung heap in which your soul is sleeping." He prodded her in the shoulder with his finger. "Wake up. Rise from the dead. And let the light shine in your darkness."

The deaf boy pushed Raphah away from her. Raphah grabbed him by the shoulders and pushed him into the lap of Mrs. Landas.

"Hold on to your son, Mrs. Landas. You're about to get him back." He then placed two firm hands upon the boy's head. Before she could speak, Raphah began to call out in a language she could not understand.

"Abba-shekinah, El Shammah, soatzettay-isthi hugiez."

He spoke at the top of his voice. Everyone in the room stood back, unsure what he would do next, frightened by the force of the words.

It was then that something strange and frightening began to happen. It felt as if the whole building was beginning to shake. The children dived under the table while the men looked at each other in complete disbelief. A loud creaking made everyone in the room turn to see the large wooden front door beginning to bend inwards. With a sudden crack it broke open, smashing against the wall. Streaks of silver and white lightning crashed in and arced across the room, earthing against the walls and ceiling with a loud thud like the sound of a freshly charged musket firing. A fine gold mist quickly filled the room. Small round globes of rainbow light danced through the air above the heads of the frightened onlookers.

Raphah, oblivious to the manifestations taking place around him, repeated the words over and over again. The young deaf boy began to shake, every muscle and sinew of his body jerking with the power that swept through him. Mrs. Landas leapt to her feet, pushing him from her as she fell to the floor, burying her face in her hands and begging for Raphah to stop what was happening.

Everyone was now facedown on the floor, covering their eyes to protect them from the incredible brightness of the golden light that filled every corner of the room. It was as if they were being forced to the ground, pressed into the floor by the weight of the glory. Each droplet of the mist appeared to weigh more than gold. No one could move: Their limbs were as heavy as lead. As the golden mist swirled around the room, they all rested in the peace that it brought. Every man, woman and child appeared to be in a deep sleep.

It was the sudden screaming and jumping around of the deaf boy that broke the silence. He had never made a sound in his life, but now he began to whoop and holler like a young dog. He shouted as loud as he could, then covered his ears to try and dampen the pain of the noise that he made.

The sound of his infectious high-pitched laughter brought Mrs. Landas out of her dreaming and from her hiding place under the table, where she had been wedged between two chairs. He jumped up and down and round and round, laughing and screaming as he heard his own voice for the first time. She looked at the boy and began to cry, holding her arms out to him and calling him by his name for the very first time.

"John, come to me, come to me. . . . Come to your mother."

She broke down in tears as she held out her arms towards

him. John smiled as he tried to speak the word *mother*. He ran into her arms. Together they cried. John was sobbing with joy and Mrs. Landas was sobbing with the delight that she was free to love him again.

Whatever had happened in that moment, she now knew that her love for her son would last forever. For so many years Mrs. Landas had felt as if she had a heart of stone, unable to love or to be loved. In those few short moments all that had been transformed. She had a heart of flesh and a feeling of great joy instead of constant despair.

As quickly as it had appeared, the golden mist vanished. The children came out from their hiding place under the table, and the men and women pulled themselves up from the floor. They all stared at Raphah, John and Mrs. Landas standing together at the end of the table, silhouetted by the blazing fire. No one dared to speak.

"How did you know?" Mrs. Landas asked Raphah as she stroked John's hair. "How did you know he was my son?"

"It was in your eyes, Mary. They are the window of the soul. Not even the hate you have for this place could stop that seed of love showing through." He wiped away a tear as it slowly rolled across her cheek. "Here is the man that you have prayed for. He can hear you and soon will be able to speak to you. He will be your future."

Mrs. Landas took the divining cards from him. "Somehow I don't think I will ever want to use these again."

With that she threw the cards and the silk cover into the blazing fire. They scattered in the flames. One card leapt from the inferno, thrust up by the hot fumes, rising in the thermal. Suddenly it fluttered and spun from the fire, falling facedown onto the stone hearth as if picked from the flames by an unseen hand.

Raphah bent over and picked up the card. He began to laugh as he held out the card for all to see.

"Not even this magician will be able to escape his fate so easily next time." Raphah slowly crushed the divining card in the palm of his hand and threw it back into the flames.

No one saw the small dark figure that crept into the room through the open door. It had the appearance of a small man with a long, white, poker-thin face and crooked sharp teeth that filled its large mouth. It looked like a shadow. In places its body was opaque, in other places quite transparent. The creature walked slowly from the doorway, staring at Raphah as it took careful, deliberate steps across the room.

The man with a red neck scarf sat at the far end of the table. He was unsure about what he had just seen, and felt quite dazed by all he had experienced. With a quick shudder of the spine, the creature suddenly stepped into the man's body. The man gave a gasp and closed his eyes, not knowing what was happening and unable to call out for help. He felt as if he were drowning as the creature smothered his soul. He could feel the creature inside his mind and could taste its dank, ghastly breath as it breathed through his mouth. He opened his eyes again, and this time it was the creature that looked out upon the world through them; it was now able to control every thought and action of the body it possessed. The man coughed and spluttered as the stench filled his lungs. The creature looked at Raphah and waited for the right moment to bring an end to his life. On the table was a carving knife. Using the man's hand, the creature took the knife and slipped it into the pocket of his jacket.

Bell, Book and Candle

Jacob Crane beat his clenched gloved fist against the black oak door of the Vicarage. It was midnight and in the nearby courtyard a large white cockerel crowed and shouted at the full moon that rose bloodred out of the sea.

The pounding echoed through the empty hallway and corridors of the house until it finally reached the ears of Beadle, who was sprawled over the kitchen table, half asleep. He was facedown in a thick slice of freshly buttered brown bread that he had been eating to dry up the several pints of warm beer that he had been quaffing all evening. Beadle enjoyed drinking, not through thirst but through the desire to feel the effects of the brew running through his veins and numbing out the pain of the world. Over the years he had become a skilled brewer. He made his own beer, mixing in the extra herbs that he gathered from his secret place at Boggle Brook. He would dry the leaves and sometimes the flowers and then mix them with the barley, wild hops, yeast and a large dollop of honey.

Tonight he realized that he had made two mistakes. One was to drink the beer whilst it was still fermenting. The other was that he had added too much valerian to the brew. All he knew was that he could hardly open his eyes as the effects of the valerian pulled them tightly shut, giving him the feeling that he would be trapped in his dreaming forever with numb lips and arms that felt as if they were made of rolled carpet.

Far more important was the belief he now had that the fermenting beer was about to make his stomach explode. As he lay drowsily, hearing the banging on the door somewhere in the distance, mouthfuls of half-digested ale gulped their way back into the world. Beadle gave a loud, retching belch that reverberated throughout the kitchen. He tried to raise his head from the table, realizing that somehow he would have to answer the banging at the door that was now becoming even louder and more insistent.

As he did so, he wiped the thick slice of bread over his forehead, believing it to be a soft, moist facecloth. The flakes of bread stuck to his skin, but he was neither aware of, nor could he really care, how he looked. He could not get the thoughts of the beautiful white flowers of the valerian out of his mind. In his half-dream all he could see as he tried to rouse himself was the small plant that he had picked on a summer's day, leaving a farthing coin pushed into the roots as payment to the Green Man, and had dried carefully by the kitchen range. He muttered under his breath.

Beadle would drink little during the day, preferring the tea that he stole from his master. He always waited until at least six o'clock before he opened the tap on the large wooden barrel and filled his cup to overflowing, again and again.

The beer allowed him to dream, to be someone that he could never be. It allowed him the freedom to think, or so he thought, although now he found that he needed more and more to gain the same blissful state as the year before. When he drank, he felt liberated from the boredom of his servitude. In his mind he would become an important man, someone who was doing more with his life than run after the Vicar. In reality, however, his merriment had caused him to become more short-tempered and even more dissatisfied with himself and his life.

Now the taste of the yeast and barley stuck to the roof of his mouth and through his dream the thumping at the door grew louder. He staggered from the kitchen and attempted to walk in a straight line along the hallway. The pounding grew even louder. He bounced from wall to wall as he almost rolled along the passageway, holding on to each door frame that he passed. The large gold raven that was set high above the front door stared down at him. In his drunkenness he was sure that the bird moved and twitched its feathers and opened one eye. He took hold of the large door handle and began to turn it. Suddenly and powerfully the door was forced open, almost pushing him to one side. The cold night air flooded into the house, and in the candlelight the tall figure of Jacob Crane filled the doorway.

"Where's your master?" Crane spoke as if he wanted an immediate answer. Beadle, still fuddled by the beer, stood with a blank expression on his face.

"Master?" He paused as if he didn't know the answer. He looked at Crane as he swayed from side to side. "I think he's in bed, or he could be out. Or he could be—"

Crane bent down and stared at Beadle eye to eye, a hairsbreadth between them.

"Fetch him. *Now!*" Crane shouted into his face. Beadle tried to focus his eyes on the end of Jacob Crane's long nose.

The reply was one that Crane would never have expected. Beadle belched a long, loud and fetid retort directly into his nostrils. The strong smell made him wince in disgust. Crane was direct in his reply. The gloved hand shot out and slapped Beadle across the face, sending him spinning across the hall and into a large wooden coat stand that fell on top of him.

"You *pig,*" said Crane in cold disgust as he stepped towards the prostrate figure of Beadle.

"Sorry, Mr. Crane, it's the beer. I can't seem to keep it down." Beadle belched again, trying to prove that it had been an accident. "I can't stop. . . . It's the ale. . . . Sometimes it gets the better of me."

"Then I suggest that you don't drink it." The voice came from the balcony at the top of the stairs. There stood Demurral, dressed in a black dressing gown and red nightcap. "Beadle, take

Mr. Crane into the study and I will be down shortly. Bring a tray of sherry."

Beadle got to his feet and looked blurrily for the door to the study. All the doors looked the same and somehow he could not recognize which was which. Crane saw the befuddlement on his face and opened the study door. He took the candle from the stand in the hallway and walked inside, leaving Beadle alone in the dark.

He went to the window of the study and opened the curtains. The bright silver light of the full moon flooded into the room, giving everything a mercurial glow. Placing the candlestick on the big round table in the middle of the room, he sat in the leather chair by the fire. He was soon joined by Demurral, who threw a pine log onto the embers.

"And to what do I owe this nocturnal visit from Jacob Crane?" he asked.

"Money, the language of life," replied Crane.

"But I have taken a vow of poverty. Why should I be interested in money?" Demurral smiled as he spoke, tilting his head to one side.

"Well, if that is the case, it should make my task easier. I have a shipment of brandy in your cellar and you want me to pay for one night's rent." He gave Demurral a stern look. "I do not want to pay you. In return for the free board and lodging for my goods, I am prepared to give you something that you want." Crane took off his leather gloves and neatly folded them across his lap. For several moments the men stared at each other.

"What could I possibly want? I have everything I desire."

"*Desire.* That is a strange word for a priest. Unsatisfied longing, lustful pleasure from gaining a possession. Conjures up all sorts of things that priests shouldn't think about. Not really the word for a man of the Church." He twisted his leather gloves in his hand. "If I were to tell you that I had two people who wanted to relieve you of one of your desires, how much would they be worth to you?"

"Theft is theft and they would have to go before the authorities and answer for their crime." Demurral edged his chair closer to Crane. "After all, they conspired to steal something very precious, something I had paid good money for. Surely it is your duty as a good citizen to hand them over freely."

In one move Crane leapt from his chair, slipped the dagger from its sheath and pressed the long, sharp blade against Demurral's throat.

"I am not here to play games, Vicar. Now do you want them for a price, or shall I let them go? You have one of them and I have the other two. For three hundred pounds you can have all of them. I don't think that for one moment they will ever see the inside of a courtroom, so you can do with them as you wish." He pulled the flat of the blade across Demurral's throat. "I hear you like to take the young ones up into that tower of yours." He paused and gestured towards the window. "I see there has been a lot of digging going on in your garden, and it is not the time of year for planting . . . but then I suppose it depends what kind of little seeds you have been placing under the earth." He held the point of the blade underneath Demurral's chin, pressing it softly into his flesh.

"Three hundred pounds will be fine. I'll have Beadle get you the money. When can I have charge of my new guests?" Demurral gulped the words, not daring to move.

Crane took the knife away from his throat and put it back into the sheath hidden in the lining of his jacket.

"I will bring them here in one hour. In return I expect the money to be waiting for me. Any tricks and you'll be joining your little seedlings. Understand?"

"Mr. Crane, I would never want to cheat anyone who has such a wonderful command of the King's English."

"Tell me, Demurral, what is it that you have got that makes them want to put their young lives at risk?" His eyes searched the room in the half-light, looking for something of value.

"It is just a trifle, an artefact brought here by an explorer, a religious relic of no real value to anyone other than a pious man like me." Demurral hesitated as he spoke, not knowing why Crane should ask such a question.

"I am a man who has travelled the world. Seeing such a thing would be of great interest to me." Crane reached into his jacket pocket and clutched the handle of the knife. He smiled at Demurral.

"I can understand that." Demurral spoke quickly. "I don't think there will be any harm in showing you what this little folly really is." He shouted over to the doorway: "Beadle, can you bring the case from my room, our guest would like to see what all the fuss is about."

Beadle had been sitting on the floor in the hallway, still recovering from the brew and the blow. He had even forgotten to get the drinks ordered by Demurral. He had forgotten where he was. He tried to drag himself up from the floor and onto his unsteady and very numb feet. In his intoxicated condition he did not know if he had answered or not.

"Beadle, you drunken ouzel, get up and get the case. My guest is waiting." The shout rang out through the house. Both men could hear the sound of Beadle trying to run up the stairs and along the long passageway to Demurral's room. Loud thuds told them how often Beadle fell, stumbling over a rug, a loose floorboard or his own numb feet.

"He has a little weakness," Demurral said as he raised his eyes to the sound of clattering above his head. "He likes to drink. He has so few pleasures in life, I would find it so hard to deny him that."

"And what is your pleasure, Vicar? Money? Wealth? Power?"

"No, no, no. I am a man of simple pleasures and I seek to do the will of him who has sent me."

"Then it's not true that you are a liar, a cheat and some would even say a murderer?" Crane laughed as he spoke. Demurral did not know if the smuggler was fooling with him. Jacob Crane had a fiery temper from years at sea. At fourteen he had been press-ganged into the Navy. He had taken the King's shilling and woken up in the bowels of a Navy cutter sailing to India. At the age of twenty-four he had jumped ship and since that time had earned his money as a smuggler and a cutthroat.

Beadle re-entered the room, dragging the long black leather case, and placed it on the table in the middle of the room. Demurral got up from the chair and lit another candle. He began the ritual of unpacking the acacia pole and the black hand. Eventually, he brought out the Keruvim. Crane looked at the small winged figure as it glowed in the light of the moon.

"What price did you give for that, then, Vicar?" He wanted to sound as if he had little interest in the value.

"Not a great deal. These native pieces have no real value. To me it is . . . er . . . of religious interest." He lifted the Keruvim from the table.

"What would you do with something like that, then?"

"Do you believe in the spirit world, Mr. Crane?" Demurral looked straight at him. Then continued to speak in a hushed tone. "A world of powers that we could only dream of?"

"I don't think that a philosopher's stone or the witchcraft of some harlot has any use in this world of ours. This is the modern world; religion is for the feeble and the uneducated," said Crane boldly. "What I have achieved in life is through the work of my own two hands and the blood of those who have stood in my way. I have no place for God or superstitious hocus-pocus." Crane stepped closer to the Keruvim, intrigued by the fine detail carved into the gold and the eyes made of pearl.

Demurral ignored Crane's remarks. "Think of a world where we were not the most powerful creatures, where the laws of time and space had been suspended. A place where power and control mattered more than love or charity." He turned the Keruvim in his hand so that it glistened in the moonlight. "Imagine having more power than God himself, being able to control the elements, the wind, the sea or even the rising of the sun. Imagine what power that would give . . . imagine what satisfaction . . . being able to destroy everyone who had ever done anything to you. Perfect revenge, and they wouldn't even know it was you." Demurral placed the figure back in the box. "I too would never be satisfied with a stone that could turn objects into gold, or the spells of a witch. The only thing that would satisfy me would be the power of God himself."

Demurral placed the pole and the black hand into the box and closed the lid. He then sat back in the chair by the fire.

"You don't desire very much then, Vicar. I thought men of the cloth were supposed to serve the Almighty, not the other way round?"

"That all depends how long he will be almighty; surely he can't hang on to his power forever." Demurral rubbed his hands together and kicked the smouldering log on the fire. It sparked and hissed as the dampness mixed with the red-hot embers.

"You're a brave man talking about your God like that, Demurral. Anyway, do you really believe in a spirit world, ghosts and demons?" Crane walked from the chair to the window and looked out over the sea to Baytown. The lights of the fishermen's cottages flickered in the darkness beneath the glowing cloud. In the bay he could see the rigging of his own ship, silhouetted against the cliffs. "It would take a miracle to make me believe in anything other than the power of the sword or the musket ball. Nothing can turn lead to gold quicker than that." He turned from the window and looked at Demurral, who was digging at the fire with a long brass poker.

"With my help, Mr. Crane, I could make you the richest man in the world. No more having to go to sea, no more putting your life at risk. You could sit back and enjoy the riches of the nations." He walked over to the window and stood next to Crane. "Look, all this could be yours and all you have to do is work for me."

"I didn't realize all the county belonged to you. I thought it was the property of the King under God." He took a step back from Demurral, who was now standing uncomfortably close. The

Vicar seemed to be suppressing excitement, as if anticipating some wonderful event that only he was aware of.

"Things change, Mr. Crane, things change. You will witness that tonight. Bring the two thieves to me and that will be the start. Come to the tower and I will show you something that will change your mind forever." Demurral stared into Jacob Crane's eyes. "You were right in what you said, the blood of those who stand in your way can often bring you all that your heart desires. It has been said that the man who loves his life will lose it and the man that hates his life in this world will keep it forever." He paused; it was an unpleasant silence. "Do you love your life, Mr. Crane?"

The Azimuth

Obadiah Demurral and Jacob Crane stepped off the stone staircase and onto a large flagstone that formed a landing at the top of the tower. Demurral tugged at Crane's jacket sleeve and pushed Beadle through the doorway. Together they entered a spacious circular room with slit windows filled with dark leaded glass. The moon glimmered through each pane, casting green and blue lights across the stone walls. In the centre of the room, standing in the middle of a circle painted on the stone floor and set between two stone columns that reached to the roof, was a wooden table covered with a linen cloth and a candlestick placed at each end. Above their heads the copper roof thudded and banged with the beating of the wind.

"Welcome to my holy place, Mr. Crane. Far more power here than in any church." Demurral flashed his eyes wildly around the dark room. He motioned for Crane to step into the darkness. "Don't be afraid, there's nothing here that can harm you. . . . Well, not yet."

Crane made no reply, keeping the growing feeling of unease to himself. He stepped into the circle and stood by the table.

"Please don't touch the altar—holy hands, only holy hands." Demurral was excited. Just being in the room brought him a deep sense of pleasure.

"So what is this place for? I thought you restricted your worship to the church?" Jacob Crane looked around the room. There were signs of faith, the altar, the circle and a six-pointed star painted on the wall in cobalt blue.

"Church is the place for reciting meaningless words to a God who isn't listening anymore," Demurral replied. "Here is the place where the answer lies. In each one of us there is a god waiting to be set free. All we need is the key to the power." Demurral ran the back of his hand over the white linen cloth that covered the table and looked at Crane to see what response he would make. Crane slid his hand into his jacket, firmly taking hold of the handle of the knife. He could feel the cold metal against his hot, moist palms. In his thirty-two years Jacob Crane had seen many things and killed many men. There was something about Demurral that made his flesh creep and his mouth dry. Crane didn't fear much in life, but being in the presence of this man knotted his stomach and unleashed the impulse to kill him on the spot.

"So what do you worship, then? Yourself or something else?" he asked abruptly, and waited for Demurral to reply.

"A god has to be worth worshipping. Personally, I never found that our God could live up to all our human expectations. We ask him to heal, and people die; we ask him to bring peace and all we get is suffering. He tells us to love our enemy and we have trouble loving ourselves. He takes all the pleasure out of life, and when we die, will we find paradise?" Demurral took in a sudden deep gasp of breath, throwing back his long white hair. He composed himself and looked at Beadle. "I have been the servant of the Almighty for most of my life, I have suffered for him, been ridiculed for him and given up everything for him. What did he ever do for me? When I came here, I found something else, or should I say . . . something else found me."

"Whatever you've found, you can keep to yourself. If this is the place where I have to bring the children, then so be it. Only make sure you have my money ready when I get here," Crane replied, knowing that whatever Demurral was doing, it was not good, and whoever he now followed, it was not God. He turned to leave, still clutching the knife in his jacket, wary that this could be a trap.

"Don't rush off, Mr. Crane. I thought I could show you something that might change your mind about miracles. You are a man of the world, a man who needs proof. Allow me to indulge myself and show you what the world is really like."

He gestured to Beadle, who was standing silently by the wall. Beadle opened a large wooden chest under one of the narrow slit windows. The metal hinges creaked as it opened and a mist of green dust appeared to rise from inside the casket. Beadle reached into the chest, almost falling in, engulfed in the fog, his puny legs straining to keep contact with the stone floor. He lost his balance and fell backwards, clutching a large blue rock tightly to his body. Getting to his feet, he carried the rock to the altar table, placing it carefully on the white linen cloth. Demurral bared his crooked, broken teeth in a gleeful smile. He placed both hands on the stone and muttered under his breath.

The rock began to split into two equal parts. Demurral lifted off the top half of the stone to reveal the perfect shape of a man's hand cut into each segment of the rock and burnished to bright silver. Very slowly he placed each of his hands into the impressions in the stones. They fitted perfectly. He declaimed:

"Stone that has listened to man but not replied,
Hear my call for the child who died.
Come to me now in brightness flame,
Child of Azimuth, I call your name."

Demurral bowed his head and stared at his hands. A sudden draught scurried into the chamber from under the oak door, blowing the dust across the stone floor around their feet. The dirt swirled round to form a tight whirlwind in front of the altar. Fragments of silver, green and purple light began to sparkle from within this ever-growing tornado. Before their eyes a young girl began to appear, first her bare white feet, then the hem of a green robe and then the rest of her body and head as if she was being pieced together cell by cell.

Crane did not want to believe his eyes. He pressed himself into the wall of the room, forcing his body as close as he could to the stone. Demurral kept his hands pressed into the quern stones on the altar and stared at the phantom that was now taking shape and substance. He kept muttering in some foreign tongue, coaxing the apparition to take form, demanding its presence.

Crane looked at the child that appeared before them. She was five feet tall with long blonde hair and bright white skin. Around the waist of the green robe was a golden belt; upon her head was a crown of mistletoe mixed with the dark cherries of the belladonna. She had deep black, lifeless eyes. They were the eyes of someone blind that stared out not knowing what they looked upon. There was something familiar about her face. Somewhere Crane had seen this child before.

"See, Crane. Even your own eyes speak to you of another world. Can you deny this?"

He looked at Crane and then to the girl. "This ghost-child can tell the future. She is the Azimuth, one who is trapped between life and death, past and present. She is the only one I can trust. The Azimuth can never lie."

Crane noticed that Demurral's hands were shaking as he pressed them into the stones. He didn't reply; he could feel the apprehension welling up inside his stomach as he tried to hold on to reality. He gripped the knife even tighter as his eyes turned from Demurral to Beadle and then to the girl. Demurral began to speak again.

"Azimuth, I call you once more to speak the truth. Tell me of the future tonight."

There was a long silence. The wind beat on the copper roof that creaked and twisted in the growing storm. Crane looked at the girl, racking his memory as to who she was. His mind cried out that he knew her, or who she had been before she had been transformed into the Azimuth. Beads of sweat trickled across his forehead. His mouth was dry with fear. He could feel his heart pounding as the blood rushed through his veins. The girl began to speak in a parched, soft voice.

"It will be as you desire. They will come here. The three you seek will be together again." The Azimuth did not move as she spoke. Her hands were held gently together as if praying.

"And what about Crane—is he to be trusted?" Demurral asked cautiously.

"A question like that will get your throat cut, Demurral," Crane butted in angrily. "I'm not so taken in by your witchcraft not to be able to part your head from your heart." Crane stepped towards the table, pulling the knife from his coat. The Azimuth held out her hand as if to stop him.

"He is a man true of heart and he will not change his intention. He will bring them to this place and leave with all that he has come for." She turned her head towards Crane. Her dead, blind eyes stared into his. "Your life is changing. You will find your heart's desire."

Crane looked at the girl, knowing that he had stared into those eyes before, sometime not long ago. He shuddered with fear, not knowing if this was a spectre or a trick of the mind. It was then that he remembered. Six months before, he had beached his ship at Baytown to repair the hull. A girl called Hester Moss had come with a basket of fish for the crew. He remembered the eyes and hair and warm smile. The Azimuth was that girl. She had vanished from the rocks, her body was never found. He was beginning to come to an understanding of how she must have died.

"Give the child her rest, Demurral—send her to her grave and let her be in peace."

"You don't understand, Mr. Crane. The Azimuth is very rare, not every child can do this and its spirit has to span horizon to horizon. It took many children to find the right one. One who had died at the right time and in the right place." He spoke casually, as if discussing the price of bread, and not speaking of murder.

"You mean a child that *you* had killed at the right hour and place. To fit in with your so-called magic. Murdered so she would end up as a slave to you, not allowed the mercy of being left in peace even when she was dead."

"What makes you think that I killed her? People can die without the help of anyone else."

Crane lunged at Demurral and grabbed him by the throat, throwing him against the wall. "I've a good mind to allow you to join her. To kill you here and now, and to hell with the money." He pressed him to the wall, one hand around Demurral's neck, the other pressing the knife into his cheek. "Promise me one thing, Priest. When this is over, you'll let her go and put a stone on her grave."

Demurral couldn't speak as he struggled for breath. He nodded his head in agreement and tapped the back of Crane's hand to let him go. Crane released his tight grip and the priest slumped to the floor, choking for breath. He turned to the Azimuth. The vision of her spirit began to fade before him. Her hands reached out, trying to hold on to this life. He called out to her.

"Hester, I'll set you free. He'll pay for what he's done to you."

Her image faded as the whirlwind blew round and round, swirling the dust. As quickly as it had appeared, it was no more. Beadle cowered by the wooden casket.

Demurral rolled on the floor by the altar table, holding his squeezed throat. Jacob Crane stood in the doorway to the tower room, knife in hand. He looked at them both in disgust.

"I'll be back in one hour and I will bring the children with me. Make sure you have the money."

Crane turned to walk away and then stepped back into the room. "One more thing. If either of you tries any tricks, my men will burn down this house with you inside. If you tell the Excise men, I will come back and see that you are both hanged from a tree, cut into tiny pieces and left out for the crows." The knife blade glinted in the soft candlelight. "Nothing would give me greater pleasure than that. Don't make me."

He stomped down the spiral staircase that led from the tower. The sound of his footsteps on the stone stairs echoed through the cold night air. Demurral struggled to his feet, holding on to the altar table. He heard the large wooden door at the bottom of the stairs slam shut. Beadle still quailed by the wooden chest, his face buried in his hands.

"Get up. Get up. He could have killed me and you just lie on the floor, too frightened to move." Demurral tore the burning candle from its holder and threw it at Beadle. He picked up the candlestick, crossed the chamber, cutting it through the air like a sword, and hit Beadle several times about the body.

"Don't you ever let that happen again," Demurral shouted as another blow thudded into his servant's fat side. "Next time protect me instead of hiding like some guttersnipe." He thrust a blow into his back. Beadle gave a squeal and begged his master to stop, which was a mistake.

Demurral began to lash out wildly with the candlestick, repeatedly hitting the wall, altar and Beadle. He screamed with rage as he thrashed each double-handed blow into its target before falling in a heap on the floor. For several moments he did not move as he sat staring blankly at the patterns made by the leaded windows.

"Go and get the boy and bring him here. We have an hour before Crane returns. We can see what pain he can endure before then." Demurral wrote with his finger in the dust on the stone floor.

"But Crane said . . ." Beadle spoke feebly, trying to recover from the beating.

"I have no concern as to what that smuggler has to say. I am the master, not him. Now do it." He threw the candlestick at Beadle, hitting him in the chest. "Get off your fat backside and do it!"

"Shall I bring the money?"

Demurral thought for a moment as he looked around the chamber, wondering what to do next.

"No. There will be no need for money, the Varrigal will see to that. There are no pockets in a dead man's shroud and nowhere to spend it in hell." He began to howl with a shrill laughter. "Now get out, Beadle, before I send you to hell to show him the way."

Tempora Mutantur

Middle-night arrived, spreading a cold dampness over the whole mine as the dank mist seeped into the workhouse. Inside, everyone slept in cramped wooden beds; the older children slept alone whilst the younger ones went top to tail in the lower bunks. The men and women rested where they could, unchanged and unwashed. Mrs. Landas had the bed nearest to the fire, separated from the rest of the room by a worn blue velvet curtain. A thick tallow candle on the long table gave a dim light, whilst the embers of the fire warmed the increasing smell of stale sweat.

Raphah dozed in his bed, in between picking the fleas from his legs and thinking of home. The sound of snoring and the whimpers of the young children constantly dragged him back from the edge of sleep. He was tired and in pain. His back burnt from the brand, his heart was filled with the anguish of being so far from home. Outside he could hear the noise of the wind rustling through the wood whilst sea breakers smashed against the base of the cliff, the sound of spray bubbling into the night.

He tried to dream, to set his mind free from this place where he was now a prisoner and from the future that seemed so uncertain. He begged Riathamus to take him from this place, to allow him to see his home again. It had been almost a year since he had left his village. His last night there had been spent under the stars with a warm desert breeze invading the forest and brushing the wispy clouds across the deep black night sky. He had been lulled to sleep by the sound of the women singing psalms and the crackle of the fire that snapped and hissed almost in time to their music.

Raphah allowed himself to think dangerous thoughts of his homeland, thoughts that he knew would bring tears for the place that he missed so much and the people he longed to embrace. He felt alone. He yearned for the touch of a friend and the warm African voice of welcome.

Raphah knew he was a stranger, separated from those around him by the colour of his skin. These people, he thought, were poor in body and in spirit. That night they had seen a deaf boy hear again and yet they still could not believe. It was as if they were themselves blinded and deafened to the signs they had seen, or perhaps had been charmed with disbelief. They would rather put their trust in a dumb spirit of divining cards and the ramblings of an old maid than in the hands of Riathamus, the living God. They appeared to be happy to stay in their poverty.

Raphah lay back into his rolled-up coat, closed his eyes yet again and slipped into dreams.

It was then that the man possessed by the Dunamez woke from his sleep. For the last long hour he had shared the mind of a creature from another world. He had been forced into the corner of his being to watch the imaginings of the Dunamez flick across his mind, completely out of his control. He had shared the scenes of each life that the Dunamez had tormented. This was a creature of death: one who revelled in the misery of human suffering, one who had flitted from life to life to possess and control, to drive mad and then chase to the edge of death each victim whose life it inhabited. This helpless victim was Samuel Blythe, farmer and indebted miner of the Raventhorpe Alum Works. He shuddered with each shared vision that the Dunamez forced him to see. They were more than the nightmares of childhood—these were like sharing the thoughts not only of the power that now controlled him but also every life that it had ever destroyed.

Blythe fought hard to regain his own mind, to close his eyes to the torments. He wanted to call out to be saved but did not know whose name to call. The Dunamez whispered to him whenever he tried to recover his thoughts and grapple with his sanity. It knew his name. It knew his deepest fears.

"Listen to me, Samuel," it now whispered softly. "Do as I say and don't resist and it will soon be over. I may even let you live." Blythe felt the voice as it echoed through him, making each nerve and sinew twitch. He wanted to reply but couldn't even move the muscles of his throat. "I will speak for you," the creature said gently. "Just sit back and allow me. After all, you have nothing to lose and all the world to gain."

The Dunamez lifted him from his dreaming and opened his eyes. Controlled by the creature, Blythe threw back the covers of the bed, got up and walked to the fireplace. He warmed himself against the fire and then peeped around the curtains to look at the sleeping Mrs. Landas.

"Fire, fire," it murmured softly. "I haven't felt the warmth of a fire for many years. You humans have so much to be thankful for, bodies that can be warmed, touched and tingle with excitement. Life for me is so cold, so lonely. Oh, to enjoy the warm embrace of another." The Dunamez reached out with Blythe's hand to touch Mrs. Landas on her cheek. "Oh, my lovely, what a pretty woman you are."

It stopped short in its whispering to Blythe, as it was then that it saw the outline of Raphah asleep on the top bunk. Blythe was overcome with a sudden change in emotion. Gone the desire for Mrs. Landas; now, overwhelming hate. He could feel the physical wrath of the creature. His body began to shake. He suffered the rush of the creature's thoughts through his mind. The overwhelming urge to scream flooded through him, only to be stopped before he could make a sound. Thoughts of murder welled up.

The Dunamez spoke to him again.

"If you do this for me, Samuel, I will leave you again as quickly as I came. Take the knife and kill him. He's not one of you, he's a stranger. He deserves to die—and you're the one to do it."

Blythe could not resist. This could not be controlled. He felt helpless, like a spectator watching some great tragedy. He walked to the side of the bunk bed, pulled up a chair from the table to stand on, then drew the knife from his jacket. He looked around the room. Everyone was in a deep sleep. No one so much as murmured. It was an unnatural sleep, as if they were all on the verge of death.

He raised his hand above his head, unable to restrain the power of the Dunamez that now controlled every muscle in his body. This was it. Now was the time. The Dunamez spoke to him again.

"Kill him now. . . . They will never suspect . . ."

Blythe wanted to scream and run. A farmer snared by his own folly, he had become indebted to Demurral for seventy pounds, but in ten months he would be a free man. If he obeyed now, he would become a murderer. He looked down at Raphah, whose soft black skin shone in the candlelight. Blythe held the knife for as long as he could, not knowing why Raphah had to die.

"Do it now." The voice grew stronger in his head. "Do it before I make you. . . . For once in your life do something that you will be proud of. . . . You've failed at everything else: Don't fail in this." The voice of the Dunamez became insistent. Blythe could feel the creature forcing his hand, wanting him to slam the blade into Raphah. He struggled against himself, holding his arm as stiff as he could and locking every muscle. It was as if his arm would be snapped in two, broken by the will of the Dunamez.

"Let go, Samuel, let go. Do what I say." The unremitting voice in his head drowned out everything else.

The door to the workhouse crashed open, waking Mrs. Landas from her hot, itchy sleep. She sat bolt upright and with one movement pulled back the bed curtain and jumped to her feet. The Dunamez flung Blythe to the floor.

Consitt and Skerry stood in the doorway in their muddy black boots and tricorne hats. They looked pitiful and ragged, covered in the damp chill of the fourth hour. Consitt didn't smile or attempt any form of welcome to Mrs. Landas. "He wants the dark boy at the tower and he doesn't want to be kept waiting."

She tried to tidy her matted hair as she crossed the room to the bunk, where Raphah was now awake.

"Don't hurt him, or I won't let you take him. He's done a lot for me, changed my life, and I won't be having you or Skerry bullying him again."

Her raised voice woke everyone in the room. Faces appeared from under dirty blankets and stared out into the gloom.

"I don't care if he's turned yer into the Queen of Sheba. Demurral wants him and what Demurral wants, Demurral gets." Consitt stepped towards the bunk bed, pushing aside Blythe, who had got to his feet and was walking to the door. "Stay here, Sam, I could be needing yer. You can come to the tower in case he tries to run off. If he does, you've my permission to give him a good hiding." Blythe tried to move away, but the Dunamez intensified its grip on him, holding him in place.

Consitt reached into his frock coat and pulled out a short, knotted club. "Wakey, wakey, my little lascar boy. Time to go and see your master." He waved the club menacingly at Raphah. "Let's not have any games or we'll have to bash yer to the ground every time you step out of line." He beat the club into the palm of his hand, looking at Raphah from under the brim of his tricorne.

"There'll be no beating, Mr. Consitt, no beating. If you touch the lad, you'll have me to deal with." Mrs. Landas pointed her longest gnarled finger at him, waving it under his nose.

"And you'll have Demurral turning you out of the place you call home for getting in his way," retorted Consitt, pushing past her. "Get down from the bed, boy. We'll get the chains off you." Still brandishing his club, he hit the side of the bunk bed with a loud thud.

"Come on, Sam. Help me pull the little blighter from his perch."

Blythe couldn't reply. The grip of the creature had him by the throat. He nodded his head as if to agree, feeling like a puppet in the control of a clumsy master. Raphah meanwhile struggled to get down from the bed. The bandages and nettle ointment heavily applied by Mrs. Landas pulled against his skin. The brand on his back scorched through his shirt with every movement of his body.

He looked at Blythe, staring deeply into his eyes. He looked away, then back again, gazing even deeper. Raphah screwed up his face and searched every inch of Blythe's skin as if he was looking for some hidden secret.

The three men led him outside into the cold black night. Raphah had grown used to the warmth and limited comfort of the workhouse. Even though the bed was itchy and full of fleas, it had been soft and moderately comfortable. Now he trudged through the cold of the night that penetrated through to the bone.

They walked up the hill through the red mud, following the narrow, winding path to the Vicarage. The full moon chased thin black clouds across the sky.

To the north and far out to sea a bright red and yellow glow hung in the sky as if the sea was on fire. Blythe held Raphah by the shoulder and with a strong hand pulled him up the hill. Skerry walked in front, complaining under his breath and cursing the day he had met Demurral. Dragging far behind was Consitt, who stopped every few paces to draw breath and look out to sea.

"It's still there, Skerry; looks like the sunrise, but it's too far to the north and too early." Skerry stopped and turned to look.

"That's been there for two days and nights. Looks like the whole sea is on fire. It's almost bright enough to read by." He turned and began to tramp slowly up the hill.

"One problem, Skerry—you're too thick to read." Consitt laughed to himself as he wheezed and panted whilst he walked. Blythe remained silent. Raphah continued to stare at him, knowing that there was something sinister controlling the man. He had seen many people who had allowed their lives to be consumed by a manifestation of evil; he had been able to sense the presence of a wraith or incubus by the look of the eyes. They would stare straight through you as if they were in another world. They hated to be challenged and were tormented to destruction by the invocation of the One True Name. Raphah knew that with the power of Riathamus he had nothing to fear from any spirit.

"You can't control him forever." Raphah spoke in hushed tones. "You have to let him go one day. After all, he's not eternal." The Dunamez did not reply. "What's your name, spirit? Tell me who you are."

Blythe pulled Raphah to him, face-to-face, tightening the jacket painfully against Raphah's shoulder. He looked up the hill and saw Skerry on the brow of the hill in the distance. Consitt lagged behind a hundred yards below them. They were too far away to intervene—now was his time. The Dunamez spoke out loud, its own voice spewing out into the night air. Blythe could feel the sounds vibrating in his throat, out of his control.

"You can't stop me, boy," he growled in a deep angry voice. "I've followed you for long enough and tonight I will have my chance to snuff out your light once and for all." The Dunamez twisted the jacket even tighter, as if trying to squeeze out as much pain as possible.

"At least you dare speak. Demons usually skulk in the darkness, afraid of the light. What kind of power or principality are you? Or are you just some *kadesh*, a lapdog of some witch?" Raphah looked straight into the creature's eyes as they stared out of Blythe's face. "What makes you think I won't call on the name of Riathamus? Will he not send a whole company of Seruvim to come and destroy you?" He paused and peered at Blythe. The incubus did not reply. "I know who you are, Dunamez. . . . Now let me go before I call upon the secret name that even you must bow before. He may even let you live."

Blythe could feel the creature tugging and pulling on his innards as it twisted and convulsed within his body. His hand snapped from his grip on Raphah and was thrust into his jacket, grabbing the long knife he had managed to hide. He pushed Raphah away and then pulled out the knife, slicing it through the air. It caught Raphah across the cheek. Unable to control himself, Blythe lurched towards Raphah, who had stumbled by the edge of the path. He fell onto Raphah, trying to plunge the knife into his chest. Raphah grabbed hold of Blythe's arm, the blade only inches away from his face.

"Think you could stop me with words, did you, boy?" the Dunamez hissed. "In this body I will take a lot of stopping. I could pick up a dead cow with these arms and soon I'll pick up a dead Cushitic priest and hurl him into the sea." The Dunamez shook as it tried to force Blythe's hand closer to Raphah. "I want to see your blood on this blade, and when you're dead, I'll dance on your grave." It slobbered as it spoke, snorting like a pig.

"In . . . the Name . . . of . . . Riathamus . . . I command you to leave." Raphah screamed the words at the top of his voice. They echoed around the mine, deep into the woods, and were carried far out to sea by the wind. Blythe leapt to his feet, stumbling across the path. Skerry turned and began to run back down the hill. Consitt scrambled up the slope as fast as his weak, fat and throbbing legs would carry him. There was a loud earsplitting cry as the Dunamez was torn from Blythe, who was cast aside like a piece of chaff. The beast stood before Raphah, bound in chains of light, unable to move as they grew tighter and tighter. Blythe hid his eyes behind one arm, shielding his face from the horrible sight of the creature. Skerry could not believe what he was seeing as he ran towards them down the narrow path.

Raphah got to his feet and looked at the pitiful creature that cowered beneath him. It stared at him through its narrow slit eyes and attempted a half-smile through a mouth so full of protruding, jagged teeth that it could hardly speak.

"Have mercy on me, I meant you no harm," it said pathetically. "If you let me, I will leave this place and cause no trouble. Let me go and find someone to carry me through their life."

"What right have you to meddle in this world? Did you give this man a chance to say no?" Raphah gestured towards Blythe as he spoke angrily to the creature as it writhed in the tightening bands of light.

"He's a human, he has no rights. They turned their backs on Riathamus just as I did. We fell from heaven, you were thrown out of the garden . . . cheated by a snake." The Dunamez laughed as it panted and gasped for breath. "What do you humans know about life? Three score years and ten, then what? Most of you are destined for Gehenna, a desert of shadows populated by ungrateful souls." It stopped speaking and looked at Skerry, who was standing petrified a few feet away.

"Let me go into *him*. What harm could I do in a body like that? He could use some brains. I could give him a life like he's never seen."

Raphah raised his hand towards the Dunamez.

"Silence, spirit. You would never be satisfied. That's why your kind were cast out of heaven. You wanted to be a god and steal the power of Riathamus. Even now you plot and scheme, hiding behind every misery you bring to the people of the world." The Dunamez winced with each word he spoke. "You remind the righteous of their past. Now is the time for you to find out your future." Raphah held out his hand towards the creature.

Blythe covered his face with his hands and crouched down behind a bush whilst Skerry dived into the thick grass at the side of the bank. Raphah raised his voice as he shouted out, the sound vibrating the air. "By the power of the Most High, I command you to leave and go to the torment ordained for your dwelling place. . . . *Go!*"

Strands of silver and gold thread engulfed the creature, spinning it around and around. Its body changed to the deepest black, the long white face was engulfed in a dark mist and then wrapped in strands of golden wire like the victim of some invisible spider being prepared for death. The creature screamed, summoning all of its strength to break out of its bonds. Then in a flash of light the Dunamez vanished completely. The night was again black and silent.

Blythe and Skerry were speechless and both too frightened to come out from their hiding places. Down the hill Consitt peered out from behind a large rock.

"Don't kill us," he called fearfully. "We won't harm you. Let us go about our business and we will leave right now."

Skerry peered out from the ditch that he had slid into, as Blythe lay back in the long grass, mumbling meaningless words to himself and hoping to wake from this horror. Raphah sat on a big stone at the side of the road and began to laugh. To him all this was a part of the living universe.

"What are you frightened of? This morning you were prepared to kick and beat me and drag me through the mud. Now you cower like children after their first nightmare." He beckoned to Consitt to get out from behind the rock. "Come on, take me to Demurral, I have unfinished business with that old dog. He has something of mine and now is the time for its return."

Blythe sat up and looked at Raphah.

"Are you a spirit like the one that took hold of me?" he asked faintly, almost too afraid to speak.

"Can one spirit cast out another? Can an army fight against itself?"

"Then by what power do you do these things?" Blythe propped himself up in the grass and looked at Raphah, who was silhouetted in the moonlight. "What kind of creature are you?"

"A man just like you with no special powers, no witchcraft, no sorcery."

"Then how did you do that? How did you know? That thing wanted to kill you—how did you destroy it?"

"It was by the power of Riathamus—the one true God. Do you not know of him?" Raphah could see that these people only believed in superstition and knew little about the truth.

"God? How can you know something that is so far-off? Why would this Riathamus want to know someone like me? I am just a farmer." Blythe paused and looked at Skerry, who was climbing out of the ditch. "Both of us were farmers; we lost everything to

Demurral. The rent got higher and higher and neither of us could afford to pay, so now we are prisoners of our debt, doormen in the workhouse." He looked again at Skerry, hoping he would speak, then went on. "Why would this Riathamus want to know people like us? God is for rich people in fancy clothes and big houses. People who are Sunday saints and get the best pews in church whilst we sit in the free seats at the back, unable to see or hear. What would God want us for?"

"Perhaps he would want you for that very reason. Have you never thought that God might love you? Have you never looked out to sea and wondered at this creation? Do you think this entire world is some sort of accident?" Raphah held out his hand to Blythe to lift him from the grass.

"Maybe in your country that is true, but here . . ." He looked at the ground. "I have thought of all those things, but then I looked at the mud on my boots, the sheep starving in the field, the rent I couldn't pay, and I realized that the only sure things in life are death and the church tax we pay to Demurral. After all, isn't he God's man? He's the Vicar, he's the one to show us the way, but all he's done is give us board and lodging in the workhouse."

Blythe got to his feet and sat next to Raphah on the stone. Together they looked out to sea. Skerry stood behind them, wondering what he should do, whilst Consitt struggled up the steep path towards them. Raphah put his arm around Blythe.

"Whatever this man is, he is not a man of God. He follows something, but it is not Riathamus. He's a thief and a liar. He will answer for these things."

Skerry now spoke, his voice faltering. "You're just a lad, how do you know so much for one so young?"

"To know Riathamus is to know wisdom, and the knowledge of him will bring understanding. That is all you need for life." Raphah smiled at Skerry.

"So how can we know him? He's up there in his heaven and we are down here in this hell."

"Open your eyes and tell me what you see."

Skerry feared he was being tricked. "I can see the sky, the sea—"

"No. Tell me what you really see."

Skerry paused and looked again. "There's the darkness and the light."

"There is something else," Raphah said gently. "Riathamus stands at the door of your life and knocks. If you hear his call and answer him, he will share your life and live with you always. He can set you free from all your poverty, free to be the person he created, not the one you have become."

Consitt came panting his way towards them, his fat legs shaking with tiredness, his face red and swollen. Raphah looked at him.

"I want you to take me to Demurral. Don't tell him what you've seen. When you leave me with him, I want you to go from this place. You will be free men. Go and start your life again, find Riathamus for yourself." He looked at Blythe. "You have known evil and been dominated by it. By the power of the Most High, you have been set free. Remember, when he sets you free, you are free indeed."

The wind blew and rattled the heather at the side of the path. The three men looked at each other and then at Raphah, wondering what to do.

"Take me to Demurral now. From the signs in the sky it will soon be time."

Raphah led them up the hill, through the darkness of the small wood, across the lawn in front of the Vicarage and past three freshly dug sepulchres cut out of the cold, black earth.

The Burning Man

Bravery comes easily to some people, but for Thomas and Kate it was bought at a price. Together they had tramped the lonely six miles from Boggle Mill to a clearing in the woods to the west of Stoup Hill. An old stone circle broke through the grass in the centre of the clearing. Each stone looked like the tip of some shrivelled finger sticking up through the earth. In the light of the moon they cast grey shadows against the tufts of heather that grew in patches.

Isabella had given Kate a long black cloak; she hugged it to herself to keep out the cold wind that blew in fresh from the sea, bringing with it a smell of salt and seaweed, and huddled closer to Thomas. They had been told by Crane to wait until he arrived and then he would take them to find their friend.

Kate was still angry that her father had conspired with Jacob Crane and helped him smuggle contraband for so many years. It was as if he had lived a lie, said one thing and then done another, Customs officer and smuggler.

She wondered if there would be any more lies, any more surprises that she would find out about as the night went on. She had lost all the trust she had in him, in fact in everyone. Life with her father was never easy. It was his drinking that had always been the problem. He would fly into a rage at the slightest thing, shout and scream and then break down in tears. For many years she had thought it was her fault, that in some way she was responsible.

Kate could never live up to his expectations, she could never be a child, never play games. Her lot in life was to cook and clean, to sew and mend. These were his demands. He wanted her to be a mother, a servant, but never a daughter.

Tonight she had learnt that he had been living a double life, and realized that her father had been slowly poisoned by the death of her mother, the guilt, the pain and now the deception. "It's not my fault, it's not my fault," she kept repeating under her breath as she thought of her father and of how he had betrayed her.

The trees clattered their branches and beat out the rhythm of the breeze. Her eyes darted around the darkness that encircled them, looking for a sign of Crane and his men.

It was not long before they heard the sound of horses. Thomas looked at her and gave a reassuring smile. He put his arm around her and pulled her close.

"Whatever happens, Kate, I will always be with you. When we were in the wood, I had a dream. I met a man." He paused, thought and then went on. "Well, he was more than a man—I think he was God. He spoke to me and my name appeared in a book. It was written out before my eyes. He told me he was a King and that if I believed in him, I need never fear death. What do you think it all meant?"

Kate could not reply at first. She could feel the welling up of tears as her throat tightened. She blurted out: "Why did we get involved in all of this? We should have known something bad was going to happen." She had tried so hard to keep herself from crying. It was a mixture of anger and fear, a sense of helplessness and predestination all rolled into one unexplainable feeling of impending disaster.

As the horses picked their way through the trees, Thomas and Kate waited for them to come into the clearing. Without warning the sky cracked with a low rumble of thunder. It shook the ground beneath their feet. A horse whinnied at the other side of the clearing and then they saw one of Crane's men ride out of the wood. He rode the horse to the centre of the stone circle, stopped and for several moments looked all around him. He looked at Thomas and Kate.

"Come forward," he shouted in a rum-coated voice. "Come forward so I can see you both."

Thomas walked towards him and gestured to Kate to stay close behind. He had a growing distrust of Jacob Crane and his men.

"Where's Jacob Crane?" Thomas asked the man.

"He'll be here right enough. He had to go and find your friend and then he'll be back for you two."

"What if we change our minds? What if we run off into the woods and find our friend for ourselves?" Thomas asked.

"What if I cut you down with this cutlass here and now, young Thomas?"

Crane stepped out from his dark hiding place at the base of a large stone three feet from where they were standing. They both jumped with fright.

"I've been here all along waiting for you to arrive. What kept you, Martin?" Crane said to the man on the horse. "Couldn't find the way out of the inn?" Crane didn't wait for a reply. "What about you two? Thought of running away already? I thought you were up for the fight. Find your friend and save the world, wasn't it? What has changed your mind?" Crane fired questions like grapeshot and didn't want an answer.

"I've found your friend, but if you want him back, you will have to do what I say." He looked sternly at them both. "Even if you think you can't, you must trust me at all times, whatever happens."

"How do we know we can trust you?" Thomas asked.

"Well, you can never know for certain what anyone will do. All I can say is that it takes fresh bait to catch a rat, but the catcher always takes care of the trap." He turned to the man on the horse. "Take ten of the men and go ahead to the Vicarage. Take up position in the garden next to the tower. I want one musket aimed at the door to the tower at all times. Don't be seen. I'll follow on with these two and the rest of the men." Crane slapped the back of the horse with the palm of his hand. Martin pulled the animal round and cantered across the clearing to the woods. The sound of other horses and other riders filled the night air as they came out of hiding and trotted into the night along the narrow pathways through the wood, over the moor top and towards the Vicarage.

"Right, you two. Ever shared a horse?" Crane walked across the clearing to the edge of the wood. "I have a mare for you, no saddle, so you'll have to hang on. She has the devil in her, so watch out. She'll have you off if she can. It's the only horse we have spare, or should I say the only one we could steal from Molly Rickets's barn."

They walked through the clearing; the great standing stones looked pale in the moonshine. Kate looked around, feeling uneasy, scared of each sound that came from the wood. She searched each dark shadow for a trace of the red-eyed creatures that had attacked them before.

"What is this place?" she asked. "I was never allowed to come here, always told that it was where the dead lived."

Crane laughed. "A story to keep you away from everything that free traders have hidden. Some say this place is like a giant clock that marks the travel of the universe, and others believe it's a place of worship for old gods, by a race of people long dead." He became more serious in his tone. "Before tonight I would never have believed in such things, but now I am not so sure."

At the edge of the clearing they found two horses tied to a tree. Crane gave a long shrill whistle and then waited. From the wood came a whistle in reply.

"That's my men; they don't like dry land, always like to have the deck beneath their feet when they fight. Let's hope that tonight they won't have to."

Crane helped them both onto the back of the mare, and leapt lightly onto the other horse. Thomas held tightly to the reins and Kate wrapped her arms around his waist. "Whatever happens, head for the Vicarage. If we get separated, I will meet you there." Crane gently kicked the side of his horse as he spoke.

The two horses and riders walked slowly into the enfolding darkness of the wood. One by one, Crane's men silently joined them as they picked their way along the winding path that led through the wood to the edge of the moor high above the sea.

Jacob Crane soon became conscious of a nagging doubt at the back of his mind that things were not right, and as the procession of riders hacked through the wood, he became increasingly aware of a sense that they were being watched. He prided himself on always being one step ahead of the Revenue men and the Captain of the Dragoons. In all his years as a smuggler he had never been caught. There had been many a close encounter, but he had never been captured. This was not always down to his skill as a horseman, sailor or fighter. Crane knew the powers of persuasion, the power of money and a cask of brandy to the right person. He knew that threats were often as powerful as action and that a reputation for murder was often all he needed to get what he wanted.

Here in the wood he knew one thing: They were not alone. He was never a man to admit to fear, but tonight in the wood, with each yard they travelled, a growing trepidation rose in his stomach. It was a sick, gnawing feeling that things were not right, a mounting apprehension that bordered on fear. The horses too were growing nervous. One by one, they began to shy and shudder with each step, to toss their heads, flick their tails and snort into the night, passing their fear from one to the other, as if speaking in some forgotten language.

To Thomas and Kate it was clear that the mare they were riding wanted them off her back so she could run into the night and escape the creature that now stalked them in the darkness. Kate held tighter to Thomas's waist and Thomas in turn gripped the reins, tugging on them as hard as he could, twisting the mare's head back to his chest. But she pulled against him so strongly that the reins slipped in his hands, cutting into his palms. She shied and tittupped about, shivering and snorting in fear.

"What's happening, Thomas?" Kate asked quietly, not wanting anyone to hear her disquiet.

"They can feel something in the air," Thomas replied. "They're frightened."

Jacob Crane turned in the saddle and spoke quietly. "Keep your eyes straight ahead. We're being followed. There are five of them on our left and about seven on the right. I think they're waiting to attack. If they know this place well enough, they'll wait until we go through the next glade before they strike." He reached out and took hold of the leather bridle of their mare. "I'll hold on to her for a while. I don't want you two running off just yet."

"What shall we do, Mr. Crane?" Thomas asked.

"Have you got that old sword you took to Rueben's?"

"He gave me it back before we left."

"Then I suggest you make ready to use it. Protect the girl and watch your back. Strike hard and never give them a second chance. Remember, lad, it's you or them."

"Who's following us?" Kate butted in.

"Could be the Revenue men, the Dragoons or something that Demurral has dreamt up for us. Whoever they are, they know how to cross country without making much noise. They've been with us since we left the stone circle." Thomas and Kate sensed that Crane's suggestion that it could be Revenue men or Dragoons was a clumsy attempt to encourage them; the horses would not have been so frightened.

The wood began to thin out as it opened up to the moor. Outcrops of thick moss-covered rock jutted from the thick black soil. Wizened trees bent by the wind spread out their knotted lifeless branches over the thickening heather. The path from the wood dropped down into a small gully overlooked by a copse of trees. Behind the rocks that overlooked the ravine a tall, lone figure stood motionless, framed by the bright, full moon.

Thomas saw it first and instinctively tugged the reins back. The mare pulled as hard as she could. Crane kept a firm hold of the bridle.

"Don't worry, I've seen him," he whispered.

"Who is it?" asked Thomas.

"Well, it's not the Revenue men or the Dragoons. They would never stand in such a place. It must be at least nine feet tall."

"What shall we do?" Kate asked, the anxiety easily discerned in her voice.

"Wait until I tell you, then ride like the wind. Don't stop. If you get thrown off, get up and run. Martin will meet you at the tower. Stay with him, you can trust Martin, he's a good man." There was strength in his voice and a reassuring tone of real concern for them.

Neither Thomas nor Kate could reply. She held on to Thomas and squeezed his waist uncomfortably hard, wanting all this to stop. It was then that the figure on the ridge burst into bright orange flames that leapt high into the air. Fragments of straw and woven, burning willow billowed out from the blaze rising up in the thermal, then fell as flakes of smouldering embers.

"It's a Wiccaman. Someone wants to frighten us." Crane let out a gasp of surprise. "Quick, run," he shouted as the first bolt shot through the dark, past their heads, hitting a rock just feet away. The quarrel smashed into pieces, shattering like glass. Then another cut through the air from behind them, hitting a tree and splintering to dust. Then another and another. The air became filled with slivers of fiery glass wands that hurtled over their heads from all directions.

"They're trying to force us into the gully—it's covering fire, they're not trying to hit you." Crane let go of the mare's bridle. "Go on, run for it, you devil," he screamed at the horse. The beast threw her head back and snorted excitedly, her ears flattened to her head, eyes rolling wildly. Her legs dug into the soft earth as she took off, nearly unseating Thomas and Kate with the force, and hurtled towards the gully, her hoofs hardly touching the ground.

As the horse galloped on, the Wiccaman blazed on the ridge above them, sending beams of orange and red flickering light across the path. On the high moor it was like another world with the silver brightness of the moon, the light from the blazing willow-and-straw effigy, the dark shadows cast by trees and stones. Air and earth, fire and water, mixed a potion so powerful that it stalled reality.

Kate hung on to Thomas as tightly as she could, her cloak billowing out and flapping behind her in the wind. The horse galloped along the narrow path that suddenly dropped into a deep black gully where even the moon could not penetrate. Thomas just managed to hold on to the reins as the mare jumped blindly over fallen branches and tufts of bracken, thrashing wildly through the undergrowth as she lost the path in the darkness. Her legs became caught in the thick entanglement of dead bracken and gorse, and as she kicked out with her hind legs to free herself from the snare of decaying vegetation, she threw Thomas and Kate to the ground.

Thomas got to his feet and quickly drew the short sword from his belt and hacked at the bracken to free the horse's legs. As he did so, she jumped away from the last brambles that clung to her hide and galloped up the bank, leaving them alone in the gully.

Thomas slumped to the ground next to Kate, who had hidden herself in the long black cloak. It was as if the silence lasted for a lifetime. They were in almost complete darkness. Neither of them moved, neither of them spoke. Thomas was out of breath and out of his mind with worry. He had set out to help Raphah for the sake of revenge. It was not out of goodness, or to help someone in need. He now understood that all he really wanted to do was to get his own back on Demurral. Yet within him he felt that something had changed and was continuing to change, something unstoppable, like the growing of a mustard seed.

He dug the tip of the sword into the ground. "We have to keep moving. If we stay here, whoever was after us might catch us. I've had too much of being ambushed in the dark." He began to laugh, not knowing why he was laughing. He just felt it grow and grow, tightening his lips and shaking his belly. As he laughed, he began to laugh at himself laughing. It felt such a good thing to do. He could feel an overwhelming sensation of joy rising from the pit of his stomach. He tried to hold it back, to keep it in, but the power of joy almost burst his side. Thomas sat back in the bracken. All he could see in his mind's eye was the face of the King smiling at him. It was then that he knew that no matter what happened, they had nothing to fear.

In the midst of the laughter he tried to speak. "Kate, we will have to go."

"I'm glad you think that it's so funny—chased till we're half dead, thrown from a horse in a black wood and then it runs off. Very funny. What will you find to laugh at next?" Kate was angry.

"I don't know why I'm laughing. I can't help it. I know that everything will work out for good. That's all that keeps coming into my mind. Everything works to the good for those who know the King. . . . It was in the dream."

"Will this dream save our lives?" she asked.

"I think it will, Kate, I think it will." He paused, then continued to speak. "I've realized since I met Raphah and had the dream that we live in a world different from the one I thought. It's as if I was blind and suddenly all the blindness has gone. I lived a life and I only thought about me, what I had, what I would do." The breeze rustled the bracken. "Now I know there is something more to life than me. I promised to help Raphah get something back from Demurral. I don't know why it is important, but I know it is."

"But what will happen, Thomas? When I came with you, I never expected to see all these things, I just thought we would break into the Vicarage and that would be it." Kate stood up and threw off the cloak. "I never came along for Raphah and what he wants to steal back, I came along because . . ." She stopped speaking and bowed her head.

"Why did you, Kate?" he asked.

"It doesn't matter now. I think I lost the reason when I pulled the trigger on the pistol and shot that thing."

Thomas looked at Kate. He could barely pick out her features in the darkness. He reached out and gently touched her cheek with his hand. He couldn't see her smile.

"We have to go, Kate. I don't know if they're behind us or where Crane has gone. Knowing him, he'll have taken them on single-handed. We'll follow the gully down and head for the Vicarage and see if Martin can really be trusted."

Kate took hold of his hand. "You go ahead, I have something to do. I'll follow you."

"I'll not leave you in the dark, I'll wait for you along the path."

With that Thomas turned and walked off through the undergrowth and down the gully. Kate picked up the cloak from the ground and brushed off the dirt and waited patiently in the darkness.

Several minutes later a solitary Varrigal appeared from the wood at the top of the ravine. It scanned the darkness with bright red eyes that saw night as day, and blackness as the brightest sun. Deep in the ravine between two trees it saw a crouched, cloaked figure kneeling as if at prayer. The Varrigal pulled back the bowstring and placed the silvery glass quarrel onto the firing plate. With bloodless precision it raised the solid, black metal crossbow and took aim. In one breathless action it squeezed the firing lever and the bolt shot through the darkness.

There was a solid thud. The bolt embedded itself in the back of its target. The Varrigal wheezed with satisfaction and, cutting its way through the bracken, stepped down the bank towards its victim. In the mud beneath two holly trees the wrinkled cloak covered a lifeless form. The Varrigal raised its sword and with one blow slashed through the woven fabric embedding itself in the trunk of its prey. From the torn fabric spilled out dry grass and crumpled bracken. Kate had gone, having left her cloak draped over the remains of a willow log and stuffed with dry grass and bracken.

The Miracle

It was two hours before dawn and already news of the night before was sweeping through the workers' cottages and around the alum works like a fire out of control.

The story of the miracle was repeated over and over again from man to woman, house to house. It was talked about in the brewer's yard and by the fermenting pits. Men stood and passed on the rumour that the dumb boy could hear and speak. Mrs. Landas couldn't stop telling everyone she met about the wonder that had happened, parading the boy around like a trophy, proudly telling all that this fine lad was her son. She had washed away the white lead powder and the beauty spot from her face, combed her hair, and in the growing dawn looked like a new woman. There was no gin with breakfast, and no pipe. She had even tried to rub the brown stains from her teeth. For Mrs. Landas, the new day was indeed the start of a new life, a life that she wanted to share with her son.

"Call me stupid," she said in her gravelly voice to the young girl in the doorway of the cottage next to the workhouse, "but I do believe I feel ten years younger." She wheezed as she spoke, her chest making sounds like the strains of some failing harmonica. "Since the black lad made my John better, I just can't stop smiling. You ought to meet him, he's a proper gentleman, a little angel. What he says makes you feel clean inside."

She looked up from the doorway of the cottage to the

Vicarage high above the mine. Dark purple storm clouds like high mountains gathered in the fading moonlight filling the sky. The incandescent light from the horizon lit the front of the Vicarage. Each of the many panes of glass reflected the red and orange glow. It appeared to stand defiant against the forthcoming storm, the tall tower reaching, Babel-like, towards heaven.

Mrs. Landas dried her hands on her apron and spoke to the girl. "I don't know what Demurral wants with the lad; I only hope he doesn't do him harm. Too many children have gone up there and never come back." She looked at the gathering storm. "I don't believe the tale that they've all been sent to sea or to London to work. Demurral's done something with 'em. I pray I'll see the lad again."

She stepped inside the cottage and closed the door behind her against the rain that had started to fall.

Raphah and the three men hid from the rain beneath the branches of a large yew tree that overlooked the door to the tower. Consitt leant uncomfortably against its trunk.

"You don't, you don't have to go in, lad," he said. "You can run off and find your friends if you want." He looked at the other two men. "We've been talking. . . . After what happened last night, we're not too sure that we're doing the right thing. We don't want to give you over to the Vicar. We want you to go and go now. You can get a boat from Whitby—take you anywhere in the world. It'd take you away from here."

The other two nodded in agreement.

"Thank you, but I won't be leaving unless I take with me what I have come for. It is worth more than gold." He pointed to the door of the tower. "Whatever happens in there, I know that Riathamus will be with me. Anyway, I have to go in. It's beyond my control."

With that, Raphah left the shelter of the yew tree and walked out into the storm. The rain fell as hailstones from the purple sky. He ran to the door alone, took hold of the hefty brass ring handle and twisted it to the right. He felt the bolt jump from the saddle and the oak door clunked open.

Slowly, he climbed the stone stairs to the top of the candlelit staircase, thinking about each step that he took. At the top he stood before another oak door and could hear the muffled voices of Demurral and Beadle as they talked inside. He paused for a second and raised his hand to knock; he wanted to show them he was not afraid, that no matter what they did, it would not turn him to bitterness or anger. Raphah knew that he was in great danger. But this was a quest he had to complete. Behind the door was the answer to all the questions he had asked himself. He had travelled many miles across land and sea to this place and to these people. This was the promise he had sworn to his father Abraham on the steps of the Temple. He would not return empty-handed.

Raphah felt his pulse begin to surge through his veins. It was excitement tinged with fear. Beads of sweat broke out on his forehead and mingled with the rain that had twisted its way through his thick black, oiled locks. He wondered how he should enter the room. What would he see? What would happen?

With great hesitation he took hold of the handle of the door and quickly pushed it open. Plumes of thick incense billowed through the doorway. Raphah looked into the darkened chamber as he breathed in the acrid fragrance of stale myrrh that had within it the smell of decay. It stung his eyes, making him recoil. In the gloom he could make out the figure of Demurral standing by the altar table. He was dressed in a long white robe, around his waist a thick, black, knotted cord. His hair was tied back into a ponytail that made his features look sharper than ever. By the altar was the acacia pole complete with stone hand. In the middle of the altar was the Keruvim, its pearl eyes sparkling in the light from the altar candles. Set against the wall were three high-backed wooden chairs with golden cords draped over the armrests.

Beadle was scurrying about the room, holding a golden bowl filled with freshly cut herbs. In his hand was a small golden sickle. They both stopped and stared at Raphah as he stood in the swirls of smoke lit by the flickering candlelight.

"I believe you want to see me?" he asked, trying not to allow his voice to falter. Demurral looked completely astonished at the sight of Raphah in the doorway. He searched the gloom behind him for sight of his men. His eyes flashed to Beadle, who dropped the golden sickle on the floor.

"Where are—?" Demurral started to say.

"Your men are outside in the shelter of the yew tree, planning what they are to do with the rest of their lives. They are leaving today. I have set them free. Their debt to you is paid in full, Demurral." Raphah could feel strength welling up inside him, his fear quickly ebbing away.

"What gives you the right to set people free? They owed you nothing, they owed me everything." His voice oozed with anger and spittle. "Cowards, the lot of them. When I've finished with you, I'll drag them back by the hair of their frightened little heads. Get him, Beadle. Bring him here." Beadle hesitated, unsure what to do. He looked at Raphah and then to Demurral. "Don't just stand there, you cretin. Get him!" Demurral shouted.

"Stay where you are, Beadle. You don't have to listen to his orders anymore. You too can be a free man. What power do you think he has over you?" Raphah stepped into the chamber and walked towards the altar.

"Don't listen to him, Beadle; he's trying to trick you."

"What do you know, Demurral? You hear but you don't understand. You see but are blind. You are so concerned with yourself that you are hardened to the needs of the people you enslave. I come here as a free man, not a slave, and I will leave with the Keruvim; give it to me now."

Demurral and Beadle looked at each other and began to laugh. The oak door suddenly slammed shut and Raphah was engulfed in the choking smoke of the swirling incense.

"You are brave, but stupid. Didn't you think I would know who you really were? Gebra Nebura told me that the Keruvim couldn't stand to be apart. It took me a long time to realize that one would be made of gold and the other would be flesh and blood. Doesn't God have a strange sense of humour?"

He picked up the golden Keruvim from the altar. "To think this is my life's work. All I have ever dreamt about, I now hold." He paused and stared at Raphah. "You are the Keruvim that I have been waiting for. Together you will give me the power to control the elements. The sea and the sky will be at my command. I can bring drought to one country and flood to another. I can cause a fleet of ships to be swallowed by the sea. Just think what power like that is worth. I'll be the richest man in the world. Kings and princes will bow before me. The power of the Keruvim will be sold to the highest bidder." Demurral almost squawked with excitement. "Do you know what gives me the greatest pleasure? Your God will just have to sit back on his throne, watch it happen and weep."

He squeezed the Keruvim even tighter to his chest. "Doesn't God realize that he's finished? People are tired of him, they've forgotten all about him. Money . . . power . . . dark arts. These are the new gods, and I hold the keys to the Kingdom."

Raphah waited for Demurral to finish speaking. He kept one eye on Beadle, who had picked up the golden sickle from the stone floor.

"Do you really think that is all that people want out of life? It won't make you immortal. You can't take these things into death."

"Death. The old man's friend." Demurral spoke in a patronizing tone. "You are more foolish than I thought. Tonight will bring an end to death. With the power invoked from the Keruvim, I will never have to fear standing before God again. The god within is far greater than the god without. That is the truth of this age. I will control powers that you know little about and you will be unable to stop me." With that Demurral reached underneath the altar. He brought out a long pistol and pulled back the hammer. The trigger gave a loud click as it set, ready to fire.

"I think this will make you obey me." Demurral laughed as he nodded to the subservient Beadle.

Beadle limped across the chamber. He took Raphah cautiously by the arm and led him to the three wooden chairs. He shrugged Raphah into the centre chair and hastily tied his wrists and feet with the golden cord. It cut into his wrists, pressing them against the hard wood.

The door to the stairs slammed shut and the sound of heavy footsteps could be heard making their way to the top of the tower. Demurral turned to Beadle.

"See who it is; we don't want to be disturbed." He barked out the order.

Beadle went to the door and reached out for the handle, but it was flung open, sweeping Beadle to one side and pressing him against the stone wall. Jacob Crane stepped into the room, giving a casual glance to the heap on the floor that was the crushed Beadle. Demurral looked surprised to see him. His eyes fell on a widening bloodstain on Crane's upper arm and shoulder, but he said nothing.

Crane looked at Raphah.

"So this is the cause of all the trouble, an Egyptian by the look of him. Wouldn't interfere with him, Demurral. Unlucky to interfere with the likes of that." Crane took a step closer towards Demurral.

"Luck comes from Lucifer. This one isn't a bright morning star. Where are the others?" Demurral demanded.

"I've come for the money. The children are downstairs." Crane spoke like a man who did not want to be messed with.

"We have a slight problem, Mr. Crane. You will have to wait." Demurral pointed to the bound Raphah in the chair. "He has taken up all our time. Beadle will take you to the house and give you the money. Bring the children; their friend is waiting and so am I."

"Don't think of swindling me, Vicar. One whiff of double cross and your servant will have a smile cut across his double chin from ear to ear." Crane gestured with his hand as if to slice his throat. Demurral pointed the pistol at him.

"What's to stop me from killing you now and keeping the money for myself?"

"Go ahead, pull the trigger," said Crane. "Then my men will light the barrel of gunpowder set at the door and blow this tower and you into the next world." He smiled. "Then we'll all know if there really is a God." He winced and clutched at his shoulder as he turned to Beadle. "Come on, slug, get up off the floor and slime your way down the stairs. The smell in here makes me want to vomit." He turned to Demurral. "When I get the money, I'll send in the children. What you do with them is your concern."

Beadle pulled himself up by the door handle and followed Crane down the stairs and out of the tower.

Raphah looked across the smoke-filled room. Demurral stood at the altar and began to lift the top from the Azimuth stone. He placed the two halves of the stone next to each other.

"Very soon, my dark friend, I will have all I have ever wanted. When your friends arrive, things will be just perfect." He smiled a thin smile.

"They have done you no harm. Why do you involve them? Am I not enough," Raphah responded.

"Enough? You can never have enough. After all, three hearts are better than one. Haven't you realized that all this is about sacrifice? Even your God knows that. A full, perfect and sufficient sacrifice for the forgiveness of sin, wasn't it?" He spoke as the metal roof of the chamber rattled in the storm outside.

Raphah was quick to rejoin. "It was more than you would ever be prepared to do."

"I know about sacrifice. All my life I have given up this or done away with that. Now is the time for me," Demurral replied.

At that, the tower door opened. Crane pushed Beadle into the chamber, followed by Kate and Thomas. Two of his men blocked the doorway.

"Here you are, Vicar, the two that you wanted and in prime

condition. Do with them what you will." Crane pushed the children towards Demurral.

"I like a man who can keep his word," Demurral answered.

"Word? He's a cheat and a liar. A sluggard," Kate screamed.

"Tie them to the chairs and get the sluggard and his men out of here. We have work to do." Demurral held the pistol up towards Crane. "No tricks, Mr. Crane; I can use one of these as well as you can."

"They're all yours, Vicar. Do what you will. I've got my money and the ship is ready to sail."

Crane turned and gestured to his men to get out of the room. He backed across the stone floor, keeping his eyes fixed on Demurral and the pistol.

"Sorry, my young friends, business is business and life is but a vapour, and a cheap one at that. Thirty pieces of the King's silver." He smiled at Kate as he walked out of the room. The last tremor of the storm shook the tower.

"Quite fitting. I like a storm, it sets the heart aquiver." Demurral turned to Beadle. "Prepare them for the ritual."

At that instant a shaft of sunlight struck the narrow windows, filling the smoke-filled room with a prism of coloured light.

Beadle shouted out, "It's too late, Master, the dawn is here, we have missed the time. It's the morning."

"One more night and we'll have lost the moon," Demurral snarled at Beadle. "Tie them well. Prepare the chamber and we'll come back tonight. I suppose it is worth waiting one more dull day for what will be." Demurral took off his long white robe and draped it over the altar. "Make sure you lock the door when you've finished; they can last a day without food—after all, it matters not whether they are fat or thin where they're going." He stepped out of the chamber, leaving Beadle to hobble around the altar, place the Keruvim in the centre and blow out the candles.

Beadle stopped and looked at Kate. His eyes searched the smooth contours of her face. He stepped towards her, dragging his withered leg. Leaning close to her, he looked in her eyes and gently stroked her cheek.

"You are so pretty, it will be such a waste. All that could have been, all that you could have done, will be vanished by the time the sun rises tomorrow."

"Leave her alone, you freak," Thomas shouted at Beadle. "Touch her again and I'll pull the warts off your face. . . ." He tugged at the cord holding him to the chair. It seemed to get tighter with every move he made.

"I'll do what I want with her," Beadle snapped at Thomas, "and I'll do what I want with you tonight. Wait until the moon rises and you'll see what he has in store for you all."

"Kate, don't listen to what he is saying. They won't dare touch any of us," Thomas said, trying to be as bold as he could. He turned back to Beadle. "We'll be out of here as soon as her father finds out."

"Her father has eaten out of Demurral's pocket for many years. Who do you think is behind all that has gone on? One day he's the Magistrate, next the priest and by night he's behind all the smuggling that has gone on for all these years. The Vicar is the power in this place, not your father. If it weren't for Demurral, you too would be in the poorhouse, chivvying alum from the alum mine, young Kate." He slapped Thomas across the face with the back of his hand. "As for you, the best thing for a Barrick is to be drowned at birth . . . then again, they usually manage to drown themselves before they get to forty." He laughed at his own wit as Thomas fought to hold back his fury.

Raphah spoke softly. "Leave him, Thomas. His own tongue will destroy him. A good word can turn back anger and it's like tipping burning coals on his head. There are more important things than his anger."

"That's right, Thomas. Listen to your dark friend. It may be the last voice that you hear in this world." Beadle picked up the candle from the altar and walked to the door of the chamber. Beside the door was a small wooden box with a brass lock. In the lid were several small holes. Beadle stepped out of the door and flicked the lid of the box open with his foot. Whatever was inside the box gave an annoyed hiss.

"Maybe this will keep you entertained whilst I am away. They hate company, and especially children." Beadle kicked the box once more and the heads of three vipers peered over the top, disturbed from their sleep. Their tongues flicked in the air as their eyes darted around the room. They bobbed their dull brown heads, trying to feel for warmth. Beadle quickly shut the door to the chamber.

He shouted from the stairway: "Good-bye, my friends. I will bring the light back when darkness falls."

The chamber felt cold. The mixture of stale incense smoke and tallow hung in the air like thick brown smog. There was still not enough light from the rising sun and, without candlelight, the chamber fell into a murky gloom. Shadow merged with shadow as it took on the appearance of an ancient tomb of a dead king. The snakes hissed coldly in their box, coiling around and sliding one over the other. Occasionally they lifted their heads over the wooden rim but did not venture any further.

Thomas stared at the altar candles and watched as the smoke rose from the snuffed-out wicks. It looked like the spiralling will-o'-the-wisp that would dance across the lake in midsummer. In his mind, he looked back to a different season. A time when he felt the warmth on his face, when the cold wind didn't beat at his back and bite at his fingers. He remembered swimming with Kate till late into the night, watching dragonflies hop and skip over the smooth water, landing on the lilies and hanging in the air like creatures from another world. They had sat for hours on the bank, watching fish catch the lumps of bread that Kate had rolled in her hands.

Together they had talked about Captain Farrell, the Captain of the Dragoons, and how he had captured twelve smugglers in one night. They had shared the secrets of their hearts for what seemed like an eternity, and he had taken it all for granted.

Thomas had thought that his life would never end, but now, high in the tower, tied to the chair and awaiting Demurral's return, thoughts of his own death flooded his mind.

Thomas was no stranger to the sight of death. He had seen the dead bodies of many sailors washed up on the shore of the bay. Death visited Baytown every day. It took the form of disease and sickness, storm and tragedy.

He realized now how precious each breath really was. He felt himself growing more and more aware of each inhalation, each beat of his trembling heart. He looked at Kate. She had closed her eyes, her head bowed towards the floor. A single tear fell across her cheek. He turned to Raphah, who was staring into the growing light that began to come into the chamber through the coloured glass of the narrow windows. Raphah muttered to himself words that Thomas couldn't hear; he could just see the rhythmic moving of Raphah's lips silently chanting over and over again. Thomas didn't know what to say. He only knew that he had to break the silence, he had to make some sound. There was a sense of helplessness and hopelessness in his heart. He felt as if all the powers of the world were set against him, overwhelming and powerful. Gone were the human adversaries, only to be replaced by the incredible fear of silence and not knowing.

"What will they do to us?" Thomas asked.

"They will kill us," Raphah replied calmly.

"Why?" Thomas could hardly say the word, his throat suddenly dried like a burnt desert.

"Why has man killed man since they left Eden? Why did Cain kill Abel? Some men have it in their hearts from birth." Raphah spoke slowly. "Others learn through bitterness and anger."

"Why us?" Thomas asked urgently.

"It is not so much us as me. I am the one he wants, not you; you should not be here and I should never have asked you to help me. I should have come alone. Your blood will be on my hands." Raphah turned to Thomas and tried to give a reassuring smile.

"But he can't kill us—people will find out," Kate cried tearfully.

Raphah looked at Kate as he spoke. "We are not the first and we will not be the last. This man will never stop, he desires the world, to rule it through some forgotten magic that in the end will turn on him and destroy him. Only then will we see the true Principality behind all this." He paused. "By then it might be too late."

"But I don't want to die, dying is for old people . . . stupid people," she said sharply. "Let Demurral have what he wants . . . he'll let us go free."

"What Demurral wants is me. He wants me dead. If I die, then he will grow stronger. As we are bound to these chairs in life, so we will be bound to him in death. Our spirits will find no rest. He will call upon us and we will have to answer, trapped between life and death, between captivity and freedom."

"I don't believe in all this. Life is only what you can see. How can he capture what is not there?" she said angrily.

"Whether you believe or not, you can never alter the truth that each one of us is body, soul and spirit. You can protest all you like, Kate, but inside you is a spirit that is eternal. You were created by Riathamus to live in this world, then be transformed in the next. This is the truth and the truth will set you free." He almost shouted, the words echoing around the chamber. "Don't fear that which destroys the body, but fear the one who can destroy your soul." As Raphah twisted his tightly bound wrists, he looked at the wooden box by the door. "One snake dragged mankind into hell; maybe three will help him escape into paradise."

The Witch of White Moor

Crane sat on his horse and watched Beadle leave the tower and walk across the gravel to the back door of the Vicarage. From his hiding place in the woods he could easily see the road to Whitby, his ship in the bay and the alum mine three hundred feet below.

The last drops of rain battered the dry leaves that clung to the branches of the trees like the hands of dead men. Crane pulled up the collar on his coat, took out an oilskin hat from his saddlebag and pulled it down over his eyes so he could just peer out from under the brim. In the saddlebag was a spyglass and the three hundred pounds wrapped in a green velvet drawstring bag that he had taken from Beadle. The large guinea coins pressed against the fabric. He held it in his hands, feeling the weight, crunching the coins against themselves. Money for nothing, he had thought.

His eyes kept returning to the room at the top of the tower. In the first light of morning he saw that a narrow stone wall connected the tower to the Vicarage and acted as a buttress. The circular roof of the tower was made of thick copper that had turned green with years of weathering from the wind and sea spray. The spines of the supporting beams had been clad with metal and looked like the points of a compass. From his years at sea he knew that they had been set to point to the four quarters: north, south, east and west. On top of the roof was a long metal pole and running from this like a thick pencil mark was a strip of iron that disappeared under the eaves.

Out to sea the sky grew lighter and more golden as daylight broke over the horizon and illuminated the dark storm clouds that sped over the waves, soon to blot out the sun from the earth. The shafts of sunlight bounced from cloud to cloud and rippled across the surface of the swelling sea. To the north the strange glow had grown brighter. It was as if the whole sky had been torn in two. From the horizon to the top of the sky the amber, green and red glow towered like a pillar of burning cloud.

Crane scanned the horizon from north to south, his eye following the line where sea met sky. He searched for a reason for the cloud: There was nothing but the peculiar glow. Crane had seen many bizarre things in his life, but the burning cloud was far beyond anything that he had ever experienced. He knew that this was not a truly natural event, that in its formation and control there was a power that would soon declare itself.

Looking out of the woods, Jacob Crane couldn't rid his mind of the night before. The vision of the Azimuth plagued his thoughts. In the light of morning he could still see her face, the pleading eyes and her desire to cling to a world now lost. He had been dragged from a world of disbelief by this one manifestation of the spirit. It had planted a seed that in several hours had begun to grow like choking ivy around his soul.

Crane knew that in his hatred for Demurral there was a trace of intrigue and admiration. It was Demurral's covetousness, his secrecy and his desire for power that penetrated into Crane's unusually hardened emotions, making him feel somewhat jealous. Jacob Crane didn't like the feeling; it meant he wasn't in control. For him there was only one way to deal with a problem and that was to get rid of it by whatever means he could.

There was one thing in the world that Crane wanted and that was money. From his teens he had seen the blessing of riches, envying all that they brought. He had watched as men had fought and died for money and betrayed even those closest to them. All for the jangle of gold coins in a velvet bag.

Somehow Demurral had managed to grasp all of this for himself. Crane would have loved to cut his throat and steal all that he had. Demurral's offer of the world echoed around in Crane's thoughts. What if it was true? If this man could give him all that he now looked upon? No more the taste of sea salt sticking to the skin or nights spent being battered from bunk to floor by the German Ocean. All this could be changed, but at what price? Crane battled with the thought of working with Demurral, of going along with what he wanted. His own greed fought against his knowledge of what was right. Crane had always been his own man, never one who liked to take orders, always ruled by his temper, never afraid to use nine inches of cold steel to win the argument. If he was to partner Demurral, then all this would have to be put to one side and he would have to do something that he knew he couldn't do . . . trust.

Crane rolled the thoughts round his mind over and over, contemplating each point and each question that churned within him. He tried to think clearly, but the memories of the night before and the eyes of the Azimuth rushed in like a storm from the sea. In his mind he heard her voice pleading with him, calling to him from beyond the grave.

From the hiding place he could see the neat grounds to the front of the Vicarage, set out in rows of flower beds surrounded by small box hedges. Within the farthest boxed border he saw three freshly dug shallow pits. He glanced back at the tower, then at his ship. Then he gave the signal whistle. From deep in the woods the reply came, carried by the wind. Several of his men emerged from the undergrowth with Martin, who looked at Crane and noticed the blood seeping through his jacket.

"What happened, Captain? Did one of those things get you?"

"Too true, Martin. Hit me from the back and went straight through. Burnt like a scalding pan." He paused. "Did we lose any men?"

"Kirkby and Randall have not returned. It seems they

stayed back to try and stop whatever was coming after you; they haven't been seen since." Martin gestured to the high moor above the wood.

"How many men would it take to strip that house of all its worth and get it to the boat?" he asked Martin.

"I don't think the lads have the heart, Captain. After what they saw last night, they're all talkin' about witchcraft and saying it was Old Meg changed into a hare that chased you." Martin looked at the other men, who remained fearfully silent.

"How often do I have to tell you that you have nothing to fear from Old Meg and the tales of her being a changeling? Who is frightened of a rabbit?" Crane scoffed.

"Something was out there last night, Captain, we all saw it." Martin looked straight at Crane. "There was the burning of the Wiccaman and then them things. That wasn't our imagination or superstition, Captain."

"Martin, you'll have me convinced if you carry on." Crane attempted to hide his feelings. "It's morning now. Things of the night have no place here. There's money to be made and a ship to sail to Holland. See to it that the lads get something to eat. We'll have to leave Kirkby and Randall to the moor. They knew the risks when they came with us—we'll crack a jar for them when we get to Holland."

"One thing," Martin replied. "We've got three new men who want to sail with us. They're alum miners, they say. We found them hiding out from the storm. Said the stranger set them free from Demurral's service. Full of all sorts of tales about what he's been up to. So full of it, they were planning to attack the tower and set the lad free. What shall we do with them?" he asked, almost laughing. Behind him, Skerry, Consitt and Blythe stepped back nervously.

Crane did not reply. He had been only half listening, having caught sight of a company of horses and riders cantering down the narrow road to the Vicarage. The sun flashed on the polished buttons and shoulder armour, the men's crimson jackets and white trousers glowing in the morning sun. The jangling of swords, buckles and chinstraps beat in time with the clatter of the hoofs of the twenty fine greys. Two lengths ahead of them was a huge black mare. Her rider wore the same uniform as the others but had a short cloak draped over one shoulder and a long musket strapped to his back. He wore a half-brimmed hat with a black feather that blew in the breeze.

"Is it . . . ?" Martin asked Crane in a hushed voice.

"It's unfinished business, that's what it is." Crane felt the wound on his cheek.

"Why should Captain Farrell be breakfasting with the Vicar?" Martin asked Crane.

"And especially when I have a tunnel full of contraband beneath their feet," Crane replied. "Twenty men with horses and all turned out in their finery with our ship sat two hundred yards off Baytown . . . what could he want with Demurral?"

"Maybe he wants forgiveness of his sins?" said Martin, stepping closer to the edge of the wood. "Gone to see the Vicar to ask him to get God to let him off slashing you across the face in Wyke Woods."

"Farrell will need more than God to forgive him. As long as I carry this mark, I'll never forget what he owes me. One lucky strike and he's bragging to the world how he took me in a sword fight. Should've killed him there and then and have done with it. One more dead Dragoon wouldn't make a great difference in the world." As he spoke, Crane kept his eyes firmly fixed on the company of men nearing the Vicarage. "I don't think we have enough men to take them, Martin. Anyway, I don't like fighting in daylight. Don't like to see the look on their faces when I run them through with my sword. It's better at night, adds a sense of drama." He laughed.

Captain Farrell rode into the Vicarage yard and tied his horse to the rail by the side of the tower. Crane watched as Beadle scurried out in welcome and ushered him inside. The rest of the men dismounted, tethered their horses and went into the long barn. In that moment any thoughts of helping Demurral dissolved like the morning mist.

"Martin, leave me with two men. I want you to put to sea. Sail across the bay and when you get in range, fire the cannon right at the Vicarage. When you've done that, turn to the north and set anchor beyond Ness Point. He won't see you there. Wait for three hours and if I don't find you, sail to Whitby." Crane took a pistol from his belt and checked the powder.

"What are you going to do, Captain?" Martin asked.

"I don't know. One thing I promise is that by midnight Farrell and Demurral will be wrapped in cold earth, sharing space in one of the graves he's had dug." He gestured to the Vicarage. "There's too much to leave behind, he knows far too much; sorcerer or not, he will need more than magic to keep him alive." He pointed to Skerry, still standing a few feet away from Martin, in the dark of the wood. "You come here. Tell me, what's so special about the African lad?"

Skerry looked at Consitt and then at Blythe. Neither said anything. Skerry dared not look at Crane—he knew his reputation and his temper—but answered falteringly.

"He's different. He can do things and say things that make people change. He's a healer, it's like he knows the inside of your head."

"So he's a witch and a sorcerer, then?" Crane asked.

"No, Captain, he ain't no witch, says they're all bad, doesn't like the fortune cards or the séances. Put Mary Landas right on that, he did." Skerry rubbed the ground with the toe of his boot. "He healed the deaf lad at the mine and got some kind of nasty spirit out of Blythe." Skerry looked at Blythe.

"That's right," Blythe said. "The thing had taken over my mind, wanted me to kill the lad. He came up and in a word commanded it to leave, and I was free."

"Has all the world gone mad?" Crane asked Martin. "Until last night I thought ghosts were stories we used to keep people away from the contraband. Now everywhere I turn, there are spirits, ghosts and the hordes of hell. You'll be telling me next you've all turned to God to protect you."

"Well, Captain," Martin said slowly, "some of us have been thinking that we'd like to hear the preacher at Whitby. We hear Mr. Wesley's coming back soon."

"Wesley." Crane raised his voice. "That man will turn you from women, drink and smuggling given half the chance. Last time he came to Baytown, I lost half a crew. You're soft in the head, Martin. I thought you'd be the last one to get a dose of religion. Let's hope you lose it like you found it—quickly. Now get on, you've got a boat to prepare. I'm going to Beastcliff; from there I'll pick up the tunnel and pay a visit to Demurral. I promised old Rueben I'd bring the children back and I'm going to keep my word. I'll take Skerry and Blythe; they know the mine and the lad. Maybe he'll change me as well," said Crane jokingly.

Martin took the men and they vanished into the dark cover of the wood. Jacob Crane kept watch on the Vicarage while Skerry and Blythe sat on a fallen tree trunk, waiting to be told what to do. They did not have to wait long.

Crane took the spyglass from the saddlebag and peered through it at the Vicarage. He could see into the room Demurral used as a study; in the bay window at a small breakfast table sat Demurral and Captain Farrell, Farrell with his back to the window; the long ringlets of his powdered wig fell over one shoulder. Demurral was clearly speaking at length, gesturing wildly and excitedly with his hands.

"You know the mine well?" Crane spoke without turning to look at Skerry and Blythe; he kept his eye fixed to the spyglass.

"Well enough. We've been there . . . too long," Blythe replied.

"Do you know it well enough to get me a barrel of gunpowder?" he asked.

"Could be done at a push," said Skerry. "I think there'll be some in the store by the fermenting pit."

"I'll need one barrel of powder, some fire rope and whatever you can get me to eat. Don't get caught, I'll meet you on Beastcliff in two hours. Now be off with you."

From his vantage point on his horse's back, Crane kept his eyes fixed on the Vicarage and the conversation that Demurral was having with Farrell. It was obvious that this was not a quiet discussion. Fingers pointed, fists banged the table as Demurral stood up, pushed his chair back and leant towards Farrell, tugging at his tunic. He was pushed away by Farrell and sat back in the chair, shaking his head. They were arguing, but about what, Crane could not guess. He rubbed his eyes—he was tired, but the ache from the wound in his shoulder kept him awake as did the gentle movement of the horse beneath him.

An uncomfortable feeling in the pit of his stomach suggested to him that he was not alone in the wood. His horse, which had been tranquilly cropping at tufts of vegetation, had stopped and thrown up its head, ears back, nostrils quivering. Crane looked around. The forest was full of the usual noises of the morning. In the field below, in between the wood and the mine, he could see Skerry and Blythe walking through the grass by the side of the hedge where it dropped down to the small brook. Far to the right was the sloped cart track up which horses dragged empty wagons to the quarry, where they dug out the shale then lowered the carts back down to the mine.

Crane was sure someone was nearby. His horse had become restive, snorting, stamping its hoofs and pawing the ground. Crane looked around again and checked the pistol in his belt. To get to Beastcliff, he would have to take the road south through Staintondale and then cut back to the sea at Bell Hill. It was a journey that would take him an hour. He could leave the horse there and then climb down the narrow goat path to the expanse of land that had at some time in the past dropped from the cliff top four hundred feet above to form an inhospitable gorse-covered plateau.

It was a place that only a few would dare to visit. There

were too many stories of people who had never returned, of their spirits walking the narrow paths that gripped perilously to the mud cliff between the land and the sea. Beastcliff had always lived up to its name. It had spawned the legend of the thulaks, creatures only too willing to enter the human world and bring with them mayhem and chaos.

Growing unusually nervous at being alone, Jacob Crane was beginning to pay more thought to legend. The feeling of being watched grew more intense. He touched his heels to the horse's side and turned to ride along the path back up and on to White Moor. He felt a sense of relief as he rode from the darkness of the wood and into the light of the sun. The storm had moved far to the south and in the distance he could see the heavy rain as it fired hailstones against the ruined castle set high above a bay several miles away.

He shrugged his shoulders at the unease he had felt in the wood and tried an inward laugh to rid himself of any fear. White Moor was a barren place with only a scattering of sheep amongst the bogs and the stone outcrops. Crane rode to the remains of the Wiccaman. It had scorched the earth. A few twigs of willow lay untouched on the ground. In the daylight it was a different place from the night before. He searched the valley where the attack had taken place and led his horse on foot as he hunted in the grass for pieces of the quarrel that had sliced through his arm and then exploded on the rocks.

In the sunlight he saw the fragments of several small, broken quarrels that looked like splintered diamonds of molten glass. So it had all been real—not imagination or hallucination caused by some strange magic. He now had proof. The wound in his upper arm and the fragments of glass scattered about the rocky outcrops were the evidence he needed.

Crane picked up several pieces of the multicoloured glass. Within each piece were amazing hues of green, red, cobalt and purple. He had never seen anything created by a human hand that could match the hypnotic beauty of this glass.

It was then that he heard the singing coming from beyond the cairn. He could see no one, but could hear the voice of a woman. She sang a sad lament, crying for the death of her child. By the cairn was an old wizened bush with no leaves and dry dead branches. It was the height of a man and every branch was festooned with messages tied on with string and ribbon. Gifts of dried bread cut into the shape of animals littered the rocks that had been piled against the trunk. The tree was covered with offerings of human hair, names written on parchment and wrapped in cloth hanging from the branches like prayers, to be blown by the wind to some deaf god. They rattled against the dry bark in the morning breeze.

The singing was getting louder, but Crane could not see the woman. He followed the voice away from the cairn, down a gully and up the other side until he saw her sitting on the rocky outcrop that jutted out of the moor like the knuckle of a large hand. He couldn't understand why he hadn't seen her before. The rock had been in view since he came out of the wood onto White Moor.

The woman continued to sing, holding her head in her hands, her long red hair falling over her face. She was dressed in the clothes of a fishwife—shawl across the shoulders covering a roughly made long dress fronted with an apron made of sackcloth.

Crane walked up to the woman and stood in front of her. He could see her rough hands and broken fingernails as she twined her hair in her fingers and buried her face in her hands. Her singing had become a drone repeating the same thing over and over.

"She's gone no more to be seen, left this land for the evergreen."

"Who's gone, woman? Why are you out here alone?" Crane asked her.

"She's gone, left me behind, taken away," the woman sang in reply.

"Look at me, woman, I may be able to help you find her," he said.

The woman shook her head violently, never looking up, hair gripped in her hand, pulling on the roots.

"She's gone and lost, not to be found," she sang again, almost screaming at him. "I'll walk the White Moor 'til she comes home again, back to my hearth and the fire that's laid."

Crane took hold of her hand and forced her to look at him. She fought to keep her eyes covered, pulling against his hands. She got to her feet and pushed Crane back.

"Leave me, leave me now," she said. "You come here and tell me what to do when all around you fly creatures wanting to take your soul. . . . As we speak, there is one who will have your heart on a plate."

The woman looked at Crane through two pure white eyes that were blind to this world.

"Woman, you are blind. How can you see these things?"

She stared at him through sightless eyes that appeared to know every detail about him. "You don't need eyes to see death, nor lips to speak of it. Now leave me. I want to sing for my girl. She may be passing and I can't miss her." The woman began to sing again, moaning like the groaning wind on a winter's night.

"Listen to me, woman. Who are you seeking? I may be able to help you, I have eyes that can see in this world." Crane lifted her head again, wanting to see her face.

"You'll need more than eyes that can see in this world. They will have to see into the next and beyond." She reached out and touched his cheek, running her finger down the wound left by Farrell's sword. ". . .'Tis you, cut by steel and driven by the devil. Hard of heart and stubborn of will. . . . In this place, on my moor, by my tree. Captain Jacob Crane, rest in peace." As she spoke, she rubbed his face as softly as she could with her hand.

"Give me no testimony of death while I still have breath in my body," protested Crane. "I am very much alive and intend to remain so."

"How long can you fight against the things you cannot see? How long can they follow you without you being caught? Give me the glass from the arrow, put it into my hand."

She reached out towards him with an open palm. Crane took the shards of broken glass from his pocket and placed them on her hand. He looked at her tough skin. It looked like battered leather. She squeezed the pieces into her fist, grinding the glass together.

"Look now, Captain Crane." She opened her hand and the glass was gone. All that was left was a red dust like dried mud. The woman held out her hand as the wind began to blow at the fine powdered glass.

"Watch this, my pretty boy, watch this," the woman sang.

With that she blew the powder from her hand towards Crane. He quickly put up his hand to protect his face. The glass bounced against his skin and swirled around him, changing colour and shape, forming into a winged black creature that flew around his head, flapping and squawking. Crane attempted to beat the creature away with his gloved hand.

"Leave it be, Captain Crane, the bird will do you no harm. It is only as real as you want it to be," said the woman.

Crane stopped beating the air with his fist. The bird flew higher and higher, rising and falling on the breeze as it stalled and dived over the moor.

"By what god do you do these things?" he asked the woman. "Why do you torment me so?"

"You torment yourself, Jacob. You are never satisfied with what you have or who you are. Your heart is restless and you're a man with no friends. Love is not a word you will ever understand and yet deep within you there is a seed of hope, a tiny mustard seed waiting to grow." She patted his shoulder. "All you have to do is learn. Go to the Rudda crossroads on the Rigg and you will see your future."

"What evil works in you? I should cut you down here and now for witchcraft."

"That would do you no good, Jacob Crane. There would only come another and then another. Look at the sky—can't you see that it will soon be time? There is a change happening in the world. Things of darkness will be commonplace, people will return to this tree to find the power within themselves." The woman began to sing for her child again.

"Why talk in riddles? Tell me who is your master," Crane said urgently and raised his hand to strike the woman. But she was gone. He looked around, but she was nowhere to be seen. He stood alone on the moor. Then he heard her voice again, singing from by the cairn, calling for her child to return. He ran to the pile of stones by her sacred tree and looked down the path that led from White Moor to the Rigg. In the distance he saw the woman walking between the stones, her shawl and long red hair swirling in the breeze. The black crow flew around her, back and forth from earth to sky, rising and falling with each note that she sang until he could see her no more as she disappeared behind the screen of rowan trees that marked the boundary of the War Dyke.

The Keruvim

Captain Farrell did not like to be shouted at. He was a military man who had to have order, preferably his order. He had taken as much abuse from Demurral as he could stomach for one morning and his patience was running out.

"I am sure you think I am a complete incompetent, Vicar, but I do know my job and the last thing you have to tell me to do is how to catch a scoundrel like Jacob Crane. After all, wasn't it me who took him near to death in the woods last week?"

"Yes," said Demurral. "I have seen the scratch on his face."

"Scratch? The man was half-dead by the time I'd finished with him," Farrell objected.

"Well, if that is half-dead then there is hope for us all. He is more alive than you and I put together and that is not the way I like it. I paid you well to kill him and you haven't done the job. Now, tell me, are you going to do it soon, or shall I get someone else?" Demurral demanded, banging his fist on the table.

"What's the rush? These things take time. Like a good wine, they should be savoured and not gulped," said Farrell, who by now was feeling the depths of his annoyance.

"Wait? Is that what you want me to do?" Demurral asked. "I can't wait any longer: I want him dead tonight and his boat blown out of the water. Every week I look out of my window and there it is across at Baytown, unloading every type of contraband that you can think of. Don't you realize that it is doing you and me out of our valuable trade? You're the man employed to stop smuggling, not allow it to go on unhindered."

"Then, I would have to arrest myself—and you, of course," said Farrell, thinking he was being extremely clever.

"Don't be stupid. Don't they teach you anything in the Army?" Demurral paused and drew breath. "You and I are in business. That business is smuggling and we have to do away with the competition." Demurral let out a sigh of exasperation as Farrell brushed dust from his bright red jacket and preened his long moustache.

"Please, Captain Farrell, do one thing. Kill him. I don't care how you do it, you can bore him to death if you want to, but I want him dead. Throw him from the cliff, have him crushed by a stampeding flock of sheep, do anything, but please KILL HIM!" Demurral roared. Beadle, who was outside the room, covered his ears.

"I thought you could do that, Vicar. After all, you keep telling me of your power and your magic. Surely you must have some sort of spell or curse to do the job for you? Isn't there a spirit of death you can conjure to scare him into hell? That way it keeps my Dragoons out of it: Blood on the uniform isn't very nice, you know." Farrell smiled at Demurral.

"You . . . you're a fop and a dandy. You're a molly, a preened skylark, no better than a tuppenny hag. I wanted someone to do this one thing and I thought you were the man. You don't go around throwing the magic at problems that can be solved by your own hands. It's special, beautiful and lovely. Sorcery is like painting a fine picture. You don't waste the paint."

Farrell looked at Demurral and then out to sea. Crane's ship lay just off the coast in the bay far below. In the morning sun it was a magnificent sight.

"What's in it for me?" he asked. "I know that there's more to all that is going on than just smuggling. What's your plan?"

He raised one eyebrow as he asked the question. Farrell knew that there was something that was being kept from him. He did not like being a soldier. He missed the life of a London socialite. Here in the north it seemed as if he were a million miles from the things he knew and loved, things he wanted to return to as soon as possible. His father had bought him the commission to save him from a failed love affair. It was just to be temporary, to save face for the family, he could soon return. Now, eleven years later, he was still in the north, on a rocky outcrop into the German Ocean, chasing smugglers, shouting orders and tramping the muddy roads from Baytown to Whitby. This, he thought, was no life for a gentleman.

"If I were to tell you a story, an imaginary tale, could you keep it to yourself and not tell a soul, ever?" Demurral asked the Captain.

Farrell was intrigued. He didn't answer straightaway. He looked around the room to give himself time to think.

"If it were a true story, then I would honour your confidentiality," he answered. "If it were a barmaid's tale, then why keep it to yourself?"

"Because this is a tale of power, with living words that can take root in our lives. Words that can change the very substance of the world. Each word is like an arrow that can pierce the heart." Demurral pulled his chair up closer to Farrell. "Each time it is told, the arrows are let fly to do their work in the world. They are beyond our control, they cannot be aimed and they will find their own target. They will always hit the mark."

Farrell nodded for him to continue.

"I take it, Captain, that you will keep my secret?" Demurral asked.

"This is more than three sniffs of a beer-stained apron. I will keep it to myself. But what if I should speak of it?" Farrell asked.

"Then the creature that you wish me to release on Crane will seek you out in the darkness and tear out your throat whilst you are still breathing." Demurral smiled pleasantly.

Farrell raised his hand to his throat and rubbed his neck.

"Then I will keep silent."

"Good. The story burns inside me. You are the only one I dare to tell what is to happen. I will leave it to you to decide the truth." He leant towards Farrell and beckoned him to come closer. "Imagine two armies facing one another in battle, one more powerful than the other. The weaker force has a captain who forsakes his charger to ride a donkey. Yet despite this his troops fight bravely and are about to overwhelm the larger force. Suddenly in the midst of the battle the captain is captured. He is taken from the field, killed and cast to one side. The battle turns and the small army is overwhelmed and rushes into hiding, scattered like sheep without a shepherd."

"Go on, and then . . ."

"Many years later there are stories that the captain is alive, somehow brought back to life by a powerful charm, and the battle is about to take place again. You find that you have the one weapon that can stop him; in fact, with this instrument you will become the commander of the strongest force this world has ever seen. You are given the power over the winds and sea. In one word you can stop time. It is a weapon so powerful that even God will bow down to you and all his angels fall at your feet. What would you do?"

Farrell wanted to laugh nervously, but he sensed that this was not a joke or sorcerer's tale. His eyes searched Demurral's face for some sign of truth. "I would, I would . . . I would not know what to do and I would pray to God that such a thing would never happen." From the look on Demurral's face he knew that it was not a story. He knew that Demurral believed it to be the truth.

"Do you have such a weapon?" he asked the Vicar, not knowing if this was a stupid question to ask him.

"Captain Farrell. You're a military man—does such a weapon exist?" Demurral countered.

"If there were such a thing, it would be worth all the gold in the world. With a weapon like that, no army could stop you. Somehow I don't think you are talking in parables. Does it exist?" Farrell raised his eyebrow again, unsure as to what the answer would be.

"It exists and it is here . . . in the tower. I have tried it once with unimaginable results. It took a ship and smashed it to the shore, breaking its back like a child snapping a twig. To think that it can sit in the palm of the hand and yet have so much power that the whole cosmos has to respond to its call." Demurral chuckled with excitement.

"How can such a thing work?" Farrell asked.

"As yet I don't fully understand. It's a matter of faith. All I can think is that it concentrates a forgotten power into a form that is unlike anything seen for thousands of years. The Keruvim has not been used since the time of Moses."

"And you have it here?" Farrell asked.

"Yes. I suppose you will want to see it?" Demurral invited.

"I would like to know what you will do with it."

"My dear friend, I will do what I want, when I want and to whom I want. I could do with a man like you to be there with me. Every general needs a captain."

"Every captain needs to be paid," Farrell replied.

"That is a minor detail. What country would you like to control?" Demurral did not appear to be joking. The excitement showed on his face. He looked like a small boy who had suddenly been given some great prize. It was something that he had to share; he needed to demonstrate his importance to someone, and Farrell was the nearest thing he had to a friend. Demurral was incapable of showing warmth to anyone, and knew it. His coldness protected him from unnecessary complications in life. He found relationships too complicated, too demanding. They had to be maintained, worked at, endured. He did not have the patience for all of this. As a small child he had owned a pet mouse, which he kept in a wooden box. For a few days he played with it, allowing the tiny creature to run up his arm and through his clothing. Then he tired of the animal. He closed the lid on the box for a final time and buried it in the garden. He never thought of the mouse again, let alone cared about how it must have died. As he grew older, it became even easier for him to ignore the sufferings of others, and indeed to inflict suffering upon them.

"Who else knows of the weapon?" Farrell asked.

"The only one that matters is Jacob Crane, but even he doesn't know its true value. Crane is a man with no belief. He's a hard-hearted scoundrel who would sell his own father if he ever had one," Demurral replied. "Once he is out of the way, we can do what we please."

"There is just one small thing that does concern me." Farrell didn't want to ask this of Demurral, but felt an urge within him to do so. "What is to stop you from killing me once you have this power?"

"Nothing. Absolutely nothing. You will just have to trust me," Demurral answered as he took a pocket watch from his waistcoat. "I have some people in the tower I would like you to meet. They tried to steal the Keruvim and now await their punishment. I can also show you something that will help you to understand what power is really at my disposal."

18

Latet Anguis in Herba

In the tower the snakes lay huddled together in the open box by the door. The cold from the icy breeze that blew in under the oak door kept them subdued except for the occasional lifting of a head above the rim to sniff the air with their long tongues.

Kate, Thomas and Raphah talked of what would happen to them when Demurral returned. Then they fell silent, each of them retiring to the world within, fighting their own fears.

Kate struggled with the rope around her wrists, and realized how securely tied to the chair she was. Helpless as she was, however, her rising anger filled her with determination not to give in to Demurral. It was this anger that fuelled her resolve to escape— either that or to inflict some deep, painful and long-lasting injury upon Demurral in her last few moments of life. In her mind she planned what she would do: She looked around the room and saw that the only things that could be used as weapons were the candle-sticks. But then something else occurred to her: When they had been betrayed by Crane, they had not been searched. Thomas still had the Varrigal sword wedged down the back of his tunic. It had been completely overlooked by Demurral and Beadle in the excite-ment of their capture. Kate pictured herself freeing her hands, reaching over to Thomas, taking the sword and inflicting fatal blows on the sorcerer and his apprentice.

She tugged at the golden cord that bound her wrists, but it grew tighter than ever and cut into her skin. It was as if with every thought of escape the cords knew what she was thinking and slowly, like coiling snakes, pulled the knots tighter and tighter. She realized that her dream of escape might not come true.

Thomas could not keep silent any longer. It had been two long hours listening to Raphah whispering under his breath and unable to know or understand what he was saying. Thomas felt deeply about the trouble they were in and believed it was his fault. He should have known not to trust Jacob Crane. When they had escaped from the valley, he should have taken Kate straight home and not waited for Crane. He felt a fool, and this captivity was his punishment.

To his mind the best way to escape was to bargain with Demurral, to plead with him for their freedom. Surely he would not refuse. Demurral had known Thomas since he was a lad. Thomas had listened to countless of his sermons, sitting rigid throughout the service in the cold and comfortless pew for hours on end. Could the Vicar ever kill someone that he knew? Thomas leant back into the chair, his hands now numb with the tightness of the cords. He realized that there was a side to Demurral that was secret, a dark, violent side that was kept away from the world. Thomas began to doubt in his own future. He had no one on whom he could call. No one to rush in and save him. He only hoped that the dream he had would come true, that he need never fear death, and that by believing in the King, he would have eternal life. This was his only hope.

Throughout all this, Raphah stared at the wall with a confident smile on his face, focusing all his inner thoughts on Riathamus. He became conscious that both Kate and Thomas were now looking at him and listening to the words he repeated over and over again.

"Blessed be the strength of Riathamus,
Who teaches my hands to war and my fingers to fight.
My goodness and my fortress;

My high tower and my deliverer,
My shield and the one in whom I trust.
He subdues my enemies before me . . ."

Raphah stopped and turned to the others. "Before you ask, it is a song to Riathamus, it is from his Book," he said. "I'm praying, talking to him; it helps to know his will."

"What does this Riathamus say? That we're all going to die?" Kate said cuttingly. "If that's all he's said, then it's pointless, you might as well talk to the ceiling or speak into thin air." She tried to shake herself from the chair; the cords tightened around her wrists. "It's your God who got us into this place, so when is he going to get us out?" she demanded.

"Have you ever tried to speak to him or do you always let your anger fill your mouth?" Raphah retorted.

"I've spoken to God many times, but he never listens," she declared angrily. "When my mother died, I asked him every day to bring her back, but nothing happened. If he's God, then why is he so deaf? Or doesn't he care for people like me?"

"He has more love for you than you have ever realized, but faith starts with an acceptance, acknowledging who you are and knowing your frailty. Then you will see the power and majesty of Riathamus. In our weakness we will find his strength, in our poverty we will find his riches. It is only in him that we will ever find peace. He is the most powerful being in the whole of creation." Raphah beamed a beautiful smile at them.

"Then why are you going to die with us if your God is so powerful?" she said.

"Many people greater than me have given their lives for him," Raphah said calmly. "We all die, it is something we cannot escape. It is more important to know where we are going when we cross the Bridge of Souls." Raphah could see that Kate struggled with his words. Her eyes burnt with anger.

"Words!" she shouted. "Just empty words that can never help, from a god of the imagination. I don't want to die, not here, never. I want to grow old and fall asleep and not wake up. Then I won't know what's happened or where I'll be. How can you prove he's real?"

"You need faith," said Raphah. "Just a small seed of faith. Something to believe and put your trust in. You've hurt for too long, you're blinded by your pain. Give it up. Let the one who can bring peace heal your life."

"How can I believe in something I know nothing about?" Kate began to cry. "I'm frightened, so frightened. I just want this to stop."

Thomas felt his insides churn with grief for Kate. He had shared so much with her in life and now he knew they would be together in death. He wanted to scream for it all to stop. To take her in his arms and protect her like she had always protected him. She had always been so strong. He felt useless, realizing that he had no power within himself to save her. Kate had always been the one who had the inner strength. The one who would encourage him to carry on, who kept him clothed and fed when he lived in the cave on the beach, bringing him meals and giving him the will to live each day.

When his father died, it had been Kate who had held him in her arms and, even though a child herself, had given him comfort. She had taken away the fear of the loneliness, the pain and loss that had overwhelmed him. She had been everything to him and now she wept beside him, her tears falling across her cheeks onto the stone floor.

Thomas knew that he was about to cry. A lump grew in his throat so that he could no longer swallow, a burning began in his eyes. He drew in a gulp of breath, trying not to weep, but this made him feel even worse. His chest heaved as he gave out a gut-wrenching sob. Red-hot tears poured from his eyes as he attempted to control the rising sense of panic that engulfed his whole body. His heart pounded in his chest as the sensation of fear made each nerve and muscle tingle. He cried for himself, for Kate, for what they were about to face. He could feel himself drowning in his grief. The snakes stirred in the box, hissing in reply.

"My deliverer, my shield and the one in whom I trust. By the power of the Word, save us!" Thomas suddenly shouted out, not knowing where the words had come from, but hoping that the King of dreams would hear him, that he would be real in this world and not just a vapour of his imagination.

All at once he felt a powerful and awesome sense of peace. His tears stopped and the agony of the fear quickly subsided. In his mind he saw the face of the King smiling at him.

Above the tower, Thomas could hear the familiar sound of seagulls calling, but then the crying and screaming of the birds took on a sudden and savage tone that sent a cold shiver down his spine. He had heard them call like this only once before, when he was far out at sea in his father's boat. He had watched as a colossal and menacing flock of seabirds ferociously devoured the body of a small half-dead whale that bobbed helplessly in the still waters. He had watched as they stripped its flesh from the bone, as the sea filled with whale oil and fragments of uneaten blubber.

Through the narrow windows of the tower he could just make out the silhouetted shapes of hundreds of seabirds wildly circling around. Their calling grew louder and louder as they filled the air, blotting out the light of the sun from the tower. They could be heard landing on the metal roof, scratching with their feet and digging their beaks into the hard surface.

"My father said that the gulls were the souls of fishermen drowned at sea, returning to the place they sailed from," said Thomas.

"My father said that when we die, we go to be with Riathamus and that those who spoke of coming back to this life fooled themselves; and so did those who listened to them," Raphah retorted sharply.

In the distance the sound of the alarm bell echoed around the alum mine. The deep, ominous *DONG ... DONG ... DONG* gave the signal that all was not well. Set on the Alum House roof, the bell tolled its mournful ring, echoing around the mine, calling for everyone to run for the safety of the Vicarage.

Kate was the first to speak as she anxiously looked outside.

"What are they trying to do?" she asked as more and more birds landed on the metal roof, their scratching sounding like a thousand trapped rats.

It was then that they felt the deep rumble. At first it sounded like thunder breaking over the distant hills. It shook the tower, vibrating the Keruvim and the candlesticks on the altar. The snakes ducked their heads back into the box as the chairs slipped over the stone floor.

Showers of white powder fell from the ceiling with each tremor, the seabirds took off in one large screaming flock, rising into the air, squealing loudly. The beams supporting the roof jumped on the lintel stones as the walls of the tower visibly moved.

"The earth's shaking!" Thomas shouted. Kate looked around her, sure she heard a voice saying her name.

"Riathamus has heard your prayer and is shaking the earth in his anger. The sea shall rise in his wrath," Raphah replied. "The birds knew what was happening before we felt the earth shake. We need to escape this place before it falls to the ground."

It was Kate who heard the footsteps painfully climbing the stairs of the tower.

"Listen . . . someone's coming," she said softly, only half heard above the cries of the seagulls. Beadle unlocked the door and stepped into the chamber, glancing at the snakes that huddled in the box. He had a look of panic on his face. Kate seized the moment.

"What's the problem, Beadle? Has your master sent you to do his dirty work?"

"He wants the Keruvim, said it'll be safer out of here. The cliffs at North Cheek and half of Baytown have slipped into the sea," Beadle answered reluctantly, not wanting to stay a minute longer in the tower.

"Then take us with you," Kate said. "Surely he doesn't want us to die if this place collapses? That can't be in his plan, can it?"

"He never mentioned you, just said get the statue and that's what I'll do," he snapped back.

"But if you take us too then he's bound to be pleased. He needs Raphah alive until tonight, then he can do the ceremony," she said quickly.

Beadle paused. He appeared confused. He looked at them tied to the chairs with the golden cords; his eyes showed his dilemma so clearly.

"If I were to untie you from the chairs . . . one at a time . . ." He paused to think. "What's to stop you from trying to escape?"

Kate looked at Thomas and Raphah. Her eyes told them not to speak: She would do the talking.

"We'll see this through whatever happens," she said. "Anyway, Beadle, how do you feel being involved in all this? You're a good man; my father always spoke so highly of you. Surely you can't go along with what Demurral is trying to do?"

Beadle looked at Kate and saw the warmth of her expression.

"Sometimes I don't know myself." Beadle attempted a smile. "It's as if something takes me over, so I just go along with everything he wants to do. I'd have no home and no job if it weren't for him."

"You could have a lot more without him," Kate said, encouraging sedition and knowing she had said enough to plant the seed of doubt in his mind. The conversation was interrupted by another tremor that shook the tower. The ceiling and the walls shook dust on their heads. Beadle made a quick grab for the Keruvim and then hobbled to the door. Kate shouted out:

"You can't leave us: The tower might fall down."

Beadle stopped and put the Keruvim on the floor. He turned and went back to Raphah.

"I suppose she's right. The Vicar wouldn't think too highly of me if you were all lost. I ask of you one thing. That you cause me no harm, understand?" He began to untie the golden

184

cords, each knot resisting his fingers as if to warn him of what would happen.

He untied Raphah, then Kate and finally Thomas. It was then that he realized his mistake. Kate deftly reached into the back of Thomas's coat and pulled out the small Varrigal sword that Beadle had failed to see. She flashed the cold metal in front of his eyes and he could see that the blade was stained with blood. He jumped back against the altar, holding up his hands.

"Please don't kill me. I'll do anything you want—just spare me my life," he said, hoping to gain sympathy. "I'll help you escape, show you a way out."

"We don't need any help," Kate said. "What shall we do, Raphah?"

The answer came as another tremor rocked the building. The seabirds leapt into the air, screaming and calling out a warning of impending misfortune.

"We can't leave him here or he'd face the same fate as us. We at least owe him his life." Raphah took hold of Beadle by the scruff of his neck. "You branded me as a slave, you had men beat me and imprison me for your master." He paused and looked Beadle straight in the eyes. "I forgive you for what you've done, let it not stand between us."

Beadle didn't reply; he lowered his head and looked passively at the stone floor.

"Pick up the snakes; they appear to know you well," Raphah commanded as he dragged Beadle by the scruff of the neck towards the door. "Carry the box. It will take care of your hands and the snakes may come in useful. I'll take the Keruvim. Demurral thought it would be powerful in his control, but he could never imagine what true force it can unleash."

Kate could hardly control her feelings; she bubbled with excitement as she shakily held the sword towards Beadle. She looked at Thomas. "He answered. You may think it thundered, but I heard his voice, he spoke to me."

Her eyes filled with tears, this time from the joy that

welled up in her heart. Raphah knew how she felt. He put a hand on her shoulder.

"We are not out of this yet. I don't know what Demurral has already released with the Keruvim. There may be creatures and forces set free that I'll have to stop." He gazed at Thomas and Kate. "You can go now, or you can see this through to the end." He looked into their faces for an answer. They glanced at each other and then at Raphah.

"We'll come with you," Kate said softly. "We're just as much a part of this as you are."

The Raven of Gold

The body of the highwayman swung gently in the breeze six feet above Jacob Crane's head. The noose dug tightly around the neck as the man dangled like a forgotten puppet. Crane looked up at the bedraggled corpse and coveted the new boots it was wearing. He was somewhat surprised that they had not been stolen. They were the boots of a gentleman, black leather with silver buckles, and now encasing the feet of a decaying corpse. It was as he inspected the body that he noticed the telltale signs of smallpox that littered the man's rotting face: the swollen cheeks, the deeply blistered skin. In that he had his answer: No one would strip the body of a man who had the pox. Crane was amazed that they had even dared to hang him for fear of catching the disease. He thought of the words spoken by the woman on the moor and now, here at the Rudda crossroads, was his answer. Was this to be his future: to die of the pox or by hanging, left dangling in the autumn breeze with no one to bury him and no family to mourn his passing?

"And what about you," he addressed the corpse. "Who mourned your death? Are we going to be brothers in the hereafter?" Crane pulled on the bridle of his horse and walked along the path towards the coast. "Peace be with you, my friend. See you in hell," he called back to the cadaver as it swung in the wind.

He walked for several minutes along the narrow lane and through Uggle Wood, then decided it was safe to remount the horse. When the first earth tremor had struck, he had decided to lead the horse, unsure as to what was happening. He looked to the north where the pillar of cloud was growing and spreading like a large fan to the east and west across the sky. It gave a strange glow that even in the morning light was stronger than the sun, though it gave no heat. He looked to the ground and saw that he had two shadows, one that fell to the north and the other to the southwest.

He rode along the rutted track and within a short time was overlooking Beastcliff. Again he felt that he wasn't alone and looked back across the field to the lane. He was sure that he was being watched. At the edge of the cliff was a small narrow path, too narrow for a horse; it dropped steeply to the plateau, curving backwards and forwards down the cliff and disappearing in the undergrowth of small trees and brambles. You could hide an army or a ship full of brandy, Crane thought to himself.

Taking the saddlebag and throwing it across his shoulders, he left the horse at the top of the cliff and made his way steadily on foot down the path. In no time he was under cover of the trees. There was a well-trodden animal track through the wood and on several of the trees he noticed strange marks deeply gouged into the bark, which worried him. He thought of what the woman on the moor had said. The face of the hanged man with its pock-marked stare had burnt itself into his memory. He took his pistol from his belt and cocked the hammer, sure that with each pace he took, someone was stalking him through the undergrowth.

He did not want to be caught by surprise by man, beast or— for Jacob Crane had been forced by circumstance to open his horizons and behold a new world of creatures and spectres that were beyond his imagination—by any other creature.

Cautiously, he followed the path through the wood. Above his head the canopy of trees kept him hidden. Looking up through the branches, he saw the figure of a man high above him on the cliff top. He stopped and took out his spyglass. His disquiet grew more intense. Through the brass-encased lens he saw a man not much older than himself, with long black hair and a small beard, and dressed from head to foot in black leather, with a white frilled shirt. The man looked down to where Crane was hiding and smiled at him and, raising his hand, gave a gentle wave. Crane looked again and the man was gone.

Soon Crane was at the entrance to the hidden tunnel that led from the cliff to the Vicarage. In the clearing he could see Blythe and Skerry. At their feet was a storm lantern and a small wooden barrel. Gunpowder!

He hastened to them. "Well done, lads, that's just what we need. It should be enough to shake old Demurral from his bed. That's if he hasn't been shaken enough today," he said.

"It was the cliff at North Cheek—fell completely into the sea—that and half of Baytown," Skerry replied.

"What about my ship?"

"After the landslide, when the earth moved, there was a large wave that came across the bay," said Blythe as he looked at Skerry. "We watched as the wave hit your ship, it lifted her up like a cork in a bottle then dropped her down again as if nothing had happened. It shook the whole of the mine, felt like the end of the world."

"That may be closer than you think, lads," said Crane as he reached for the gunpowder. "Let's get into the tunnel and give the old dog the surprise of his life, or should I say death?"

He stepped inside. The roof dripped with water and the walls were covered with a thick slimy moss. The three men walked into the tunnel. Crane stopped and looked back into the daylight. He waited.

"A problem, Captain?" asked Blythe.

"Just waiting. I think someone has an interest in our journey. I want to see if I am being followed or if the affairs of the last two days are softening my mind."

Under the protective branches of the yew tree and surrounded by the thick bushes, Kate kept the sword pointed at Beadle, who was holding the box of snakes at an unsteady arm's length. Raphah and Thomas looked out from the undergrowth, trying to see the Dragoons.

"Which way do we go, Thomas?" Raphah asked. "Through the house and into the tunnel, or down the path to the mine?"

Thomas thought for several seconds, weighing up each option. "The house and then the tunnel. It'll give us greater cover, but we'll have to get by Demurral."

"I'll help you get through," Beadle offered.

"No, Beadle." Kate spoke sharply as she held the sword towards him. "I don't think we can trust you. We'll take you with us, and once we're free from the house, we'll let you go. Keep quiet or I will take off your ears and make them into a purse." She laughed, feeling she had found a new strength; now that they were free from the tower, escape could be possible. Kate thought of her home high on the cliffs of Baytown. She wanted to see if it was still there and find her father.

Raphah looked at the cloud spreading its glow across the sky.

"We haven't got much time, maybe two days at the most," he said. "Demurral has done something to the world without even realizing it when he used the Keruvim. He could even have released the Glashan. If they are free, they will find us in time."

"What are Glashan?" Thomas asked.

"They are creatures that I have never wanted to meet. Creatures so evil that you could not even dream what they could do in this world. Before the start of time the Glashan rebelled against Riathamus. They tried to conquer the home-land, but the Seruvim fought against them and many of them fell in battle. The one who leads them was cast to the earth; he has tempted men since that day. The power of the Glashan has been bound since the time of the Great Capture, when Riathamus defeated them at the Battle of the Skull. Their leader was a creature called Pyratheon; he has wanted the Keruvim since its creation. My family has always guarded it from him, but one of our own helped to bring it here and sold it to Demurral." Raphah spoke quietly. "There are two

Keruvim in the world, one is made of gold, the other of flesh. Today we stand in your midst."

"So that's why Demurral wants to kill you," Kate said.

"Yes, and if he does, then the Glashan will again fight Riathamus. The Great Capture will be over. Demurral believes the Keruvim to be a magical trinket that he can use at his whim. Pyratheon would never allow him to control its power. Demurral is in more danger than he knows."

"What will happen if Demurral does this?" Thomas asked.

"It is written that the moon will turn to blood, the sky will grow dark and the earth will be struck by a falling star that will poison the seas. There will be plagues upon the earth and wars and earthquakes shall destroy every city. The earth will then fall into the captivity of Pyratheon for one thousand years. It would be better that we should all die than go through those times." Raphah stepped deeper into the shade of the yew tree for fear of being heard by unwanted ears. He beckoned for them to draw closer. "Demurral will suffer for his greed; Pyratheon will demand all that is due to him. He will try to capture the Keruvim before the end of the full moon."

"How can he be stopped when there are only three of us?" Kate questioned Raphah as she kept her eyes fixed on Beadle.

"There is a feast that is kept in this land called Samhain; some call it Halloween. On that night the gate that holds back the Glashan from this world is at its weakest. I have to be out of the country by then and I have to have the Keruvim with me. Pyratheon is limited in his power; he cannot be in two places at once. He is not all-powerful and relies on the work of his followers; their fortune cards, séances and witchcraft are all part of his deception. They that do his will shall be destroyed with him," Raphah said, holding the Keruvim close to his chest.

"Then we'll have to get you to Whitby. We can be there by tonight and have you on a boat first thing in the morning," said Thomas. "Let's hurry; Demurral won't even think we'd use the house to get to the tunnels. From there we can get to the beach and at low tide we can walk to Baytown."

To himself, he thought that this was easier said than done. Twenty Dragoons sat in the barn between the yew tree and the back door of the Vicarage. Inside, Captain Farrell and Demurral would be in one of the rooms that led off the long passageway that led past the kitchen and then down to the cellar and into the tunnel. Beadle could not be trusted. With one shout he could alert the Dragoons, or if he waited until they were in the house, he could call for Demurral and then there would be no escape.

Thomas took the sword from Kate and prodded Beadle.

"One word out of you and I'll have to run you through with this—do you understand?" He tried to sound as menacing as he could. "I'll do it, Beadle: My life depends on it."

Beadle looked at the three of them. They were dirty and tired. It was obvious that Raphah was feeling the pain of the brand to his back and the blow to his head. Something inside made Beadle feel responsible. He knew he was to blame in part for the hurt caused to the lad. It was not a feeling that he liked. It disturbed him. He looked at Raphah, and remembered what he had said just before they left the tower.

"How can you forgive me when I hurt you so badly?" Beadle asked.

"It is what Riathamus commands," Raphah replied.

"But I don't know you or like you. I would have been prepared to hurt you even more, so how can you say that you forgive me for that?" He kept his whining voice as low as he could, the wart twitching nervously on the end of his nose.

"If I didn't forgive you, then I would not be true to myself. Bitterness eats away on the inside. I could easily hate you forever for what you have done to me, and what you would have done, but what good would that do? It would make me as wicked as you and your master. You have held Demurral's coat for too long whilst he went the way of evil. You have done nothing to stop him and in your complicity you've got blood on your hands."

The words stung Beadle like a willow whip across the back

of the legs. He had no reply and no clever words.

"So what's it to be, then?" Thomas asked Beadle. "If you speak out, you'll get the blade in the back, then I'll cut that wart off your nose and mount it in a brooch."

"I give you my word, for what you may think it's worth, that I will keep silent," Beadle replied.

"We can't trust him, let's tie him to the tree and leave him here and go our own way," Kate whispered.

"Something makes me want to take him with me. If we get found in the house, we can always trade his life for ours," Raphah said.

"I'll show you the way to the tunnel. I promise to give you an hour's start before I tell Demurral. It'll take me that long to walk from the cliff, you can be sure of that," Beadle interrupted just as Thomas was about to speak.

"On that we have your word?" Raphah asked. "Then we take you with us. Show us the way. If you betray us, then you will answer to Riathamus."

"You'll also answer to this blade," Thomas whispered quietly into Beadle's ear. "I may be a lad, but in the last two nights I have learnt to be a man. *He* may have forgiven you, Beadle, but my wrists still burn from the ropes you tied them with."

Together they set off from the cover of the yew tree and the thick bushes that surrounded it and walked across the gravelled yard to the back door of the Vicarage. There was no sign of the Dragoons, other than their horses, at rest in the barn. Beadle walked slightly ahead, still carrying the wooden snake box. Thomas walked behind him, the sword up his right sleeve, ready to slide it forward as quickly as he could at the first sign of trouble.

Beadle took them into the house. Walking as quietly as they could, they were soon in the passageway that led to the kitchen, the cellar and finally the tunnel. There was no sign of Demurral; the house was deathly quiet. Cook was not swearing in the kitchen. There were no sounds of her throwing the pans into the sink. The house had an eerie sense of emptiness.

"There's no one here," Beadle muttered quietly. "They'll have gone to see the cliff fall at Baytown. They'll be at the front of the house."

It was a deep comfort to know that nothing would hinder their escape. The falling of the cliff had meant that the mine had been cleared of people and horses. Everyone stood on the cliff top watching the mudslide across the bay and the increasing brightness of the expanding red cloud.

The long passageway smelt nastily of cold meat and rotten fish. It was dark and dismal with no real source of light. Every few yards were small candles, placed on wooden holders set into the peeling walls, that flickered as each of them passed by. They cast long shadows against the sodden walls. At the end of the passageway the light of the window brought the red glow of the cloud into the house. It reflected from the large golden mirror set on the wall and glimmered on the gold leaf of the raven's wings. Beadle stopped and gave a sign for them to be very quiet.

Fearful of being discovered, they walked as quietly as they could as they left the passageway and went out into the light of the hall. The door to Demurral's study was closed; the staircase that led to the upper floor was empty. The large statue of the golden raven that kept guard above the front door looked down into the hallway. They began the long walk from the front door along the hall that led to the kitchen and eventually down into the cellar. There was a low rumble as yet another tremor shook the house. Their pace quickened, keeping time with their pounding hearts. The excitement made their mouths go dry and their legs feel weak. Each of them fought against the uncontrollable urge to scream and run.

Raphah turned and saw the look on Thomas's face. It spoke of a growing fear. He looked at Kate, who was biting her lip, her brow furrowed with anxiety.

It was then that they heard the thud coming from near the front door. Beadle was the first to turn. A look of utter horror swept across his face. The golden raven had crashed to the floor and was now picking itself up and shaking its feathers. It was alive. Its golden eyes stared out of its golden head and looked directly at them, as its great gold beak pecked at the air. It shook its golden feathers, took two giant steps towards them and began to spread its wings.

Without a word they all began to run, Beadle struggling with his withered leg. Soon he was a distance behind them, the large golden raven bearing down upon him as if he were a fresh rabbit in the field waiting to be snapped up and torn to shreds by its powerful golden beak.

"Keep running, I'll try to stop it," Beadle shouted. He threw the box of snakes at the raven. The three vipers slithered out on the wooden floor only to be ripped apart by the giant bird. Beadle tried to run faster along the hallway. As he did so, he opened every door that he passed on each side to hold the raven up.

They could hear the *bang-bang-bang* as the huge creature smashed each door, knocking them out of the way. Thomas stopped and turned to look back. He saw Beadle hobbling as fast as he could with the large fumbling bird getting closer and closer. Sword in hand, he began to run back to Beadle.

"Don't be a fool, lad, save yourself," Beadle shouted frantically. With that he dived through the open kitchen door and slammed it firmly shut. The raven jumped at the door, slashing at it with its metal talons, which rasped at the wood, sending splinters across the hallway. Thomas could hear Beadle piling chairs against the door to protect himself from the onslaught. "Keep running—go to the cellar," came the muffled voice of Beadle, only just audible above the crashing of furniture and the shredding of wood.

Thomas couldn't leave. He knew that within a matter of seconds the giant bird would be through the door and tearing Beadle to bits.

"Come and get me, you fat chicken," Thomas shouted at the bird and waved the Varrigal sword above his head.

The raven stopped clawing at the door and turned and looked at him. It stood six feet high and almost filled the width of the passageway, its long metal claws digging into the wooden floorboards as it made ready to pounce at him.

He began to panic. Raphah and Kate had run to the cellar. He was on his own. It was then that he heard a voice speaking into his heart.

"I will be with you always, even to the end of the age." It was the voice of the King.

The raven charged at Thomas, who was taken by surprise at its speed. He stumbled back, unsure of what to do or how to fight against such a creature. He lashed out with the sword, hitting the metal feathers of the bird but with no effect. The bird grabbed him by the front of his jacket, picked him up with its beak and began to toss him from side to side, smashing him against the walls of the passageway. Thomas dropped the sword as his head hit the corner of a door. The raven threw him to the floor with a thud, stepped forward and placed an enormous talon on his body, bending its head lower to begin ripping at his flesh with its sharp beak.

Barely conscious, Thomas heard the chant of the Seruvim.

"Holy. Holy. Holy. Lord of Hosts.
Heaven and earth are full of your Glory."

A vivid bright light that seemed to penetrate his flesh surrounded him; he opened his eyes. He was at the bottom of a long stone stairway encircled by Seruvim. At the top of the stairway the King looked down at him.

"Do you want to fight on, Thomas, or come home to me?" It was a soft, warm voice that filled Thomas with peace. "The choice is up to you. I stood at the door of your life and you heard me call; now you can come and eat with me."

Thomas felt an overwhelming compulsion to leave the world behind and to go to the King. He looked back and saw his life frozen in time. He could see the entire Vicarage as if all the walls had been removed, and the contents of the rooms and the people left completely still, as if time had stopped, like a doll's house in some child's game. The raven was poised to strike above his body in the darkened hallway. Beadle was at the door of the kitchen. Raphah and Kate were halfway down the flight of stairs into the cellar. Demurral and Captain Farrell and two Dragoons were in the tunnel, about to step back into the cellar. They had been inside when the tremor had struck and had hidden in the tunnel.

From his place at the gate of heaven Thomas could see that Kate and Raphah were about to be caught by Demurral. The raven would kill him, then go after them. They would have nowhere to run but into the arms of the waiting Demurral, the Captain and his men.

"Let me return and fight; I must warn them. If I do not go back, then the task will not be completed. Please, My King, let me return," Thomas said.

"Very well, go, but act quickly. You will have to strike before the raven. At its heart there is a force of evil, which has given the creature life. Strike to the heart with a pure blow in my name."

With that, the bright light, the Seruvim and the stairway vanished. The damp smell of the hallway quickly filled Thomas's nostrils. He snatched up the Varrigal sword, which had fallen to the floor. The raven jumped into the air, talons outstretched, ready to fall and rip into his chest. Thomas opened his eyes and screamed as loud as he could.

"In the Name of the King . . . be gone!"

He thrust the sword into the breast of the creature as its talons crunched into the flesh of his shoulders. The sword broke through the metal, stabbing into the heart of the large bird. It let out a long, loud, shrill caw as it slackened its grip and fell to one side of the hallway. The metal began to dissolve and bubble before his eyes, burning the wooden floor and steaming against the damp of the walls.

Thomas saw the creature change from a bird into a man. He had a large nose, dazzling white face and bright red hair. He was dressed in a leather tunic, breeches and boots. As he fell to one side, Thomas saw that his teeth were made of solid gold. From his breast oozed a deep blue essence that pumped from his chest with each beat of his failing heart. In his final moments of life he looked at Thomas with piercing catlike eyes. It was a defiant stare filled with hatred as the last beat of his heart took him from this world.

"Thomas!" screamed Raphah. "What have you done?" Raphah stopped and looked at the dead body on the floor. "He is a Glashan. That was the creature. The Great Capture is over. If they are here, then Pyratheon will not be far away."

With that the door to the kitchen flew open. Beadle scrambled over chairs, pots and pans, brushes and a whole pile of implements that he had stacked against the door.

"You've killed it—saved my life," he sobbed.

"Demurral and Farrell are in the cellar with two men," Thomas said. He turned to Beadle. "Is there another way into the tunnel?"

Beadle gestured for them to follow him into the kitchen. They crossed the flagstone floor to the pantry at the far side of the room. Beadle pulled on the cooling stone set into the wall. A door the size of a small man slid open in the wall. Beyond were three stone steps that fell into darkness. From a shelf Beadle took a lamp and, with a tinderbox, lit the wick, turning the lamp up as bright as he could.

"This way will take you to Beastcliff. Beware of that place, there are creatures there that Demurral has in his control. Get to the beach as fast as you can." He looked at Raphah, who was clutching the golden Keruvim. "Leave this land and take that thing with you; it has no place here."

"Come with us, Beadle—you can come too," Kate said as she tugged at his sleeve.

"No. I'll stay here and answer to Demurral. I will have to

close the secret door from this side, so I can't come with you. Now go: He will be here soon."

Thomas clutched the sword and the lantern and led the others into the darkness. Beadle pushed the cooling stone and the door slammed shut. He brushed away the fallen pieces of plaster and, ignoring the feet of the Glashan in the doorway, began to tidy the kitchen. Hearing footsteps from the hallway, he braced himself for what would happen next.

Pyratheon

For a long moment there was complete silence, except for the *drip-drip-drip* from the roof of the tunnel. The light from the lamp lit up the damp stone walls and the stone slabs that made up the slanted floor.

The tunnel smelt of the sea, rock pools and dead fish mixed with the dampness of fresh mud. It resounded with each foot-step and was as cold as death. Thomas held tightly to the lamp and the sword. He did not want to be taken by surprise. Kate walked between him and Raphah, who placed a warm hand on her shoulder as he followed, looking back every now and then into the blackness.

"No one speak," Thomas whispered as quietly as he could. "In a tunnel like this the noise will travel for miles." The sentence echoed like the whispers of ghostly children.

They followed Thomas as he walked down the slope, hoping that he was going in the right direction. He knew that as long as he was walking downhill then they would come to either the cliff or the beach. If they found the cliff, they would be safe. If they found the beach at high tide, they would be trapped in the cave with no means of escape other than waiting for the sea to subside.

Thomas knew this well. A few years before, he had been cut off by the tide that flooded the sands and rocks beneath Beastcliff. He had managed to clamber onto a pinnacle of rock that jutted out of the cliff and had clung there for several long hours as wave after wave seemed to reach out for him to drag him into the depths.

That had been the day he had found the tunnel to the Vicarage, and had found too his first keg of brandy hidden amongst the rocks by the water's edge. Since that time he had been a regular visitor by day and night. He had rowed from the beach to a boat offshore and back again, then tramped high into the tunnel with caskets of tea, silk and gentleman's medicine. This was a thick green fluid in dark bottles that smelt of dead cats. His father had said it was made from wormwood and would drive you mad. This, he had been told, was Demurral's favourite drink.

In the tunnel the sound of the sea could be heard far below. They stopped and listened. Kate thought she could hear the scratch of men's boots on wet stone. She dared not speak, but tapped Thomas on the shoulder, and in the half-light pointed to her feet then to the tunnel.

Thomas nodded. He too had heard the sound of footsteps far off in the dark. He signalled for them to walk as quietly as they could. As he led the way, Thomas looked for anything on the floor of the tunnel that might make a sound. He kept on thinking about the creature he had killed. He felt proud but also frightened. He struggled with the vision he had had of the King; it felt so true, as if he had really stood at the gate of heaven. It was more than a dream. If the Glashan were real, then there would be others that would come after them. He knew that they wanted Raphah and the Keruvim. Thomas mulled this over and wondered if his loyalty to Raphah would overcome his own fear of death.

The sound of metal clanging against stone then echoing through the tunnel brought them to a complete standstill. They had nowhere to hide. Whatever was making the noise was coming towards them. In the distance they could see the light of a storm lamp reflecting off the wet walls. Thomas quickly trimmed the lantern until it was just a small glow and then covered it with his jacket. They were in complete darkness. The light that came towards them grew brighter and brighter. The creature wheezed and puffed as it walked up the steep incline of the tunnel. Every now and then it would cough and spit, almost retching in the darkness.

Thomas drew his sword, ready to strike, leaning against the wall of the tunnel. He could still feel the marks in the rock where the tunnel had been chiselled from solid stone. The beast shuffled up the stone floor, making the sound of several feet stomping against the damp rock.

Kate held her breath, unsure of what she would see. She pressed herself into the wall of the tunnel, as if trying to find some small crevice or crack into which she could disappear. Raphah stood with his back against the tunnel and spoke silently to Riathamus.

The glow from the creature's lamp came very close and then suddenly veered to the right. It had taken the passage, only yards from them, that ran to the cellar door. Thomas could hear the coughing and spluttering moving up the tunnel away from them into the distance. Mingled with their enormous relief that the creature had turned before it found them was the dread that surrounded them like so many unseen hands grabbing at their thoughts, a terror heightened by the smell of the tunnel, the penetrating dampness and the long, shrill echo of each footstep.

They waited for what seemed like a lifetime and then Thomas took the lamp from under his coat, turned up the wick and began to lead them down the tunnel. He knew that soon they would be out of the darkness and into the fresh air of Beastcliff.

A small patch of light was visible a hundred yards below them. It was the entrance to the tunnel. The red glow from the cloud merged with the golden sunlight, forming a beautiful yellow and red ochre glow that shone on the walls. It brought with it a sense of relief as they quickened their steps, wanting to run towards the light. Raphah held the Keruvim close; in his heart he believed there was a chance of getting the statue back to the Temple. He had travelled so far, and here, in what he had been told was a civilized land, he had found hostility, hatred and ignorance. He had met with a people who beneath a profession of faith still believed in the power of spirits. People who clung to the old gods but dressed them in new clothes; who called them different names but still believed in their power.

It was then that they heard the muffled coughing getting closer and closer. Raphah turned, and there saw to his horror the light of a lamp coming back down the tunnel. Thomas looked to the entrance and silhouetted against the light was the figure of a tall man with sword in hand. They were trapped.

From behind they heard men's voices coming closer. Thomas looked back and then down to the entrance. He could not think how they could escape. Kate grabbed hold of his shoulder.

"What can we do?" she asked desperately.

"They have us," Thomas said. "All we can do is either fight or give up."

"There is another way," said Raphah as he took out the Keruvim from inside his coat.

"You can put that back," the voice shouted from the entrance. "You won't be needing any help from that God of yours." It was Jacob Crane.

Behind them the wheezing got stronger as Skerry and Blythe approached. Blythe was completely out of breath and wearily dragged his feet along as he walked. They echoed through the tunnel, amplified by the cold stone walls and their imaginations.

"We came back for you," Blythe panted as they approached in the dim lamplight. "Captain Crane came to set you free, but it looks like you've done the job for yourselves."

They followed Thomas to the entrance of the tunnel. Crane waited, leaning against the wall and holding his wounded shoulder. He could see the look of anger on Kate's face, and he knew that a broadside of venomous words would soon follow.

"You left us," she screamed, "left us to die in that tower!"

"I left you to buy some more time and lucky I did. Captain

Farrell and the Dragoons arrived. That old soak had sold me to Farrell. If I'd waited around, I'd be in irons by now and on my way to the gallows at York." He pointed to his cheek. "I have some unfinished business with Captain Farrell. The plan was to leave you here until tonight, then come back for you. I have ordered my ship to fire a broadside at the house tonight, just when the Vicar is settling down for dinner."

"There is something you should know," Raphah interrupted. "There are creatures that have been released by Demurral. They too want the Keruvim."

"One tried to kill us in the house," Thomas butted in.

"So, what are these things, my young lascar?" Crane asked. "In the last two days I have seen so much I don't understand."

"They're the Glashan, fallen Seruvim and followers of Pyratheon. They intend to capture the Keruvim and wage war against Riathamus. Heaven and earth are in great danger. Demurral is being used by them and I don't think he even knows of their existence," Raphah told him.

"So, how do I know if I see one? Can they be killed?" Crane asked.

"They have green eyes, like a cat's, and they can change shape," said Raphah. "They look like people. The only way to tell them is by the eyes. If you have faith, they can be destroyed; if not, then they will overpower you."

Crane took the pistol from his belt and aimed it at Raphah.

"Can they take a piece of lead and still survive? Can they endure the cutlass and not bleed?" he asked.

"Yes, they can," said Raphah. "These weapons are of this world. What you need is far more powerful than lead or metal fashioned by man's hand. You need that which comes from Riathamus and cannot be seen."

"A pure blow in his name?" Thomas asked.

"Yes, in his name," Raphah replied.

"You leave me confused," said Crane. "I'll fight these Glashan with the things I know. If that's not good enough, then

I'll die. You fight them with your riddles and we'll see who wins."
He lowered the pistol and looked at Raphah. "I know I have to
help you escape. Since you've been here, the world has changed.
Maybe when you've gone, things will get back to normal and I
can get back to my business."

"If we don't stop the Glashan and Pyratheon, then you won't
have a world to carry on your business in. What you have to
understand is that Demurral has opened the gates of the Great
Capture. The Glashan are free again; they will take over this
world and then attack Riathamus." He looked at the faces of those
gathered around him. In the glow of the lamp they looked at him
as if he were speaking in a foreign language, as if their minds
could not grasp what he was trying to say. "There are two
worlds—one visible, the other unseen. In this world we are ruled
by time, by the rising of the sun, the stars and the tides. In the
other we stand outside time: Past, present and future are all the
same. A prayer today can affect an event yesterday; a curse tomorrow can be like an arrow fired into the past. Pyratheon wants to
overthrow all of this."

"But that is what Demurral said to me—that he wants to
control the elements," Crane said, pressing his hand to his
wound, which was becoming increasingly painful.

"You are hurt," Raphah said. "You need to be healed for the
fight ahead."

"What I need is a jug of rum and a soft bed," Crane replied.

Raphah ignored him and placed his hand on Crane's forehead. He closed his eyes and for several seconds stood silent;
then he began to speak quietly to himself. Crane felt a powerful
heat radiating from Raphah's hand, rushing through his body.
He began to tremble as the heat set every nerve on fire and
vibrated through each sinew. He felt as if he were standing
beneath a hot waterfall that gushed into his body, cleansing and
scouring each thought and desire. Instinctively he placed a protective hand over the wound, to find to his surprise that the pain
had gone. Pulling aside his clothing to inspect the injury, he

found only fresh, undamaged skin. To a man of action, with no time for fanciful thought or theory, it seemed what he had thought impossible was now grabbing at him, turning his world upside down. He searched for an explanation but found none, and felt himself beginning to panic. The madness was closer to him than he'd thought.

Such uncomfortable thoughts were soon driven from his mind, however, as, before any of them could speak, a sudden draught rushed through the tunnel. In the distance they heard the resonant clang of a heavy metal door closing. "We have little time," Raphah said. "Each one of you has seen something of this other world. You have to decide on whose side you wish to fight. If you are not for Riathamus, then you are against him; there is no neutrality in the kingdoms of heaven and hell."

"I never thought I'd see the day when I would be asked to stand for God. Can't he fight his own battles?" Crane asked.

"Don't think he will leave us helpless. He has given us one who will fight with us, back to back in the thick of battle. He will be with us and the Seruvim will fight in the realms we cannot see."

"Well, lad," said Crane, "you're either insane or this world has completely changed. Two days ago I would have seen you in the madhouse for talking like this, but now I'm sure that there must be some truth in what you say. We can fight only against what we see. You'll have to show us that which is unseen, our eyes are blind to the things you talk of and my heart has been hardened to your God by too many years of fighting and stealing."

The sound of marching feet echoed in the tunnel. They resounded and grew louder and louder as echo built on echo, pounding through the tunnel.

"Dragoons," said Crane. "Quickly, into the wood."

"This is the place of the Varrigal," Kate protested. "They may be here again."

"Whatever they are, they can't stop us; we have three pistols, a barrel of powder and two swords. That's enough to take on twenty Dragoons," Crane said. "Now come on. Into the wood. We'll hide there and leave a surprise for whoever is following us."

Thomas was the first out of the tunnel and into the wood. The clearing had a fresh feeling. The morning dew clung to the blades of grass, the trees hung over the entrance like a deep green curtain. He stopped by the holly bush and looked out into the glade; he could see no one. He waved for the others to follow. Crane stayed by the entrance to the tunnel and wedged the barrel of powder into some tree roots that had knotted themselves in and out of the rock. Taking a length of the fire rope that had been dipped in lamp oil and coated with iron filings and black powder, he ran a length from the barrel to a tree stump several feet above the entrance.

The sound of marching feet could be heard getting closer and closer.

"Not much further." The voice was familiar to Crane. "Draw your pistols. They may be anywhere down there." The words reverberated through the tunnel.

Crane smiled. Captain Farrell, he thought to himself. If only he could time the explosion, it would be so fitting to blow the tunnel right above his head. He waved for the others to hide away from the entrance. Thomas, Kate and Raphah ran a little way along the track and hid amongst the dried bracken. They could see the entrance to the tunnel behind the holly bush and could hear the men approaching.

It was Kate who saw the first red coat appear from the holly bush. He was a small man whose uniform fitted badly. He shielded his eyes from the glare of the sun and looked around him before going back into the tunnel.

Captain Farrell then came into view, large hat and feather blowing in the breeze. In one hand he had a pistol, in the other a rapier, its blade flashing cold and clean in the light. She watched Crane light the fire rope, which flashed blue sparks and hissed and smoked deep blue smoke.

Farrell turned to look, unaware of what was happening. The

fire rope burnt quickly, covering the several feet in a matter of seconds. Crane ran for the cover of a sturdy oak tree, pressing himself as close as he could to its bark as the blast from the explosion ripped through the woods.

Farrell was blasted backwards into the sharp leaves of the holly bush and then covered in large clumps of sodden earth. The thunderous roar sent shock waves that tore at the branches of the trees and blew back the dead bracken. The entrance to the tunnel had completely collapsed with the power of the exploding powder keg. All that could be seen was a crater of imploded mud, and shale filled the space where the entrance had once been.

The Dragoons were stuck in the tunnel. Their only escape was to go back to the Vicarage. Farrell, now separated from his men, lay on the flattened bush, covered in dirt. His bright red tunic was stained with mud and his fine hat with its feather was nowhere to be seen.

Crane stepped out from behind the cover of the oak tree. Embedded in it were fragments of wood and stone that had been blown like shrapnel from the explosion. He walked towards Farrell, looking down on him from the mound that formed one side of the crater. Taking out his pistol from his belt and with sword in hand, he stared at Farrell, still stretched out, stunned by the blast.

"Stand and deliver, or the devil he may take yer!" Crane shouted at Farrell. "No jar of whisky for you, my fancy friend. No helping hand to pull you from that tree." He stepped down from the mound and walked towards the Captain, who struggled to get up from the holly bush. "Stay where you are, I'm not finished with you yet. I hoped that you would have been killed with the explosion, but now I am going to have to do it myself." He looked at Farrell. "What do you want, pistol or the sword? I promise either way to make it as slow and lingering a death as possible."

"Take my money; leave me to live," Farrell muttered painfully. "I promise I won't follow you."

"I'll have your money and your life: There is no bargaining to be done. You came for the lad and now I've got you." Crane cocked the pistol and put it to Farrell's temple, pressing the rim of the barrel into the flesh. "Say good-bye to Jacob. The next time you see me will be in hell." His finger went to squeeze the trigger.

A hand fell on Crane's shoulder. Surprised, he turned to see Raphah.

"There is another way, Captain Crane—he doesn't have to die."

"Keep out of this, lad, it goes too deep for you to be involved," Crane snapped at him. "He dies now, it's only right. If I let him go, my men will think I've gone soft. I'll have every one of them trying to take over. If I kill him, they'll know I mean business."

"So you would kill him to save face—what kind of a man does that? He's not some dog to be shot when it's outlived its use, he's a man, flesh and blood like you and me." Raphah put his hand on the pistol. "There'll be others who'll come after you if you kill him. You'll have to kill them and keep on killing until they kill you."

"He's a Dragoon. Farrell knew what he let himself in for when he took the King's shilling. He knew that one day it could end like this. Did he think of me when he tried to swipe my head off in the woods?" Crane clicked back the hammer of the pistol.

"You don't have to act as he expects you to. You can be free from that. A kind word turns away wrath. Giving him his life isn't a sign that you're weak; it shows that in your power there is also mercy. If he's involved with Demurral, then there may be another way of getting what you really want."

"Blythe, Skerry!" Crane called. "Tie him up, he's still drunk from the blast, so he'll cause you no trouble. We'll leave him here, it won't be long before they find him." Crane leant over and looked at Farrell straight in the face. "I give you the right to live. Don't go telling people fancy tales about nearly capturing me, because if you do, I'll finish the job. Go and tell your master that the stakes are now higher. I want half of what he's stolen from the people and I'll be out of these parts for good. Tell him to leave it in gold at the wishing tree on White Moor at midnight tonight. If he tries to take any of my men, then I'll give word for my ship to bombard his house and blow it to pieces. Understand?" Crane took the pistol away from Farrell's head. "Tie him to the thorn tree, make sure he's uncomfortable."

Blythe and Skerry dragged Farrell to his knees and then across the glade to the thorn tree. Using the rest of the fire rope, they bound his arms tightly to some low branches and his feet to the trunk. He hung there like a life-sized puppet. Skerry found the Captain's hat, now torn and tattered, and put it on Farrell's head, pulling it down over his eyes so he could not see. Crane gestured for them all to walk silently down the track that led to the beach.

Within a few minutes they were standing on the muddy point that overlooked the bay. It was low tide and a vast expanse of sand stretched into the distance. On the other side of the bay they could see where the cliff had fallen. It was as if a large chunk of the headland had been scooped out by a giant and thrown into the sea. Strewn across the beach and mixed in with the mud, clay and stone was the wreckage of the houses and shops of King Street, which had toppled. Crane's ship lay at anchor in the bay. Two miles of sand separated them from the safety of his boat and the escape to freedom for Raphah and the Keruvim.

"If we go by the beach, then Demurral can watch us all the way," said Crane cautiously. "If we split up, then we'll have a better chance of getting through." He turned to Thomas. "You take the lad to Rueben at the Mill, I'll go for the ship. Martin should be there by now. We put to sea at six o'clock, I can't wait for you." He pointed to a deeply rutted path used by the miners to take the alum to the ships that put into the shore and then took it to London. "Go that way, stay clear of the mine and get to the Mill as fast as you can. Rueben will get you to the ship. I'll take my crew this way; we should make it in the hour. Good luck."

"I don't believe in luck," Raphah said. "It leaves so much to chance."

With that the three quickly made their way to the steep track that went from the beach into the wood. Thomas turned and watched as Crane and his two men walked along the beach, keeping as close to the high cliff as they could to stay out of sight of Demurral and the Dragoons.

In the wood Captain Farrell hung from the thorn tree by his hands and feet. He was aware that there was someone standing close by. The hat pulled over his eyes prevented him from seeing anything. He heard a twig break underfoot, a hand rested on his shoulder, warm breath danced across his neck.

"Who is it? Who plagues me with their games?" he growled, angry of his capture and humiliation.

"It is I," said the soft feminine voice, "the one you love and left behind so long ago. At last I have found you."

"Elizabeth, is it you?" he asked, unsure if he was dreaming. "If it's you, then take this hat from me so I can see your face."

"If you insist," said the voice, even softer and lovelier than before. He felt his neck being gently stroked by long warm fingers.

The hat was ripped from his head and he opened his eyes to see. In shock he gave a sudden, long and shrill yell. There before him, dressed from head to foot in black leather, was a Glashan, its long white hair and goatee beard blowing in the soft morning breeze.

"Oh, Captain Farrell," it said sweetly in the voice of Elizabeth. "How good it is to see you."

The Glashan laughed and slapped Farrell across the face.

"Human beings, human dirt," it growled through its golden teeth. "What rot. Just look at you, torn apart by greed and lust, you're so confused, you don't even know your own heart. You slave every day for possessions that mean nothing and in the end you have to leave them all behind when death kisses you gently and calls you to her breast."

The creature grabbed Farrell by the ears and stared at him through its catlike eyes.

"You, my friend, will be used for what you do best." It clicked its long thin fingers and with that appeared the small squat figure of a Dunamez, which scratched around the forest floor like some wild pig, jumping around excitedly.

"Quiet, he'll be yours soon enough," the Glashan said to the Dunamez as it panted in anticipation. "Let's savour what we are going to do. We can't rush Captain Farrell, he'll want to see everything."

With that the Glashan stepped back and beckoned the Dunamez to step forward. Before Farrell could scream, it stepped into his body, choking his breath from him. He was overwhelmed by the stench of its breathing as it stretched out inside him.

The Twisted Oak

The light from the cloud penetrated the depths of the forest, giving a strange glow to the fallen leaves strewn across the ground. It crisscrossed in dark shadowy patterns on the forest floor, giving the appearance that it was fighting against the sun to cast blacker shadows.

Thomas, Kate and Raphah walked along the path, the only sound the crunching of dry leaves underfoot. Thomas held the sword in his hand. Raphah hugged the Keruvim tightly beneath his coat. He felt that its rescue had been too easy—it had fallen into his possession without a fight; the forces that desired its power had released it without an ounce of blood being shed.

Kate kept watch, looking in amongst the trees for the slightest sign of the creatures that had chased them along this same path. They passed the tree where the Varrigal had attacked them. She could see the deep sword cut where it had tried to kill Thomas only to miss and sink the weapon deep within the bark. The tree had begun to rot, the bark had turned to a soft pulp, which was oozing out from the cut and spreading like gangrene. The tree, sagging and drooping, looked as though it was melting as the rot crept through each fibre. A noxious smell filled the air. They covered their mouths with their hands and walked quickly by.

"That could have been you," Kate said to Thomas.

"It must be something in the metal of the sword," Thomas replied, looking at it, wanting to cast it away. It somehow felt wrong to carry the weapon, as if it had a power that he should not be a part of.

"It's the creature that brings evil," said Raphah. "Where there is life, it will bring death; where there is growth, it will bring decay; and where there is light, it will bring darkness. It is a reflection of Pyratheon. The creatures can do only what he desires."

"So what about Demurral? He thinks he can control them," Thomas said.

"It's as if they are on loan. He can use them, but they do not belong to him. He is deceived into believing he has the power, when in reality he too is a puppet. People who use these forces never really understand the true energy behind them," said Raphah. "They think that they are the masters when in reality they soon become the slaves. Pyratheon gives them what they want . . . until he wants them."

"But I thought that Demurral followed God?" Kate interrupted. "How can he leave all that behind?"

"It's so easy. Many people start off on the right path, then greed or envy start to burn into their hearts. Soon the things of the world take over and they are far from where they started. Power has always been more sought after than love and yet the true power comes when we find the one who can bring us perfect love. We must cling to that with all our hearts."

Thomas listened to Raphah as he walked. The path through the wood overlooked the bay. He knew that a new future lay ahead of him. There would be no going back to his old life. Whatever happened, he knew his life would be away from this place. As he looked across the sea to Baytown, the view appeared to have changed. He could not tell if it was because of the strange light from the cloud or if something within him had opened his eyes so that he was seeing it in a new way. He felt sad yet excited. It was as if he was changing, growing and becoming a man. He gripped the sword, trying to make sense of all that he had seen. In the daylight and the open air the world of darkness was so far away and yet he knew that even behind the veil of light the forces and powers that sought their destruction still lurked, waiting for the moment to strike.

The path through the forest dropped into a small valley; a twisted oak tree spread out its branches like the roof of some large Gothic cathedral.

It was Kate who saw the man first. It was as if he had appeared from nowhere. He was walking slowly ahead of them with his head down. He clutched a long shepherd's staff in his right hand and over his shoulder was flung a goatskin bag. A large felt hat covered strands of black hair that fell in long ringlets down his back and over the dirty grey frock coat edged in yellow that was obviously too big for him.

She tapped Thomas on the shoulder and pointed to the man.

"What shall we do?" Kate asked.

They stopped walking and huddled together. It was Raphah who replied.

"Let us keep walking; he looks like a shepherd. Thomas, keep that sword to hand. If he is more than a man, strike out and then we shall run. Kate, always keep ahead of us and don't fall back."

The man had stopped and sat down on the trunk of a fallen tree that lay across the long ditch that ran by the side of the path. He had taken the bag from his shoulder and now rested it on his lap. He had brown, weather-beaten skin. With his right hand he wiped the sweat from his forehead.

"Don't be shy," he called to them. "I don't like to be followed; well, not through these woods. You never know who may be after you."

Thomas tried to hide the sword behind his back, not wanting the man to see what he carried.

"You might need that one day, lad, there's no need to hide it from me," the man shouted. "Why don't you come here and join me? I have fresh bread and salted fish—you can have as much as you like."

It was hunger that prompted Thomas to turn to the others

and gesture for them to follow. They walked cautiously over to the man, and Kate leant against the tree. Thomas stood two arm's lengths away, the sword firm in his hand.

"It looks like you three are hungry," said the man. "Here, have some of this bread."

He took the loaf between his two big, strong-looking hands and broke it in two and then into four, handing a piece to each of them and keeping one for himself.

"Do you want some fish? It's been well smoked and tastes of leather, but I've been told it does you good."

He offered them a small piece of brown, dried fish. The meat clung to the dark lined skin and smelt of oak chippings. Thomas took a handful and greedily pushed it into his mouth. It mixed with the wad of bread to form a delicious smoky sop that gave off the fragrance of burnt wood, yeast and fish with each chew.

"You all look hungry. You must have come a long way," said the man. He looked at Raphah. "From the look of you, you must have travelled the furthest. Wouldn't expect to see one like you in these parts." He stopped speaking and waited for Raphah to reply. There was something familiar about the man, which bothered Thomas. He knew he had seen him before, but he could not remember where or when.

"Are you from these parts?" Thomas asked. "I can't remember seeing you before, yet I seem to know you."

"I'm a shepherd, come to look for some of my sheep that have lost their way. You've seen me before. You're Thomas Barrick, your father was a fisherman; and you, young lass, are Kate Coglan, daughter of the Excise man. See, I know you both so well. Where are you going?"

"We are going to a friend's house," Thomas replied, realizing that the man had avoided the question.

"The only friend I would choose in this forest would be Rueben the Boggle. He's a good friend of mine, a man who can be trusted. I've known Rueben since he was a babe," said the man.

Kate looked at his face; he looked no more than thirty years old. He had young eyes that burnt bright blue in the dark frame of the weathered face.

"He's twice your age—how could you have known him as a baby?"

"You see, Kate . . ." The shepherd paused. "It's like what your grandmother said when your brother died. It's not the length of life or gold of kings that makes a person rich, it's the love that we gather on the way."

It was as if Kate had been stunned by a sudden and numbing blow. She shuddered and fell back against the fallen tree trunk, gasping in astonishment. These had been the words spoken to her by her grandmother every night before Kate went to sleep. They were the last words she had ever spoken in this world. They were private words shared in love, words that had kept away the fears of the night, words that Kate had repeated and repeated like a prayer. He could not possibly know them. She felt he had stolen them, eavesdropped into the most precious moments of her life. And yet they carried the same infectious feeling of love and warmed her heart as if they had been spoken for the first time.

"How did you know?" she whispered.

Thomas and Raphah looked at Kate but did not grasp the significance of what had been said.

"So what about your journey? Is Rueben going to help you?" the man asked.

"How do you know Rueben? You *can't* be older than he is," Thomas said.

"I know so much of what goes on in these parts. You just have to listen to the wind or stand silently in the wood and you hear the voices calling. There are no secrets, nothing can be hidden from me."

Thomas stared at his face, knowing that he had looked into those eyes before.

"So what about you, Thomas: When will you learn to swim? You can't rely on that caul you carry, or this lad, to pull you out whenever you fall into the sea."

Thomas looked at Raphah in amazement.

"My family never swim. You have to trust your boat. How did you know Raphah pulled me out of the sea? Was it you that pushed me in?" Thomas asked angrily.

"You're like your great-grandfather, he had a fiery temper just like you. He knew me just before he died. Called out to me and I was with him. . . . You're straight out of the Barrick mould," said the man.

"How could he have called out to you? He was ten miles out at sea in a storm. They never found him, all they brought back was the empty coble." Thomas felt so angry. It was as if this man could pick a moment from your life and tease it before your eyes.

Raphah didn't speak as he looked at the man. He too found something familiar about him, something that he had seen before or an inflection he'd heard before in his voice. The man had a dark skin that looked burnt from years of toil under the sun. Around his eyes was a myriad of lines that spoke of hours of laughter. His face was one open smile with white teeth that flashed brilliantly when he spoke.

The man broke another piece of bread and handed it to Raphah.

"You look hungry and far away from home. Whatever has brought you here must be important to you," he said.

"It is far more important than some people will ever know or understand," Raphah replied. The man laughed.

"You want to serve your master with all your heart, do you?" He looked at Raphah, who was readjusting his jacket over the Keruvim. "What have you got there?" he asked.

"Nothing," Raphah snapped, quickly taking a step back from the man. "Nothing of any importance." The Keruvim flashed its pearl eye in the sunlight.

"And that is your prize?" asked the man.

"My prize is worth more than this," said Raphah as he took another step away from the man.

"Are you frightened that I might snatch it from you, that I'll take it like a common thief?" the man asked. "The cattle on a thousand hills belong to me, not even Solomon in all his glory had the wealth that I possess."

"Solomon?" Raphah looked at the man, unsure if he had misheard what he had said.

"Solomon," the man replied quickly. "The great King, the one who built the temple to place in it what you carry."

Raphah showed his surprise.

"You know of Solomon, your people are descended from him. It is your task to keep the creature that you hold on to so tightly from the world. You have done well to save the Keruvim from those who would use it for evil."

Raphah, Thomas and Kate all stared at the man. It was as if in that moment they had all come to a sudden realization that they were in the presence of someone who was mighty and powerful and yet came to them in the rags of a poor shepherd.

"You are . . ." Raphah could hardly speak.

"I AM WHO I AM. That is all you need to know. You must go quickly from here, do not go to the Mill. Go to the seaport to the north. There you will find a church at the top of the cliff. Go there. It is important that you arrive before midnight tomorrow. In that town you will find a man who knows me and that man will put you on a ship for France. Keep trusting me; I will send the Seruvim when they are needed."

The earth on which the man stood began to glow, his clothing began to change, his appearance softened and he smiled.

"I will be with you always, even to the end of the time," he said as he was surrounded by swirls of golden light that blew like millions of thin strands.

From out of nowhere a violent wind began to blow from the sea. The trees of the forest rattled against one another as pieces of timber and branches blew through the air. The swirling wind picked up the dead leaves from the forest floor and blew them round and around, forming a great impenetrable mass of browns, reds and green. The leaves battered against their faces and

Thomas curled up as small as he could against the forest floor whilst Raphah and Kate huddled in the crevice between the tree trunk and the rich earth.

The sound of creaking, snapping and breaking branches filled the air. The crash of wood against wood echoed through the glade as branch smashed against tree. In amongst the highest limbs of the trees darted tongues of blue and red fire that flashed and sparked as they hit each branch. The noise of the whirlwind, the flames and the crashing branches almost burst their ears with its savagery.

Thomas looked up, dirt and tree bark splattering into his face. He tried to look at the man who stood in the centre of the whirlwind, completely transfigured. No more was he dressed in the clothes of a shepherd. His clothes shone like bright silver, his face was as radiant as the sun itself. Thomas hid his gaze from the brightness. In a moment the man was gone and all that was left was the goatskin bag propped against the side of the tree. There was complete silence, complete peace.

Raphah was the first to pull himself from the refuge under the tree trunk. He dug his way out of the leaves and branches that had been heaped on top of him by the whirlwind. Kate scrambled out, gasping for air. Thomas lay facedown on the ground, his hands covering his head to shut out the noise of the wind. He pulled himself to his knees and looked at Raphah and Kate.

"Was that . . . ?" he asked, unable to finish his sentence.

"It was Riathamus, I just know it was," Raphah replied shakily, shocked by the experience.

"How can you be sure—it could have been one of those creatures in another form," Kate said, picking the dry leaves from her hair. "He could have killed us with that storm. Where is he now, how can you be sure it was him?"

"I just know, don't ask me how. It was his voice, something in his eyes. It was the way he knew so much about us," Raphah answered.

"Then we'll have to do as he says. Whitby is a good walk; it'll be dark within two hours and we'll never make it before night-fall," Thomas announced as he got to his feet.

Kate picked up the goatskin bag. It was made of one piece of skin folded over and a thick leather strap twisted its way from end to end. She peered inside. It smelt of fresh grass and treacle, cinnamon and hot bread. She closed her eyes and breathed in the glorious sensation. She began to smile.

"What's inside?" Thomas asked.

Kate looked in the bag, where there was another small loaf of bread, several more pieces of salted fish wrapped in a muslin cloth, some gold coins and a small silver flask. Rummaging in the deepest part of the bag, she felt two pieces of stone. When she took them out of the bag, she saw that they were identical, the size of a goose egg and completely clear like glass. The surface of each stone was brightly polished and they weighed much more for their size than she thought was normal. She showed them to Raphah.

"What are they?"

"I have never seen anything like them before," Raphah said as he took one of them from her outstretched palm and looked at it closely. "If they are from Riathamus, then they will have a power and a purpose. Put them back in the bag—there may be eyes watching—I have a bad feeling about this place." He looked around the wood, watching for any sign that they had been followed. "I think we should carry on with our journey. Which is the best way?"

"If we leave the wood, we can get up onto the White Moor and then on the road to Whitby," Kate said. "It would be best to avoid Baytown. Too many people know us."

"What do we do with the bag?" Thomas asked.

"We take it with us. It has everything we need for the journey. It has been given to us for a reason and I feel that the reason will make itself clear, very soon."

22

Seirizzim

By the light of the candle on the kitchen table, Beadle tried to ease the bruising to his face with a small, wet rag that had been used to wipe the bacon fat from the cooking pan. Each dab of the greasy, dirty cloth sent a scorching pain through his skin and deep into his face. He had been beaten around the head for several minutes, several long and painful minutes. He had been beaten in punishment for losing the prisoners, beaten as a way for Demurral to vent his anger, beaten with a frying pan, kitchen chair and when they broke and were no longer any use, Demurral used his feet to punish his servant.

Beadle had poured himself a large mug of his strongest beer. It sat by him like a large vat of fermenting soup: thick, cloudy and with a head of almost solid froth. He picked up the mug and carefully put it to his lips. The froth covered his nose. He breathed in and at the same time gulped the warm beer. It stung the inside of his mouth and clung to the side of his throat as he swallowed. He looked up from the table and through his bruised and closing eyes he could see the body of the Glashan still slumped in the hall. Demurral hovered behind him, only just restraining himself from hitting Beadle again, making do, for the moment, with ranting at him instead.

"You're a fool for letting them get away. It was important that I had them," he screamed. "Now they've gone and taken the Keruvim with them. It's all your fault and you will pay for it before the day is out." He glared at the little man. "I've a good mind to put you in his place, to have *your* blood instead of his. What would you say to that?"

"I'd say it would be a relief," Beadle quietly muttered under his breath.

"What? What did you say?"

"It would be understandable. I'm so sorry," Beadle pleaded. He had lost heart. The thought of spending the rest of his life with this man made him feel sick. He wanted to run but knew he would get only a few paces before Demurral caught him and finished him off. He now wished he had gone with the others, left for a new life. Kate had said he had the potential to be someone different, someone far better.

"Then drag that creature to the cellar. I want to see what it is," Demurral barked.

Beadle got up from the table, battered and bruised, and walked over to the creature. Grabbing it by the boots, he dragged it along the stone floor and then down the cellar steps. He paid no attention to the noise it made as he pulled it along the floor, nor did he see the slight rise and fall of the chest as if it were taking small, gentle breaths of air. He didn't see the flickering of the Glashan's eyes, nor the slight twitching of its fingers.

Upstairs, Demurral went to answer a hammering at the front door, muttering angrily to himself as he walked along the passageway. As he took a sturdy walking stick from the stand next to the door to give a sharp blow to whoever it was that was knocking so loudly, he glanced up and saw that the carved golden raven was no longer there.

"Be quiet, man. I'm coming as fast as I can," he shouted.

Opening the door and peering out, he saw Captain Farrell, his uniform torn from the blast and his face charred with powder burns. Demurral didn't speak. Farrell staggered past him and into his study, falling into the chair by the fire.

"Get me a drink . . . I want a drink." It was the Dunamez in Farrell that shouted. "A jar of whisky, nothing less."

Demurral went and came back with the whisky. Farrell took

the brown jar and raised it to his lips, gulping down the liquid.

"That's so good," said the creature, trying to use Farrell's voice. "Haven't tasted that in years," it added as it wiped a sleeve across Farrell's face. "Sit down, Priest, I have a message from someone who wants to speak to you."

Demurral sat in the chair opposite.

"I see that the accident you've had hasn't made your London manners any better. Still as full as yourself as ever you were. From what your men said, I thought you would be dead."

"He will be soon," the Dunamez said in its own voice. "And so will you if you don't listen to me. You have brought a new dawn to this world and either by your conscious efforts or by your stupidity have allowed something wonderful. We have passed from the age of Riathamus into the age of Pyratheon."

"Farrell, don't play games. What do you know of Pyratheon? Who told you of him?" Demurral asked.

"Your friend is unable to speak," the Dunamez said, giggling. "He is completely trapped in his own mind. I wear him like a coat, and a very shabby one at that."

"Then, creature, tell me what you have to say and be gone out of him," Demurral barked at the Dunamez.

"Be gone? You almost sound like a priest. Riathamus I know, the Seruvim I know, but Demurral is someone who has little power and then that is given to him only by the one who controls the world. You're a puppet." The Dunamez laughed. "I have come for the Keruvim. I am to take it to Pyratheon. Where is it?"

"It is nearby." Demurral thought quickly. "And is in safe hands."

"Then get it for me and I will be done with you. There are some pleasures of the flesh that I would like to enjoy and that I can only do when I walk in Farrell's boots."

Demurral got up from the chair and walked over to the window. He looked out to Baytown; the glow of the cloud was brighter than ever.

"It's not as simple as that. The Keruvim is not here. There

was always the chance it could be stolen, so I have taken it to Lord Finnesterre at Stregoika Manor. He has promised me to take good care of it and I will collect it from him tomorrow," Demurral said, hoping he would not be seen to be lying.

"You'll go today and be done with it," the Dunamez spat through its teeth, almost bursting out of Farrell in anger. "Pyratheon will be here tonight and I wouldn't want to be the man who kept him waiting."

"You are not a man, so what kind of a creature are you?" Demurral asked, trying to avoid the subject of the Keruvim.

"One who walks through time, never dying, but never really living. I am a spirit that likes the comfort of flesh and blood. There is something so wonderful about being able to touch, smell and taste. You humans don't know how wonderfully you were created, you take all those things for granted. I can know them only when I inhabit one of you." He paused and looked at Demurral. "And you will never know how weary a life it can be."

"But what about your powers, what can you do?" Demurral asked.

"Is power all you think of? I leave power to others; all I desire is to experience the wonders of this world, to eat and drink and gather around me . . ." The creature stopped speaking and, turning Farrell's head, listened. "I think your servant is calling you."

"I can hear nothing," Demurral replied.

"He is in the cellar, I can hear him screaming. I think he is about to die," the Dunamez said calmly.

Demurral rushed from the room, followed by Farrell, who walked at a stately pace, the creature admiring the passageway.

The sound of muffled screaming could be heard coming from the doorway to the cellar. It was Beadle. Within moments, Demurral had raced down the stairs and was beating at the locked cellar door.

"Let me in, man. What's happening?" he shouted as he banged at the door. There was no reply, only muffled grunts coming from inside.

Demurral kicked at the door lock, which flew open, and stared into the blackness of the cellar. He could sense a presence other than Beadle's. In the darkness he could hear Beadle groaning and moaning, but he knew there was someone else there, someone very close by.

"Come out, man, or I'll draw my sword and come and get you," Demurral lied, hoping to call the bluff of whoever was in the darkened room.

From out of the darkness a brandy casket flew through the air and hit him in the chest, sending him reeling backwards to the feet of Farrell's Dunamez. The creature looked calmly down at him. "I wouldn't go in there if I were you. You can always get another servant, they are so easy to come by," it said.

"But I need him," replied Demurral as he got to his feet.

"Then you had better have my sword," the creature said as it handed him Farrell's rapier. "Be careful, you might cut yourself," it added sarcastically.

Demurral stepped warily into the pitch-black room. He could hear Beadle sobbing to his left. He looked around the cellar, trying to see in the darkness. Ahead of him he knew that there was the doorway to the tunnel, and around the walls boxes and barrels of smuggled contraband were stacked. To his right came a sudden sharp noise of something clawing against the stone wall. Like some giant cat, a black-clad entity leapt from the corner of the room. It took hold of Demurral by the ears and flung him to the ground; he hit the stone floor and dropped the sword, which spun and scraped across the stone slabs into the corner of the room.

Farrell looked on from the safety of the doorway as the creature grabbed Demurral by the head and lifted him from the ground, its cat eyes flashing in the darkness. Demurral grabbed hold of the spectre and tried to push it away. It threw him through the air and he slumped against the stone stairs in the doorway. The metal door to the cellar opened and the creature was gone, the sound of its running echoing through the tunnel in the damp darkness.

The path to Whitby twisted from the safety of the forest into the bright wilderness of White Moor. Now exposed to the elements, they tramped like tired sheep with their heads down against the wind along the narrow path between the tufts of thick heather. The afternoon sun was fading in the west, making the light of the cloud that rose from the sea in the east seem even brighter.

Far below them they could see Baytown clinging to the side of the cliff, the high tide washing at the debris from the landslide. In the bay they could see the ship being made ready to sail. Its three masts each carried a lantern strapped to the base like three stars shining in a black sea.

Then, from out of the clear sky to the west, there came a sudden and violent storm of thick, white hailstones. They hit the ground, smashing like giant white eggs against the rocks and beating against the heather. They could be heard shattering against the branches of the trees and bouncing from the pathway. They pelted the three as they walked along, knocking Thomas to the ground.

Kate and Raphah pulled him to his feet and dragged him to the shade of a large rock. There, they huddled together, covering their heads with their coats against the icy beating, while the storm grew stronger.

"We'll have to get off the moor," Kate shouted, trying to make her voice heard above the noise of the storm and battering hailstones. "There's a house down there in the valley, I can see its lights . . . we could shelter in the barn . . . we'll never get to Whitby before nightfall."

Together they ran down the track from the moor, keeping the lights of the house in their sight. Thomas had a growing sense of disquiet. He had been to the house once before, when he was a small child. It was the house of Lord Finnesterre.

The sky cleared and the cloud glowed brighter than the moon as they ran the last few paces to the entrance to Stregoika Manor. It was a beautiful, large, daunting house with seven high chimneys reaching up into the night sky. Wisps of smoke billowed from each one and in the bay window that overlooked the lawned gardens burnt a red candle. In the centre of one lawn was a tall stone that looked as though it had forced its way up from the ground to twice the height of a man. It was like some ancient pillar, the mark of a forgotten people, its purpose forgotten to the world.

The house was made of cut stone and from the side looked as if three houses had been joined into one as successive generations expanded the building along with their wealth. On three sides it was surrounded by trees, but to the east it overlooked the sea and the moor. From the front door of the house was a complete and unbroken view of the Vicarage and the mine five miles to the south. The garden of the house was littered with the white, melting hailstones. There was an eerie silence, with not even the sound of birdsong. The glow of the cloud had turned from red to a sullen green; and to the south, far out to sea, the full moon peered over the horizon. As they walked to the door, Thomas pulled on Raphah's coat sleeve.

"I don't know if we are doing the right thing. My father told me stories about this house. He said it wasn't a good place." He turned to Kate. "You know that, don't you, Kate?"

"All I know is that I could do with a warm bed. All we're going to do is to ask to sleep in his stables, then in the morning we'll be off to Whitby," she replied coldly.

"We should have done what Crane said and gone to see Rueben, then gone to the boat. It would be over by now and we would be out of this place." Thomas had begun to doubt that Riathamus had really appeared. He began to wonder if some wood spirit had tricked them, that it had all been some shared dream. "I have a bad feeling, Kate. We'll stay at the gate—you can go and ask his lordship for room in his stables."

Thomas and Raphah went to the gate. Raphah bent down by the stone gate post and appeared to hide something in a gap in the dry stone wall. Kate went to the large wooden door that protected the entrance to Stregoika Manor. It was twice as tall and four times as wide as she was and was studded with large black nails driven deep into the wood. It had a brass door handle and, set in the middle of the door at arm's length, a large door knocker in the shape of a goat's head.

Reaching up, she took hold of the door knocker and gave three loud knocks that clattered through the silence. Kate waited. Presently she heard the sound of someone walking on the tiled floor in heavy boots. The door was opened slowly and there before her was a small man with a red face and white sideburns and an exceedingly wide, friendly smile. He was dressed in a fashionable pair of breeches, a red hunting coat and black riding boots.

"My goodness, what are you doing out on a night like this?" he said in a warm voice. "You'd better come in; you'll catch your death." He gave Kate a friendly smile; his eyes sparkled in the candlelight. Coming from the house was the smell of coffee and cinnamon; Kate had smelt it only once before, at the Griffin Inn by the market square in Whitby. She had been given a taste from her father's mug as he sat and talked with the landlord; it was bitter and powdery and coated the roof of her mouth with the flavour of burnt biscuits. On that day she had fallen in love with the strong aromatic smell. It made her think of faraway places, it was exciting, intoxicating and sophisticated. Coffee was a drink for the rich, the thinkers, the artists, and was worth its weight in gold. Here at Stregoika Manor the smell of coffee beckoned her to come in, it spoke of safety and comfort and took away every ounce of fear. She looked into the man's eyes and finally knew she had found someone who would help them.

"My friends are at the gate. We're in terrible trouble. Please can we stay in your stables for the night?" she said to the man without thinking. She didn't stop to wonder why the door had not been opened by a housekeeper or other servant.

"Of course, my dear girl, come in." He then shouted to Thomas and Raphah, "Come and join your friend. There is room by the fire and food on the stove, come in and get warm."

His voice sounded friendly and calming. Dark clouds began

to come over the sky from the west and moved towards the fire cloud, almost engulfing it. The moon fought to give its light to the world, but soon the thick, dark blanket enveloped the sky. Reluctantly, Thomas nodded to Raphah and they walked to the door of the house. They were welcomed with the same warm smile, and as they entered the house, the man shook each of their hands with a double handshake.

"Welcome, welcome to Stregoika Manor. This has been my family home for three hundred years. My ancestors travelled here from a land far to the east, a land of mountains and forests, and we have been here ever since." He spoke quickly to Raphah, his voice like a creaking gate. "We too were once visitors and our family always offer a warm welcome to the stranger at the gate." He ushered them into the large ornate hallway. "Forgive me, I haven't introduced myself. I am Lord Finnesterre. And who do we have here?" he asked through white teeth and a beaming smile.

It was Kate who introduced them one by one. She shivered as she spoke and dripped the now melting hailstones over the floor.

"To the kitchen, I think, before we all end up swimming," he said quickly. "There's a fire there and some warm water to get you washed." He looked at Raphah. "I've never met one of your kind before; you'll have come far and have many stories to tell. After you're cleaned up and fed, we can sit by the fire and you can tell me where you are from and what you are doing here."

Finnesterre led them to the kitchen of the house. It was a broad room with stone walls and a large stone fireplace as tall as a man. In the hearth a raging fire burnt brightly, flickering against the wall and shooting sparks, smoke and flames up the wide chimney.

"Stand by the fire, it'll warm you through," he said.

They stood as close as they could to the heat without getting burnt. Their clothes began to steam as the moisture evaporated, and it looked as if their clothes were on fire. Thomas stared into the flames as they warmed his face and pulled his skin tighter over his cheekbones. He felt hungry, his mouth was dry, and the smell of the coffee was almost intoxicating as it boiled in the cauldron that was suspended in front of them. The charred pot with its thick black lid bubbled noisily.

"I like my coffee to boil," said Finnesterre. "It gives it a smoky flavour."

He bustled around the kitchen, moving pans and putting bread on the oak table. For the Lord of the Manor he seemed to have done these things many times before. Although the kitchen had been well swept and the cupboards cleaned, there was no sign of any servants. The three gave little attention to what he was doing. They silently stared into the flames, each thinking of what had gone before and what was to come.

Kate dreamt as she looked into the fire. The flickering of the flames allowed her mind to leave that place and to float in another world. She looked upon images of streets and houses; the spire of a great church rose up and then vanished, changing into the swirling sails of a ship. She held her cold hands out towards the flames and was aware of the overpowering feeling of sleep rising up her legs and numbing every muscle.

"Come and sit at the table," said the bright voice behind them. "It's not much, but it'll keep you going." Finnesterre smiled a warm and friendly smile.

On the table was a loaf of fresh bread, cheese, apples and cold meat. Finnesterre placed a hot pot of coffee and four cups on the table. It was like a ritual. He placed the cups to form a perfect square and then poured the dark liquid into each cup. The hot steam swirled in the half-light, like the vapours rising from a witch's cauldron. They had an eerie glow in the candlelight and whirled around his hands as he carefully poured the coffee.

"Is this coffee?" Kate asked, wanting to be sure.

"It is, my dear girl, I'm afraid I'm quite an addict. Coffee, chocolate and the occasional glass of wine are all that I can call my sins," he said as he sat at the table.

"Sir," said Raphah, "I do not wish to be rude, but I cannot have this drink. Its effect is not one that I desire."

"A wise man always knows what he shouldn't have," Finnesterre said curtly. "But he should never push his views on others." He smiled through his teeth as he pushed the cups towards Kate and Thomas. "I'm sure you two would like to try some of this wonderful elixir, wouldn't you?" He paused. "What brings you to Stregoika Manor?"

Thomas took hold of the cup and sat back in the tall-backed chair. He had never been one for talking, but the warmth of the fire and the hot bitter coffee made his mind race. He felt comfortable with Finnesterre, almost at home. His fears had subsided and were now replaced by the desperate urge to share all that had happened with someone who he thought wanted to listen. He did not sense Raphah's growing unease.

For the next ten minutes Thomas told him of their adventure, from the moment they had entered the tunnel, the Keruvim, the escape and the trek across the moors.

"My goodness!" Finnesterre exclaimed. "And to think all this happened so close to my home. Where is the Keruvim now?" he enquired casually.

"It's lost," Raphah interrupted before the others could speak. "Before we got here, I must have dropped it on the moor. I checked my coat at the gate and it was gone. When we leave here, we will have to go back and find it."

"You never said," Kate snapped at him.

"I never had the chance," he replied.

"Well, such an item should not be lost for long. You wouldn't want such a powerful thing to fall into the wrong hands again." Finnesterre patted Thomas on the back. "You are a brave lad; you should all get some sleep. I'll have no talk of you sleeping in the stables, you can have the servants' room at the top of the house. I am all alone. Sadly no one will stay with me for long; they always say they don't like the house. Come, bring a candle and your food and I will show you the room. I lit a fire for your arrival—" Finnesterre stopped short as if he had said too much, stood up from the table and beckoned for them to follow him.

They left the warmth of the kitchen for the icy cold of the back stairs that led to the top of the house. On each landing was a doorway to the rooms on that floor with a key in each lock. Finnesterre took them higher and higher until they were in the eaves of the house. The wind rattled the stone tiles and blew in through the wattled and whitewashed ceiling into the long thin room that was the servants' quarters. Four beds filled one half of the room, leaving little space to walk. A large rug covered the wooden floor and a fire burnt brightly in the small fireplace.

"You can make yourselves at home. I'll leave you be and see you in the morning," Finnesterre said as he stepped back to the door. "Don't worry about any noises you may hear. There are always owls and foxes outside and sometimes they sound quite human. This house rattles and moans, but it means no harm." He stopped speaking and a worried look came over his face. "It'd be best that you stayed in the room. I wouldn't go walking the corridors if I were you. I would hate you to have an accident."

With that he bowed politely and stepped out of the room, closing the door behind him. They waited until the sound of his footsteps going down the stairs could be heard no more.

Thomas looked at the beds in disbelief. He had never slept on anything so wonderful. The sheets were white and crisp and the blankets had no sign of lice to prickle his sleep. He fell back on to the mattress and wallowed in the delight of the softness of the feathers. Soon Thomas and Kate had left this world and were dreaming, whimpering and twitching their limbs like worn-out spaniels. Raphah sat on his bed and in the candlelight he listened to every noise in the house, waiting for something he knew would come.

Lubbock's Drum

Crane heaved himself onto the deck of the *Magenta*. A rolling swell made it difficult for him to stand upright. He held on to the rail and looked up. The ship was ready for sail. The crew pulled on the halyard ropes, and by the mainsail, the cannon was being powdered and made ready for firing. The wind tugged at the sails and the ship lurched forward, beating against the waves. Crane took in a deep breath; on land he always felt confined, almost claustrophobic, but here at sea he felt he was a free man. He reached into his pocket and took out a small silver coin and in one movement tossed it into the sea.

"Thanks for safe harbour," he said under his breath as he paid off the Selkie, hoping that the sea spirit would look after the ship until its return.

"Right, men," he shouted. "We'll head out into the bay and cut as close as we can to the cliff, then clear for action."

Martin came from below deck and greeted his captain.

"Did they make the ship?" Crane asked.

"No sign of them, Captain. I had two men waiting for them and Rueben, but we can't wait any longer. We'll have to run on this tide or stay until the morning." Martin walked with Crane to his cabin.

"I just hope that Demurral never caught them. When we cross the bay, we'll lay up and give the old soak something to think about," Crane said. "They'll have to make their own way."

The *Magenta* rose and fell with each wave. The wind in the sails quickly pulled her through the water and out into the bay. Crane could see the lights of the Vicarage in the distance, high on the hill. Far below, the chimney of the alum mine belched out its dark, acrid smoke.

Crane and Martin stood at the cabin door and looked towards the Vicarage. In his heart Crane knew that the action he was about to take would make him an outlaw forever. He knew that as soon as the cannon fired, he was a condemned man. Farrell would see to that, and Demurral was sure to lie through his teeth. But, Crane thought, the satisfaction of blasting the house from the cliff face far outweighed the cost of spending the rest of his life away from this land. There would be other ports, other countries, and maybe, just maybe, he would find what he was looking for.

Crane looked around the deck. Around him men were heaving ropes and pushing the cannon into position.

"I want some music. There's nothing better than a song and the sight of cannon fire. Where are Lubbock and Fingus?" Crane shouted. "Get those two bogeys out here now, I want music."

Lubbock and Fingus were both drunk and seated on a coil of rope, oblivious to all that was happening. Lubbock had a thick leather strap over his left shoulder and by his feet was the large pigskin drum he had stolen from a Dragoon. In his lap Fingus had an old violin that he kept in a black velvet bag. At the shout from the Captain they both jumped to their unsteady feet.

Fingus was a small man with spider-thin legs and a long nose. His long feet got in the way as he took the violin and bow from the bag, stuck it under his chin and began to play. Lubbock took up the drum and began to beat out the rhythm faster and faster. Some of the ship's crew began to clap as Fingus danced and played the violin. He spun on his feet, crashed into the cabin door and then fell to his knees while still playing a raucous tune in time to the rapid beating of Lubbock's drum. As the ship rolled, Fingus was thrown from side to side but still kept playing. His tune got faster and faster. Some of the men began to dance. They twirled each other arm in arm and spun round and round. Fingus danced as fast as he could on the deck. Crane kept a constant eye on the cliff and the Vicarage high above. By the side of the ship two dolphins broke cover from the waves and leapt into the air.

Lubbock's drum beat louder as Fingus sawed the bow across the strings faster and faster. Spray from the sea began to break over the decks, and to the north the glow from the cloud broke through. In one sudden moment the music stopped.

"Make ready to fire," Crane shouted as the Vicarage came into range of the heavy cannon. He waited for the swell to lift the side of the ship nearest to the cliff. The vessel tilted in the waves. *"Fire!"*

The night air was filled with the smell of burning powder. A bright red pall blasted from the cannon into the black sky. There was a loud roar as the ball flew through the air towards its target. Then, with unexpected force, the roof of the Vicarage blew up, scattering the grey tiles through the air and sending a shock wave to the ground.

"Fire!" Crane shouted again to the crew manning the second cannon. The shot groaned into the night like an unseen fist. It smashed into the corner wall, sending bricks and stone crashing to the ground.

There was then a *crack-crack-crack* of muskets being fired and flashes like small sparks could be seen on the cliff top. Musket balls pelted the rigging like hailstones.

"Go for the muskets," Crane ordered. He waited for the roll of the ship. *"Fire!"*

The first cannon fired again, aimed directly at the small group of riflemen on the cliff top. In the shadows from the moon and cloud, Crane could see the ball hit its target, sending clods of soil up into the air. The firing stopped.

"Fingus, play me something cheerful, I want to celebrate," Crane said calmly as he walked into his cabin. The crew gave a loud cheer and Fingus struck up another tune to the beat of Lubbock's drum.

The sound of the cannon fire had echoed across the valley. In Stregoika Manor, Raphah leapt from his bed and ran to the window. In the distance he could see the smoke and fire of the Vicarage glowing like a soft, red candle on top of the dark hill.

"Quickly," he said in a hushed voice to Thomas and Kate. "Demurral's house is on fire."

Thomas woke clumsily from his dream and staggered to the window, pulling Kate with him. Together they looked out through sleepy eyes at the sight in front of them.

"What's happened?" Kate asked.

"Whatever it is, I don't think Demurral will be pleased. He'll come looking for us and we are too close for comfort," Raphah replied.

"Look," Thomas said, suddenly pointing through the window into the garden.

Walking through the trees and out onto the lawn was a long procession of black hooded figures. They walked towards the standing stone and formed a circle around it.

Thomas stepped back into the room to blow out the candle and rejoined the others at the window.

"What are they doing?" he asked as they watched the figures join hands and slowly begin to walk hand in hand anticlockwise around the stone.

"They're witches," Raphah said. "They are walking against the sun. They are summoning a power for evil."

"How do you know what they are? They could be doing anything," Kate objected.

"I have seen them many times. They're trying to use the stone as a centre for power. It is buried deep in the earth and —"

"Why walk around a stone?" Kate interrupted.

"They believe it brings power from the earth that they can use—but all along Pyratheon is using them," Raphah said.

They looked on as the crowd of hooded figures began to chant. They began to walk faster and faster until their walking turned into a dance, their voices getting louder and louder. The circle of dancers let go their hands and began to twist and turn as they went around the stone. One of the figures stopped dancing and, taking a long shaft of wood, walked up to the stone and began to hit the side of the rock.

"One, the wind that springs from the west,
Two, the earth that brings forth life,
Three, the fire that consumes our breath,
Four, the water that brings our healing,
Five, the moon that lights our path,
Six, the sun, the greatest light,
Seven, the master we summon this night."

The figure shouted the spell at the wind as he hit the rock with the staff. He then thrust it into the ground and stepped back from the stone. The staff burst into bud, young shoots sprang from the old wood. It became a living tree before their eyes. From the trunk grew thick branches and from the branches fresh green leaves. White flowers tipped each branch, the blossom giving way quickly to small red apples. All but one apple dropped from the tree and were swallowed up by the earth. The last fruit hung on the smallest branch, bowing it low. With one hand the figure lifted back the hood from his face. It was Finnesterre.

There was no need for the three to speak his name. Kate and Thomas just looked at each other in total disbelief.

"We must leave here as soon as we can. They must never get the Keruvim, and they are closer to it than they would ever imagine," Raphah said.

"Look," Thomas exclaimed as he saw what was taking place below.

In the garden the other figures began to take the hoods from their faces. In amongst them was Demurral, standing next to Finnesterre, and by him was Captain Farrell, whose face appeared blurred as the Dunamez trembled slightly in and out of his body, merging its face with his.

At that point the stone began to make a low rumbling noise, vibrating the earth around it. Demurral looked at Finnesterre and smiled. A mist began to rise from the ground, forming a white curtain around the circle and reflecting the moonlight. Two Glashan appeared from the wood and walked into the centre of the circle and stood next to the stone. The whole gathering was becoming obscured by a blanket of fog that had appeared, to hover over the garden. By the standing stone the earth split in two, and out of the ground marched a company of Varrigal with their burnished shields, short swords and snake helmets. They formed an outer circle around the coven as if to protect them from a hidden adversary.

Demurral took the acacia pole and black hand from under his cloak. He held it upright and then stabbed it into the ground. Immediately it began to glow white-hot.

"Both of the Keruvim are near," he said. "When the moon strikes the stone, it will be time." He looked up to the bedroom window high in the eaves of the house. "They sleep soundly," he commented to Finnesterre.

As he spoke, a deep hush fell over the gathering. Demurral turned to see the phalanx of Varrigal quickly part and a tall figure with bright red hair and dressed in armoured leather walk into the middle of the circle. The Glashan fell to their knees and bowed their heads before him, not daring to gaze upon his incredibly beautiful face.

Finnesterre and Demurral stood silently, not knowing what to say. They both looked at him, not daring to ask his name and wondering if their thoughts could possibly be true.

"For people so eager to speak to me, you both appear to be lost for words."

The man spoke with a surprisingly warm voice, his words appearing quite tender. "I am always willing to come and listen to those who follow me and it is so . . . nice . . . to meet you." He looked at them and smiled. "There is no need for you to introduce yourselves. I know who you both are, I have followed your lives with great interest and my helpers have told me all about you and your desires. I believe, Parson Demurral, that you once followed the ways of . . ." He paused and looked at the sky. "I wonder what he is thinking, moments away from being deposed of all his power. I have waited many lifetimes for this . . . and look—we even have the tree and the apple. All we need is an Adam and an Eve and the Keruvim, and we will have the fall of man and the fall of God, once and for all and this time forever, without any interruptions from Riathamus," he shouted, his voice deepening and growing angry, his face contorting as if in pain and then suddenly calming and regaining composure.

"Gentlemen, I am sorry. Please allow me to introduce myself. I am Pyratheon; that is my true name. I am the one behind every deity that is not him. I am whatever distraction I could think of to call myself and get your kind to worship me. I've been called many things in my time, but I prefer Pyratheon; it was the name given to me by my father."

"You—you are different from what we expected," Finnesterre said quietly and fearfully.

Pyratheon laughed. "You expected a horned beast with a spiked tail covered in scales?" He looked at Finnesterre. "I thought so. My dear, dear Finnesterre, I was once a Seruvim, I led the worship in heaven, I sat at his feet. Do you think that he would allow something ugly to serve him? Wickedness came to me like an unexpected joy and I seized the opportunity and if it hadn't been for Riathamus, I would have succeeded." He looked at Demurral. "Sadly, Demurral, you'll not have all the power for yourself. You have underestimated what you have begun. I could never leave the running of the world in the hands of a human. Your kind often has fits of compassion and mercy; even the most despicable people have that dreaded seed of love that melts the heart. It was the flaw in your creation. Without the ability to love, you would have so much potential. Sadly, none of you is beyond redemption, so you cannot be trusted with much. When I set up my kingdom, you will get what you deserve and what is right for a man of your standing." He looked around the coven circle. "Where are the three?"

"They are in the house," Finnesterre replied.

"Then, Lord Finnesterre, I suggest you fetch them." He paused and thought. "No. I will send the Glashan, they don't like to make mistakes or let people escape." He signalled to the Glashan, who left the circle and walked towards the house.

Raphah watched as they crossed the lawn, their black figures silhouetted against the white mist.

"That is Pyratheon. I know it is. We have to get out of here—they'll be here soon. We can take the stairs, go on to the main landing, then out of the kitchen door and escape into the woods," he said.

"What if they catch us?" Kate asked.

"Then what Pyratheon desires may come true. Riathamus gave us a promise in the woods, that he would never leave us or forsake us, and that he would send the Seruvim when needed. He knows what we are facing, we must trust him."

They heard a loud slamming of doors coming from downstairs and heavy footsteps walking along the hallway.

"Grab the bag and run," Thomas exclaimed as he ran towards the door.

Kate grabbed the bag and the three ran out of the room and down the first flight of stairs until they reached the middle landing that led on to the bedroom corridor. The key had gone from the lock and the door was firmly secured. To their horror the door from the kitchen opened and there, in the semidarkness, stood a Glashan looking up at them.

"We're trapped," Thomas shouted as a second Glashan stepped onto the staircase and began to walk towards them. He felt a surge of cold run through his body as if his blood had turned to ice. His breath stuck in his throat as he frantically looked at Kate and Raphah, not knowing what to do. The Glashan walked slowly towards them up the stairs, holding out its black leather-clad hand.

"There must be a way out of here," Kate said desperately as she fumbled in the bag for the two crystals.

"Back to the room, quickly," Raphah shouted.

They ran as fast as they could up the stairs and through the door of the servants' room. Kate slammed the door behind her and Thomas slid the beds across the floor to barricade the door. They piled the frames and mattresses as high as they could and slid the cupboards from the walls and propped them against the pile of furniture that was now their only defence against the Glashan.

"What now?" Thomas asked, hoping beyond hope that there was still a chance of escape.

"Peace," Raphah said calmly. "We will ask Riathamus for his peace, I know he will give that to us and help us to escape from this evil. Sit on the floor, close your eyes and think of him."

The three got down on the floor and closed their eyes. Kate clutched a crystal in each hand. The Glashan began to pound at the door but were held back by the barricade.

"Think of him," Raphah said. "Let him speak to you."

In the midst of the chaos all three began to concentrate on Riathamus as the Glashan hammered on the door and tried to smash their way into the room through the wood. Even with all the noise and the fear, Thomas and Kate slipped into a place of complete peace. It was as if they were deafened to the noise of the world as their minds were drawn deeper and deeper into his presence. In a moment the fear subsided and a sure and positive hope filled their hearts and minds. They did not question what was happening, or why; they just allowed this strange new experience to gather up their thoughts and lead them to wherever it wished to go.

Kate clutched the crystals; it felt as if the hard surface of each stone was melting in her hands. In her mind she saw the panelled wall of the room. Her eyes were drawn to a small piece of wood that jutted out from the corner of one of the panels. As she looked, she saw the panel open and it led to a staircase.

"A tunnel," she cried. "A secret tunnel. We can escape!"

Her voice quickly brought them back to the present. At that moment a black-gloved hand smashed its way through a panel of the door and started to grab at anything it could. Another hand smashed through the wall next to the door, sending white plaster scattering over the floor.

"Quick," Kate said urgently. "I know the way out." She jumped up and looked around the room. There on the far side under the eaves she saw the small panel of wood set into the oak panelled wall, just as she had seen in her mind. She flicked the catch and a panel sprang open. There before them was a secret passage, once used to hide from the Excise men, leading from the room into the darkness.

"We can't go down there, we have no light," Thomas protested as a leather fist appeared through another hole in the wall. Kate held out the crystals before them.

"Look, they're glowing. We'll have enough light from these stones to see our way," she said as the glow from the crystals lit up their faces. Behind them the door began to give way under the assault from the Glashan. The room shuddered with every blow and the barricade moved forward slowly as the door opened wider. "We'd better get going or else they'll catch us," she added.

With a final kick the door gave way and the barricade collapsed into the room. The two Glashan jumped over the debris and into the room, their eyes searching every corner in the darkness. The three were nowhere to be seen. The room was empty. The creatures looked at each other. The taller began to crawl on the floor and sniff with his long nose, searching for the scent of the escapees.

By the light of the crystals it was easy to make their way from the servants' room through the low passageway that seemed to be built into the walls of the house. As they ran, they noticed doorways into other rooms and store places cut into the floors for the hiding of contraband. The passageway dropped floor by floor until they smelt the strong odour of stale water and earth. The air grew colder in the tunnel, as did the dampness. The floor of the tunnel turned into a shallow stream of fresh water; every ten yards metal grates had been cut into the roof. They were out of the house. The light of the moon shone in through the metal covers and above them they could hear voices.

"Eat from this," Pyratheon was saying, "then I will know if you truly are for or against me."

"But what will it do?" they heard Demurral ask, his voice unusually tentative.

"It will give you an understanding of what the world is really like and commit you to me forever. That is what you've always wanted, isn't it?" Pyratheon replied. "You, Lord Finnesterre, can have the second bite; don't worry, it does not lose its power and there'll be plenty for both of you." He smiled. "Once you have eaten from the tree, there will be no turning back and when the three are dead, then the assault on heaven will begin."

Demurral looked at Finnesterre. "I'm not too sure if this is right. I am just a human being and these are things that are not of this world." Suddenly all his confidence was ebbing away like the tide. For the first time in his life he began to see the consequences of what he was about to do. Finnesterre grabbed the apple from the branch of the tree and took a large bite.

"See, nothing to it," he said as he chomped on the mouthful of apple. "Why worry? It can do you no harm. We sold ourselves to him years ago, Demurral. Now is not the time for fear and cold feet. Come on, man, the world is waiting."

He handed the half-eaten apple to Demurral and as it changed hands, they both saw the apple become whole again before their eyes. It was completely remade, completely perfect. Demurral reluctantly bit into the apple. As they swallowed each mouthful, the world suddenly began to change. Demurral had the feeling that his body was growing and growing. The trees of the wood greeted him with their whispering; he could almost hear the words that they were speaking. Every branch and every leaf looked as if it were an individual living creature. They each shone with a brilliance that he had never seen before. The leaves were no longer the drab green that he had always thought but were now shimmering shades of blue and purple that fluttered in the moonlight. He wished that he could understand what they were saying, because he knew that they were trying to speak to him, trying to give him some long-lost secret. A seagull circled overhead, which drew his eyes from the trees to the sky. It was then that Demurral realized how small he really was. He could feel himself getting smaller and smaller as his eyes scanned each brilliant star. He could feel a rising sense of complete oneness with everything around him. He wanted the moment to go on forever. This was the experience he had been searching for, this was being near to his god, and now he knew his name . . . Pyratheon.

A soft breeze blew gently across the lawn. The grass beneath his feet began to move and sway with every breath that he took. He felt as if he was slowly being absorbed into the whole of nature. He looked around the gathering of the coven and stared into the eyes of each person there in turn. This time, as he looked at them, he saw the lives that they lived, the lies that they told, the people that they really were. He had an insight into each sordid reality. He looked at his hands. They appeared to shimmer with a silver light.

"This is being alive," he said. "This is really knowing life."

Finnesterre had curled up on the grass and was weeping like a small child. All he could see was the cold blackness of the darkest night. He was alone; a child, aged six, left in his room with no light. His father's voice boomed a warning in his head. "Get out of bed and the ghosts will get you." He was crying, trapped in his bed, wanting to be with his mother, knowing that she would bring safety from all that he feared in the night. He was held by his fear and again lived each terrible moment. As he lay in the wet grass, he could hear the voices that he had heard so long ago. Voices that spoke of the things he did not want to hear. They whispered and touched his ear as they spoke with sharp words. He held his hands to his head, trying to plug his ears, hoping to stop the sound, hoping to stop them from talking. It was then that he found that the voices were within his head, trying to get out. The voice of his father shouted even louder. "Call yourself a boy? You act like a girl, look like a girl. I wanted a son, not a fop; I wanted an heir, not a dandy who always wants his mother."

It was as if his experience had been shared with all around him. The coven stood silently looking at them both. Pyratheon stared at them through his soft and beautiful blue eyes.

"Such is this tree," said Pyratheon. "For one it brings enlightenment, the other fear. Don't worry, Finnesterre, it will not last. The spirits of the past cannot tempt you forever."

In the tunnel the three kept as silent as possible. Kate hid the crystals in her coat for fear of their bright light shining into the darkness outside. They slowly edged their way along, ankle-deep in the cool stream. The tunnel became narrower and smaller. They crouched as they walked and after a few more paces the tunnel abruptly stopped. Above their heads was a large stone, long and flat like the marker to a grave. To one side of the stone there were steps to the surface. Kate let the light from the crystals spill out from under her coat. It shone on the walls of the tunnel that had been daubed with what looked like red paint. She looked at the stone. "I think this might be the stone by the path to the front door—away from where they are." She ran her hand around the stone and on one side found a big hinge. "If we push on this side, the stone will open," she said.

Thomas gently pushed on the side. It gave a reassuring click as it eased open. Raphah looked out through the narrow slit and could see the gathering of the coven by the corner of the house near the standing stone.

"Come on," he said quietly, "we can get to the wood before they see us."

Quickly the three climbed the steps of the tunnel and ran into the wood. Raphah crept along the bottom of the wall to the gate. He knew he would be close to where Pyratheon stood waiting. Just then the Glashan burst from the door of the house and ran across the lawn to Pyratheon. Raphah snatched the Keruvim from its hiding place in the wall and fled back to the wood.

Demurral happened to glance at the divining hand on the acacia pole and saw its lifeless colour.

"The Keruvim have gone!" he shouted. "Quickly. Let's be after them."

"My dear Demurral. It will take many lifetimes for you to understand. Let them go, they will soon be found. Bring the Azimuth, she will tell us where they have gone."

24

Vitae Veritas

In the light of the early morning, the three tired bodies trudged their way over the final stretch of Hawsker Moor to look out over the estuary from the high cliffs that surrounded the town of Whitby.

They had run, walked and slept, hiding in bushes and hay barns, one of them always keeping watch to make sure that they were not being followed. Now, finally, they were at the end of their journey, and they had the Keruvim. The fears of the night vanished with the onset of day; the bright glow in the sky to the north was the only sign that things were not as they should be and that the power of Pyratheon still pervaded the world.

The harbour below was filled with sailing ships, some larger than Thomas had ever seen, some so small that he thought they would never withstand the journey to Baytown, let alone to the Continent or London. The vessels were crammed together and packed into every available piece of water. In the dawn light they looked like black logs trapped in the harbour, the residue from some recent flood.

The smell of smoke and cooked herring helped them to feel that their journey was nearly over. It reminded them that they were hungry and it took their minds from the nagging fear that had followed them throughout the dark night. Wispy spirals of smoke came from the chimneys of the houses huddled to the side of the cliff, below the stone church that looked out over the town.

Behind the church the crumbling remains of an abbey dominated the skyline. Thomas could see the roof of the infirmary where they had taken his mother after the fire. He had no way of knowing if she was alive. In his own way he had committed her to the care of another, to one who would be there for her when he in his human weakness failed to be. As he looked at the red tiled roof, he wondered about her fate, but even now there was no time to consider looking for her.

"If we can get to the church, we might find the man that Riathamus told us about," Thomas said as they left the open moor and walked for the first time on the steep cobbled bank of the donkey path.

Raphah replied, earnestly, "The one we seek will find us, and he will not be like we expect. We will have to be careful: Pyratheon will not let us go so easily."

They followed the narrow path down the steep bank, through alleyways and tiny yards of fishermen's cottages, until they eventually reached the marketplace. In ten feet they left the peace of the passageways for the bustle of the street. Within seconds the powerful aroma of the street with its fish stalls, fresh meat and bread overwhelmed them. The whole of the road that led to the church was packed with people who pushed and jostled each other as they tried to make way through the crowds.

Kate hung on to Thomas's arm as he and Raphah walked the last few yards towards the entrance to the Griffin Inn. The sign above the door swung in the gentle breeze of morning, the white horse entwined in the golden griffin flashing backwards and forwards.

Once inside, the three huddled at a table near to the fire. The room was nearly empty. By the door three old men sat with filled clay pipes that smoked like the white chimney pots. The old men were sharing a mug of beer and half a loaf, passing the mug from one to the other and occasionally staring at Raphah. Behind the counter a fat young woman moved plates from one side of the bar to the other and then back again. Along one wall a long window at the height of the street let in the golden glow from the cloud as it reflected off the whitewashed paint of the narrow alley.

The woman looked up from the pots and came over to the three.

"Can I be getting you anything or are you here just for the heat?" she asked Raphah sharply. "We don't usually get your kind in here, and you can't sit there without buying, so what will you be having?"

Raphah frantically checked the pockets of his coat for money. They were completely empty. Kate dipped her hand into the goatskin bag. She closed her fingers on two large round coins and without looking slapped them onto the table. The woman stared at two gold sovereigns. Kate took in a deep surprised breath as Thomas stared at the treasure before his eyes.

"My friend is a merchant, he has travelled here from far away and we all want something to eat," she blurted out. "We'll have bread, cheese and three cups of your finest chocolate," she added in tones of confidence she never knew she had. As the woman walked away, Kate called her back. "Tell me, I've never seen anyone like you before, where are you from?" The woman didn't reply but quickly scurried away to the kitchen.

It was Kate who saw the man smiling at them from the darkest corner of the room. He wore a French hat and sat back in his chair with his feet on the table and a glass of red wine in his hand. She had not seen him when they had entered. She was sure that she had looked in that part of the room before and that the table where the man now sat had been empty. She *knew* that no one had come into the inn. They had been alone in the room with just the three smoky old men in the corner. She looked again and the man was still there, smiling. He had the kind of eyes that made Kate know that he wanted to speak, that at any moment he would get up from his chair and walk across the room and sit down.

The man looked at her and laughed to himself; it was as if he knew what she was thinking. He pushed the hat back from his forehead, leant forward in the chair, got to his feet and walked over to the table, just as Kate had seen in her mind. Kate saw him look at the two gold coins, then at the goatskin bag on the table.

"That's a very fine bag you have there, young lady," he said in a fine English accent. "I know a man who once had a bag like that. Told me that he had left it in the wood and wondered how it was being used."

Thomas did not turn around. He clutched the sword that he had well hidden in his coat. The man put his hand on his shoulder. "I hope you don't mind me joining you. Whitby is not the place to be with so much money and so few friends, and not even Varrigal metal can protect you from some around here."

Thomas let go of the sword and put both hands on the table, trying to cover the coins with his sleeve. The man pulled a chair from another table and sat between Kate and Thomas.

"I'm not here to steal. I just thought I would come over and share breakfast. I hate eating alone and the company has been so . . ." He nodded to the old men who sat in the cloud of tobacco smoke. "Aromatic." He grimaced and laughed.

"We are travellers," Raphah said, "and we are seeking a boat to take us from here. Do you know of such a ship?"

"Travellers? That is such an interesting term. I was a traveller once, saw many things and many different people. I even went to the land where you are from; but that was a long time ago. Now I just go where I really have to. I like to spend my time thinking. Remembering the past is such a wonderful thing. In remembering you can often see the things you missed at the time. It's as if the mind can contain everything you have ever seen, smelt, tasted or even thought, and in the business of our lives so much of what we are is forgotten." He paused and looked around. "I wonder, if we had several lifetimes to live, would we be able to find out the truth, the *vitae veritas* of why we are all here, or can that be achieved in just one chance meeting?"

"You appear to know so much about us and we so little about you," Raphah said, tightening his grip on the Keruvim hidden under his coat.

"I am sorry, the thought of good conversation and sharing your breakfast has taken away every ounce of manners. I am . . ." He paused, his mind searching for a name, his eyes flickering around the room. "Abram Rickards," he said as he read the name from the sign above the door. "But you can call me Abram."

"Well, Abram, please join us. We have money for breakfast and have not had the pleasure of sensible company for some time," Raphah said, sensing that the man would not go away until he had eaten. Kate and Thomas looked at him, unsure of what to say. They both knew that somehow this man had an insight into their lives. They did not know if he was from Riathamus, or was yet another adversary who sought to intrude on their company and then forsake them to Demurral or Pyratheon.

Abram Rickards looked every inch a gentleman, but Thomas knew that this was no guarantee of integrity. Demurral looked every inch a priest, but he was as far away from goodness as one man could possibly be. Abram took off his hat and placed it on the table. The woman came from the kitchen and placed the food in front of them, not looking at them as she did so, keeping her gaze to the floor.

Abram took the bread in his hands and broke it and gave each of them a small piece.

"In France," he said, "the latest fashion is to dip your bread in the chocolate and allow it to soak."

"How do you know so much about us, Abram?" Thomas asked.

"I know little, really. Meeting you is such a coincidence."

"Your friend who lost his goatskin bag, did he know who found it?" Thomas asked.

"All he told me was if I ever saw one similar, I was to enquire of the keeper as to where they were going and to help them in all that they had to do," he said quietly.

"Did your friend say where those who had the bag were to be found?" Raphah asked.

"No. He told me to look out for them where they would need help, help in finding a boat, help in protecting them from certain things," Abram replied.

"Does your friend have a name?" Kate asked him, trying to catch him out.

"He has many names, some are known to the world, others are secret only to him. His name is really important; but knowing him is all that really matters."

"So what do you call this friend?" Kate asked again.

"I call to him every day and have called upon his name since long before you were born. I AM, Riathamus or just the longing of the heart are names for him." He stopped. "We have played enough games for the morning. I know you don't trust me and only time will prove to you who I am. He sent me to find you and now I am here. I have secured a place for you on a ship to France. You must all leave. It will not be safe for you to stay." He reached into his coat pocket and leaned forward. "If I can show you one thing to prove to you who I am, then look at this." He opened his hand. Inside was a crystal egg just like the ones they had found in the bag. "I know that you will now understand everything I have said. We must leave, I have been staying at a house nearby and you must come with me."

He threw five pennies onto the table as they all got to their feet. Kate put the golden coins back in the bag and threw it across her shoulders. None had noticed the growing fragrance of smoke in the room. It had gusted around their feet like a winter fog and now filled the room to the height of their waists. As they turned, it wafted up like a rising cloud. The old men could not be seen in the thick mist of the smoke. They saw the look on Abram's face.

"Quick! Out of the door—this is dragon's breath. The Glashan are nearby. Quickly, run."

Abram took a chair and struck out into the fog at waist height. They heard the first scream come from the mist and then saw the figure rise up like a serpent from the deep, blocking their way to the door. Two other heads sprang quickly from the smog, each staring through catlike eyes.

"You go nowhere, Raphael, they belong to us," said the first creature.

"They belong to Riathamus," Abram replied.

"Then let him come for them himself if he dare, or does he still send you to do his work for him?" the creature sneered.

The mist grew deeper and thicker like a blanket of black fog. Soon Kate could not see. She grabbed hold of Thomas by the arm.

"Kate, the crystals," Abram shouted. "Throw one at the wall."

She quickly reached into the bag, took hold of the smooth crystal and hurled it as hard as she could at the wall. There was an earsplitting crack followed by a blinding flash of light and a thunderous roar. Everything in the room shuddered with the blast. The three were blown from their feet and landed on the other side of the room in a heap. The mist had completely vanished and the creatures had gone. Abram was unaffected by the blast and stood by the door with a smile on his face.

"It worked well, my dear girl. The Abaris crystal has many uses and it is up to you to find them out." He looked at Raphah. "Soon you will be able to see Glashan even when they come in disguise. Now you see how important it is for you three to be out of this land. Pyratheon will want you dead, because then he will have even more power."

"He called you Raphael—I heard him call you by that name," Raphah said.

"What's in a name? All you have to know is that I am here to help you. There are things I must do. Quickly, get to your feet, there may be others after you and I have to get you to the safe house."

"Why can't Riathamus just come and stop all this?" Kate asked as she struggled to her feet.

"His ways are not your ways, his thoughts are not your

thoughts. Sometimes we can never understand why he is or what he does. I have known him for so long and even I don't understand him sometimes. All I can say is that he is in control no matter how dark or hard life may become. His word says that you in this world look at life as if through a clouded mirror, you see but a vague reflection of what life is really like. This is all you know and you put all your hope in this life, but there is a greater life to come for those who follow him. Now quickly, we must go," Abram said as he helped Thomas to his feet and looked around the room. From behind the counter a fearful face peered out. The fat woman looked terrified as she looked at the scene of destruction that had fallen on the inn.

Kate reached into the bag and brought out the two gold coins and put them on the counter in front of her.

"For all that has happened and for your silence. Tell no one of what you have seen: They would never believe you anyway," she said.

The woman reached out for the gold coins and bit each one to check if they were real. She smiled a worried smile, hoping that her guests would leave soon.

In the street they were overcome by the noise of children running, people shouting and wooden carts clattering over the stone cobbles. Shouts rang out from the quayside where the tall masts of ships and their rigging towered over the cottages. Several women carrying baskets of fish bustled past, swearing about the night before and their scoundrel husbands who had come home drunk having spent all they had caught. Children in rags, shorn and shoeless, sat at the feet of a fisherman arguing with a tangled net as they played with cast-off pieces of twine and rope. A priest in pious black passed by and stared into Kate's eyes and smiled. She did not know who to trust anymore. Life had become so unpredictable, surreal, sinister.

Abram ushered them along the street, past the windows of busy shops and through the crowds of people gathered to buy and sell whatever they could.

"It's not too far—by the bottom of the church steps. There is the house of a follower, a good man, one whom you can trust. I have been staying with him for some time. You will be safe there." Abram spoke in a confident way. The three felt the warmth of his voice touch their hearts and give them hope.

Kate looked at him and noticed that he had no lines on his face, he was old yet looked so young, so wise and yet had something childlike about his voice. She followed him through the crowded street unaware of anyone else. She kept her eyes fixed upon him, as if she knew that as long as she gazed upon him, she would be safe.

"The Abaris crystal, what did it do?" she asked as she followed on behind with Thomas and Raphah.

"It is something that humans know little about. Riathamus has given all things to the world. A cure for every disease in the plants and trees. The sweetness of honey to lift the sadness of winter, bitter nuts to take away incurable growths and Abaris crystal to send fallen Seruvim back to where they belong," he replied as he pushed his way through the noisy crowds with the three following.

"So will they return?" Raphah asked.

"They will be summoned back by some fool. Since Demurral used the old magic, things have not been right in the two worlds. There was a time when Seruvim and man seldom mixed, now the worlds are being slowly drawn together." Abram pointed to the lustrous cloud. "That cloud is like a gateway between the heavens and the earth. There are dark creatures that have found their way into this world and need to be stopped. Riathamus is preparing for a battle and I must keep you three safe."

They came to a blue door set up three steps in a large brick house. It had two upper floors and a cellar. Above the door was a sign that read JOAB MULBERRY, NOTARY PUBLIC. The cellar of the house was a shoemaker's shop. Opposite, built on the harbour side, was an alehouse, down the side of which a narrow alleyway ran into the lapping seawater.

Abram turned to them as he stood on the bottom step. "You can trust old Mulberry; he has a good soul."

They went into the house. The front room, with a wide bay window overlooking the street, was full of files and papers, scattered around the large desk that dominated it.

Joab Mulberry sat at the desk and looked up over a pair of small, round spectacles on the end of his nose. As they entered, he got to his feet. Thomas noticed how tall and thin he was as he stood in his immaculate black suit with yellow waistcoat. The neatly trimmed grey beard that clung to the sides of his thin face could not hide his infectious smile. He gave a boisterous laugh as he greeted them.

"So you three are what all the fuss is about. Oh my soul, to think half the angels in heaven have been searching the land for you and you turn up here at my house with my good friend . . ." He paused and looked at Abram, waiting for a name.

"Abram brought them here for you, Mr. Mulberry, just as I said I would," Abram said quickly.

"Safe and sound, Abram, safe and sound?" Mulberry asked.

"Just one little problem, but the lass has some Abaris crystal that soon put a stop to that," Abram replied.

"And our friend here all the way from Africa. Always something new comes out of Africa, and we find him here in Whitby." He smiled as he welcomed Raphah. "So what's it to be? There'll be a bit of a wait until the ship sails tonight. You can all rest upstairs and then tonight you'll be on your way."

Abram turned to the three. "You will be safe here. It would be foolish for the Glashan or the Varrigal to come here. Joab has fought against these creatures before and is a man of great valour."

"You flatter me, Abram. I am just a follower of the Way like our young friends here. Can I see what you carry, my lad?" Mulberry asked Raphah.

Raphah looked surprised. He glanced at Thomas and then Kate and wondered how this man knew about the Keruvim.

Reluctantly he pulled the golden statue from his coat and held it out before him. Mulberry stared at the Keruvim, his eyes wide open.

"It is a thing of beauty," he said. "I can see why they want to take it from you."

"It's not the beauty that men want, it is the power," Raphah replied. "They think it will bring them money, wealth and happiness. All that it will bring is an outpouring of what is in their hearts. If a man is wicked, he will reap wickedness; if he is good, then he will find goodness. My people have protected this since the time of Moses. We thought we were far enough away from the world to keep it safe, but greed has a way of finding all things of worth." Raphah looked at Mulberry. "Many people have died for this creature, they have searched the ends of the earth and it was one of our own that finally betrayed us."

The door to the house opened and footsteps could be heard in the hallway. Raphah quickly covered the Keruvim with his coat. A middle-aged man dressed in a ragged coat came into the room. He was unshaven and dirty with short stubby fingers that gripped tightly to a rolled-up cap.

"Sorry, Mr. Mulberry, I came about the stealing. I'm sure they're going to get me for it and I don't fancy my chances against the rope," the man blurted out as his eyes searched each face in the room.

Mulberry looked at Abram as if to ask him to take them out of sight. This was an unexpected visitor and not one that Mulberry wished to welcome in this company. Abram ushered the three from the room.

"Come, my friends, we have taken too much of Mr. Mulberry's time. Let us refresh ourselves and talk later," Abram said as he stood with his back to the man, trying to protect the three from him.

"I know you," the man said as Thomas walked past. "You're Thomas Barrick of Baytown. I saw your mother not an hour ago in the infirmary. What a state she was in, dying I would say, calling out your name and wanting you to go to her, crying like a baby. Here you are with no cares in the world, keeping the company of gentlemen. Some son you are."

"Whatever he is, it is none of your business. Now state your case to Mulberry or be gone." Abram's voice had changed. His anger was almost visible as his hand reached out to push the man out.

"Leave him to me, Abram. I will take the case," Mulberry said. "It may be more than the gallows that he is running from."

The upstairs room overlooked the harbour. The words of the man echoed around Thomas's head. He could not get his mother from his mind. He paced the floor from window to door, biting at his fingernails. He was so close to her; in ten minutes he could be with her, holding her hand, listening to her voice, being there when she needed him the most. Now he felt like a prisoner, trapped in some room and not knowing the reason for his imprisonment. At midnight he would leave this land, as if washed away from his old life by a tidal wave of change. It had all happened so fast. He felt he was a reluctant participant in a strange battle that raged around him and had changed his life forever.

In the fading light of the afternoon he looked at Raphah and Kate as they sat on the bed quietly talking to each other and occasionally laughing. Thomas felt separated from them by the nagging words of the man. He did not know if his mother was still alive and he felt the tug of love pulling at his heart, overwhelming all of his thoughts.

He heard Kate asking Raphah what Africa was like. She seemed to accept all the changes so easily. Thomas felt angry that she was prepared to leave for good and had never even mentioned her father. He was jealous of Raphah, someone who could bring healing to many lives yet hadn't even offered to heal his mother.

Thomas looked at the Keruvim that had been placed on the candle stand by the door. In his resentment it looked to him like an arrogant little idol boasting of its power through silent lips.

Thomas looked out the window to the street below. The thief was there, looking up. Their eyes met. The man beckoned and started to walk to the steps. He turned and waved for Thomas to come with him.

It was dark when Abram came into the room, holding a candlestick and a tray of tea. He gave a warm smile to Kate and Raphah. His eyes searched the room. Thomas and the Keruvim were gone.

The Sword of Mayence

The cold night air stung his face as Raphah stepped from the warmth of Mulberry's house into the near dark of Church Street. He looked to his left, where a flight of a hundred and ninety-nine stone stairs ran up to the church high above, now etched out against the sky in the silver of the full moon. There was no one else in the street. All was quiet except for the lapping of gentle waves up the alleyway by the alehouse.

He pulled up the collar of his coat and turned down the cuffs to cover his hands, then turned and signalled to Abram and Kate to follow. They slipped from the house into the shadows of the long, high wall that ran up the hill at the side of the church stairs. It was a broken cobble road that in winter ran like a small stream from the abbey to the harbour, but tonight the stones broke from the dry earth like the skulls of the dead woken from their slumber. The steepness of the hill forced them to walk slowly to the infirmary that formed part of the walls of the ruined abbey. They stalked the shadows, not knowing if they were being watched or what would await them. Thomas had gone and taken the Keruvim with him. The infirmary was the only place where Kate thought he might be, and now they followed her hunch in the hope they would find them both safely.

Abram led the way up the hill, a long black case in the shape of a cross strapped to his back. Kate clambered behind him, trying to keep up with his surefooted strides. It was as if he flew rather than walked, each step appeared not to touch the ground or leave a trace in the patterns of mud that clustered around each cobbled rock.

Halfway up the lane they saw a man standing in the darkness, the glow of his pipe half lighting his face and showing the cap pulled down to his eyes.

"A Glashan," Abram whispered as they approached. "A sentry guarding what is ahead. Keep walking and we'll see if he follows." Abram nodded to the man as they passed by. The man nodded back, pipe in mouth, eyes firmly fixed to the ground.

For Kate and Raphah the last few paces made their lungs fit to burst. At the top of the hill they turned and looked down on the town. It was so peaceful, so beautiful, yet the darkness hid a corruption and an evil that lurked in every street and now followed a little distance behind.

To their right was a short path that led to the front door of the infirmary. By the door a metal brazier lit the way, casting flickering shadows across their path. Behind them the Glashan leant against the wall and watched as they walked to the entrance. The door opened easily and they stepped into the hall. A single candle greeted them with a tallow light. From a room at the side they heard someone approaching.

Out of the darkness stepped a tall, gaunt woman with broken teeth and a thin smile. She stared at them without speaking for a while.

"Too late for visiting," she then snapped. "There are sick people here who can't be disturbed. Some of them are dying and they won't want the likes of you trying to keep them in this world."

"We come in search of our friend," Raphah said. "You may know him; his mother was brought here some time ago from Baytown."

"They're in the end room by the fire," the woman snapped again. "She ain't got long, she may still be alive if you hurry; but don't be staying all night because I like to have the comforters gone and them all tucked up by midnight."

They walked cautiously past the beds of the sick and dying like a procession of mourners, first Raphah, then Kate and then Abram. Raphah looked at each bed with its candle on a small table, each patient strapped tightly in by well-folded blankets with corners tucked firmly under the straw mattresses. Some of the patients reached out as they walked by, holding out hands to be touched; the sound of choking and coughing filled the long room.

"Ignore them," the woman shouted above the noise. "Like little children they are, just wish they'd get on and die." They were comfortless words.

It was the sound of Thomas's voice coming from the room that heralded their arrival. He sat at the side of the bed, sobbing, his hands clasped together as if he were praying, the Keruvim placed at the bottom of the bed staring blindly. He didn't look up from his tears or turn to greet them.

"It didn't work, Raphah. I brought it here to heal her and it didn't work. It's all a lie; there's no power, there's no goodness. I've shouted at Riathamus and he's as deaf as the statue, either that or he doesn't care if she dies." He turned and looked at them through tear-filled eyes. "She's all I've got and now even that'll be snatched from me."

Raphah noticed a small brown pot of salt sitting on the table by the bed. By the side were a piece of stale soaked bread and a sprig of bitter herbs. Thomas noticed him looking.

"It's for when she dies. I'll dip the bread in the salt and eat it with the herbs. I'll take her sin into me, she'll leave this world clean and she can go to the dead life without being purged and tortured for what she did wrong." He sobbed. "It's the least I can do for my own mother. More sins won't make much difference to me. I'll be in the dark place for eternity when I die."

"Don't do it at all. It is written that the souls of the faithful go straight to be with Riathamus. What you have been told is a tradition made by men. Don't fool yourself with this silly magic. All you've seen should prove that to you," Raphah said.

"Why don't you pray for her, Raphah? You pray for everyone else, why not for her?" Thomas cried.

There was an unwelcome silence in the room broken only by the rattle of each breath that his mother strained into her body. She reached out to touch his face. Her eyes never opened and as she laboured for breath, she appeared as one drowning, reaching out for a hand to save her.

"Do something, Raphah. . . . Abram, help him. . . . Help me. This is my mother—she needs you. Where is your faith now?" Thomas pleaded.

Abram didn't reply. He took the long black case from his back. Flipped the clasp and stood it upright against the wall just behind him.

"I'll pray for her, Thomas, but this illness could be to death. It may not be his will," Raphah said gently.

Raphah leant over the bed and placed his hand on her head. It was surprisingly cold for one who looked so racked with fever. As he touched her skin, a strange sensation ran the length of his arm, as if he had touched something foul. He pulled his hand back from her clammy flesh.

Thomas's mother began to breathe heavily and a deep cough barked in her throat as she struggled to gulp the stale air. She was dying. She clutched Thomas's hand tightly, squeezing his flesh with her fingers and twisting his hand in hers. Her head rose from the pillow and her eyelids opened to reveal the whites of her eyes staring out of deep, drawn sockets.

"She's dying," he wept. "Can't you help her for my sake? I thought you were a friend." Raphah did not reply. He looked at Abram, who shook his head then looked out of the door of the room, concerned that something was not as it should be.

She pulled Thomas closer and closer to her face as if she was trying to give him one final kiss, a last reward for his faithfulness. He reached out to her, trying to hold her head in his hands, to cradle that which once showed him so much love. She opened her mouth as if to say one last word, the wrinkles of her hard life began to fade as death consumed her. She smiled one last, loving and tender smile.

It happened in a split second as she bit at his neck with the ferocity of a lion, her long gold teeth sinking into the soft skin, trying to capture the vein as she scratched at his face with her long sharp nails. Her once blind eyes suddenly glowed a deep cat-like green as she leapt forward, still clenching his throat in her mouth, and pushed him to the floor with amazing strength.

"Glashan!" Abram shouted as he grabbed the long thin sword from the case and lashed out at Thomas's mother, striking a blow across her back. The blade sang through the air, leaving a trail of fiery vapour. It struck the Glashan, cutting through its back and snuffing out the flame.

The door to the infirmary burst open as three more creatures spilled into the long room and ran towards them. Thomas got up from the floor, blood oozing from the wound in his neck.

"It's not her. The thief tricked me and I believed him," Thomas shouted as he kicked away the halved corpse of the Glashan that struggled to keep hold of his leg.

"We're trapped in here," Kate cried.

"It's time to fight for your lives," Abram shouted as the Glashan stood before them. "Kate, do you have the Abaris crystal?"

She looked around the room for the goatskin bag and realized that in the haste to find Thomas she had left it in the house.

"It's at Mulberry's . . . I forgot it . . ."

"Then we must fight with what we have and make our way to the church." He dipped the point of the sword onto the cold stone floor. It melted through the stone without effort. "Well, then: With the Sword of Mayence, Varrigal iron, the Keruvim and the hearts of the faithful, let this battle begin," he exclaimed as he took the sword and began to swing it round and round his head. "Come under the sword, we'll fight close quarters; whatever you do, keep to me. Whatever you feel, keep your eyes fixed on Riathamus. Now come on; we fight to the door."

Abram shouted out a long, loud cry in a language that none could understand. It sounded above the moans of the dying like the shrill call of some giant bird in full flight or the call of the leviathan rising from the deep. They charged at the wall of Glashan that stood between them and freedom. Abram swirled the sword, striking out at the attackers. The Glashan struck back with long, spiked staffs. One leapt onto the blade with no care for his death as it effortlessly sliced through his flesh several times. Another lashed out with a long knife that sucked the air from Thomas's lungs as the blow glanced past his face.

One by one the Glashan were struck down by Abram as the four made their escape. At times the fighting was so intense that Kate feared that with each step she would be cut to the ground. The sound of the Sword of Mayence whirling above her head and the screams as it sliced through flesh and bone made her tremble with fear.

Abram got to the doorway as the three sheltered beneath the protection of the sword.

"Run for the church. Get to the sanctuary by the altar, nothing can harm you there. I will follow," he said as without warning more Glashan rose from the bodies of the sick and the dying and came towards him.

"Where are they coming from?" Raphah shouted as he fell backwards out of the door.

"They use the moment of death as a doorway to this place. Now run quickly, you must get to the altar."

They ran for all they were worth, Thomas clutching at the wound to his neck and Raphah holding his branded shoulder, which burnt with more fire than ever, the pain visible across his face. Kate was pushing them both to run faster. Behind them the sound of battle grew louder and louder, the screams of the Glashan cutting through the cold night air.

Before them the church door stood open and the glow of the candles could be seen through the stained-glass windows. They ran through the gravestones of saints and sinners, fishers and freemen, until they reached the tall oak door. Raphah looked up. Above his head was a painting of a white stag impaled with an arrow. The stag wore a crown and a holly wreath around its neck, whilst all around hands stretched out to it from the darkness.

Kate pushed them along into the church. They turned to the right and went through two wooden doors. Before them was a long aisle lit by candles that hung over each box pew. In front of them was a tall three-tier pulpit with a wooden canopy and a solitary red candle lighting the black prayer book that lay open on its cushion.

Thomas shuddered. Here was the chamber of his dream; this was the place of fear. He found he couldn't move. It was as if an unseen force had gripped him. He tried to speak, but his tongue stuck to the roof of his mouth. Kate pushed him and he stumbled towards the sanctuary steps that were covered with a thick red carpet.

"We're nearly there, come on, Thomas, we'll be safe soon, they can't get us in the sanctuary," she said.

"No—but I can," came the voice from the pulpit. "Glashan and Varrigal may be bound by the law of sanctity, but I am not." It was Demurral, high above them.

It was exactly as Thomas had seen. He was petrified and stood rooted to the spot.

"Give the Keruvim to me freely and I will let you go. If I have to take it from you, I assure you that you will all die here," Demurral said as he began to come slowly down from the pulpit step by step.

"Come into the sanctuary," Raphah shouted. "I'd rather die where I choose to than where that dog wants me to."

Behind him was the wooden altar set in the pitch darkness of the chancel. This was sanctuary. . . . Kate pulled Thomas across onto the first step. It was as if he was suddenly released from tightly binding chains. The holiness of the place had broken the power of Demurral's grip on him. They felt as though they had crossed the border into a new world, a world of peace and freedom.

Thomas sprang to life with a newfound bravery and pulled the Varrigal sword from his coat. "He will come for us," he declared, "but he will not take me again!"

Defiantly, he stood on the top step and waited for Demurral to approach.

"So you think a sword can stop me, do you?" The priest walked the final few paces to the steps.

"Do not cross that line," Thomas said staunchly. "This is a holy place and not for people like you." He thrust the sword out towards Demurral as he spoke.

"Bravery. One minute fear, the next you will take on the world. How will you stand against this?" Demurral waved his hand above his head. Every candle in the church guttered for a moment, as if its light were being sucked into some dark hole. In the gallery above the door the pews were suddenly filled with a whole army of Varrigal, dressed in death black and staring down through bloodred eyes.

"Lock the doors!" Demurral shouted. "They will not leave this place alive, even if we wait until Christmas."

He waved his hand. "Think again, give the Keruvim to me." A Varrigal aimed its crossbow directly at Thomas's head. Thomas looked up and saw the creature begin to pull back the lever.

"If I give the word, the quarrel will drop you to the floor, dead. I could do with someone like you. Beadle is past his best— given to fits of compassion. You would be better suited to the job. Come with me, follow me."

"I follow no one but Riathamus." Thomas felt the strange words burst from his mouth and bring tears to his eyes. "If I die here, I die well. Do what you will, I fear neither you nor death any longer."

Demurral gave an almost unseen signal to the waiting Varrigal. The quarrel leapt from the bow and darted through the air. Time stood still. Thomas watched as the bolt slithered through the ether towards him. He smiled. He could hear nothing but the sound of the quarrel spinning.

The bolt shattered abruptly as it hit the air of the chancel. It exploded in midflight, showering Demurral in shards of broken crystal that clinked across the stone floor.

"See," shouted Raphah. "This is the place of peace. Nothing from Pyratheon will harm us here."

"Speak of the devil and he shall appear . . ." The voice came out of the darkness from the direction of the altar behind him. Raphah turned. There stood Pyratheon.

"How?" Raphah asked.

"You forget I was once an angel. I stood in the presence of God. I may not like it here, but I can cope for a while." Pyratheon walked towards Raphah. "So you are Raphah, the healer, keeper of the Keruvim. A mighty work for someone so young, so pretty and so naïve. Now give it to me and stop your fooling." Pyratheon held out his hand. Raphah stood his ground. "Don't mess with me, boy, or you'll die."

"Then I die," Raphah said calmly.

In a fit of sudden anger Pyratheon lashed out with his fist. The blow struck Raphah on the face, blasting him from his feet and through the air. He crashed against the wooden door. The Keruvim fell to the ground at the feet of Pyratheon; Raphah crumpled into a lifeless heap on the cold stone floor. They could see the golden shimmering over the body as his soul clung to the last few seconds of life.

"At last, after five thousand years it is mine."

He bent down to pick up the statue. Thomas ran the seven paces and jumped through the air. As he landed, he plunged the sword as hard and as deep as he could into Pyratheon. They fell to the floor together. Demurral rushed up the steps and seized hold of Kate. Pyratheon got to his feet, the Varrigal sword embedded in his chest. Thomas grabbed at his legs. Pyratheon stooped down and with one hand lifted him off the ground and held him with an outstretched arm away from him, then tossed Thomas across the floor towards Demurral.

"Take him—he will come in useful. Give her to the Glashan," said Pyratheon.

Through the stained-glass windows of the church the light of flaming torches flickered against the stone walls. A slow *thud-thud-thud* echoed through the night air as the door vibrated to the beating of a hundred men.

"Stand back," came a cry as the fuse of a cannon hissed.

The explosion blasted against the door, sending splinters of wood through the church as the iron ball smashed through at point-blank range and then spun and bounced into the church, crashing against each box pew as it hurtled towards them.

The Varrigal leapt from the gallery, swords in hand, as the first men stormed through the broken church door, screaming and lashing out at those who stood before them. Jacob Crane and his men stepped into the church, swords and pistols at the ready.

The Varrigal fell back until a wall of swords pushed them from the aisle. Jacob Crane walked towards Demurral. He lifted the pistol and aimed it at his head.

"Let them go!" he ordered as he pulled back the hammer.

Pyratheon laughed in disbelief. "Who is this man?" he asked.

"A smuggler, a pirate, an irritating carbuncle," Demurral spat.

There was a sudden whirring of machinery as the working of the church clock lifted back the hammers to strike midnight against the bass bell.

"I'll give you till the last bell has sounded and then I'll blow your head off your shoulders," Crane said calmly as he took aim.

"It is not that simple," said Pyratheon. "You can kill him if you want. He is expendable. There are so many greedy fools, one less won't make a difference to me. In one minute the world will change beyond my wildest dreams."

The first bell struck. Pyratheon lifted the Keruvim above his head and closed his eyes. Kate struggled against the hold that Demurral had around her neck.

The second and then the third bell rang out. Crane's men

held back the Varrigal, who fell silent, waiting expectantly for a divine moment in time.

Four, five, six bells reverberated through the church and across the roofs of the houses below. Pyratheon began to whisper, his lips moved slowly. Crane lowered the pistol as he watched. Kate broke free and ran to Raphah.

The church began to shudder as the Keruvim pulsed out a blinding light. The night sky faded to day; the sun rose, then set and rose again. The tides washed in and out of the harbour, rising and falling with each moon. It was as if the whole earth was spinning faster and faster through space.

With each beat of the bell it was another day, another dawn, another night. Seven, eight, nine, ten, eleven times. On the final clang, as the hammer struck the bell, the church fell silent. All that could be heard were the screams of panic coming from the streets below.

All light had gone from the world. The sun, moon and stars had vanished from the sky and an icy coldness hovered over the surface of the deep waters.

"It is finished," Pyratheon said triumphantly. "I am, I AM." He laughed. "Riathamus is dead."

He threw the Keruvim to the floor. It spun across the stone and landed at Raphah's feet.

"Then it won't matter if I kill your servant," Crane shouted as he pulled the trigger of the pistol. The hammer fell. There was a muffled thud as the ball rolled slowly from the barrel and dropped to the floor.

"Everything has changed, Eternal Law is now mine to dictate. The Battle of the Skull has been overthrown."

There was complete silence in the universe. Pyratheon looked around, not knowing what to do next. He had waited so long for this moment and now felt a deep sadness that the battle was all over. He was overwhelmed with sudden and unexpected feeling of grief at the loss of Riathamus.

The moment was broken by the sobbing of Kate as she held

on to the lifeless body of her friend.

"It's not over. Listen to me. It's not over," she said time and time again as she pressed his hand close to her body.

"The crying of a child. How touching that the first thing I should hear in my new world is the crying of a child," Pyratheon said as her sobbing echoed around the church.

Kate's tears dripped onto the Keruvim. She lifted it up and placed it into Raphah's hands.

"You kept this all your life, now keep it in death," she said.

Without warning, the small door that led out of the chancel and into the churchyard was effortlessly sliced in two and the Sword of Mayence appeared. Abram pushed aside the fragments of the door and stepped into the sanctuary.

"Raphael!" said the surprised Pyratheon. "You are . . ."

"Still alive. The Glashan kept me longer than I expected. Your meddling has gone too far this time. Riathamus will not be pleased."

"Riathamus is dead; he is gone, the bright morning star has flickered and shimmered its last on this world. So go down on your knee," Pyratheon demanded.

"You fool yourself. This was not the place or the time for the last destruction. You have meddled with time. Come to the cliff and see what is happening to your world," Abram said as he looked down at the body of Raphah. He then spoke to him as if he were alive. "I have a gift. To you from the master. He knew of this time."

Abram knelt and breathed on Raphah. "Receive that which hovers over the waters," he said as he placed his thumb into the middle of Raphah's forehead.

Kate watched in awe as she saw the life and warmth flood back into his cold body. Raphah looked up.

"You bring me back just when I stood before the King. I thought my work was done," he said.

"The King is dead. Is none of you listening to me? *Dead.* Finished," Pyratheon shouted again and again.

Abram lifted the Sword of Mayence and pointed it at Pyratheon's throat.

"Go to the cliff and see your world," he said.

One by one, they left the church. Raphah held the Keruvim tight as he walked through the gravestones, helped by Kate. Thomas walked on behind with Demurral, Crane and Pyratheon. It was darkness so thick that it was like black water pressing against them.

They fumbled and groped blindly from gravestone to gravestone to where they could hear the voice of Abram calling them to draw closer. Demurral crawled like an old dog being led on by the voice of his master.

Not a single star shone. The bright cloud had vanished and the moon was no more. In the gloom they could hear the frightened screams of the people far below. Darkness covered the land.

Abram stood on the cliff edge. He was radiant and the only source of light that they could see.

"See," said Pyratheon, "it is just as I said. The light of the world has gone forever. Let no one believe he is still alive."

"You deceive yourself. Look, follow the light of my hand."

In the distance a small speck of light began to appear. First it was like a pinhole in the blackness, a point of pure white light. Slowly, it began to grow as the whole horizon began to expand with the growing radiance of the rising sun.

"See, Pyratheon, you just played with time. The Keruvim was never yours; while Raphah was dead, it had no real power. You needed them both but your own anger deceived you, your lust for death engulfed you. A light shines in the darkness and the darkness will never overcome it. See, he is coming, the bright morning star shines upon the earth and your days are numbered."

Abram lifted the sword above his head to strike at Pyratheon, but he was gone—melted away like a fleeting shadow. So too were the Varrigal. And as all stared at this spectacle, Demurral slipped away, running through the churchyard like a scurrying rat, never looking back.

"You need say no more, all is new," Abram said. "Take these people from this land. Go quickly, for Pyratheon will try again and the Keruvim must be returned. Go now."

With that Abram was transformed before their eyes. His clothes burnt with the brightness of heaven, his hair was polished gold. A single ray of the sun touched his forehead and in that moment he was gone.

The *Magenta* broke free of the harbour and glided into open water. There was a fresh breeze and a clear sky. On the deck of the ship the three stood looking back to the cliffs, the ruined abbey and the church high above them. Crane stood behind them and smiled. He knew not what lay ahead, but in his heart he was a changed man.

In the distance the sea began to slowly bubble and boil, a curtain of thick brown fog rolled in from the horizon. Beneath the cry of the seagulls could faintly be heard the singing of the Seloth . . .

Praise for *SHADOWMANCER* and *WORMWOOD*

"[*Shadowmancer*] goes where 'Potter' didn't, tapping into spiritual themes that credit God as the force of all good."
—*Newsweek*, March 29, 2004

"More supernatural shenanigans from the *Shadowmancer* man—this is even better." —*The Independent* (London)

"Wormwood...the bright star shall fall from the sky..."

Panic fills the streets of London on a night in 1756 when the earth suddenly lurches forward and starts spinning out of control. Is the end of the world at hand? Is there any hope left?

$17.99
1-59185-626-4

Tersias

Coming in 2006...DON'T MISS IT!

The story of a blind beggar who suddenly develops the gift of "seeing" and illustrates the dangers of spiritism.

$17.99 • 1-59185-802-X (Hardcover)